Jacob Høigilt is Associate Professor of Arabic language and culture at the University of Oslo. He is also Senior Researcher at the Peace Research Institute, Oslo. He was previously Senior Researcher at the Fafo Institute for Applied International Studies. He is the author of *Islamist Rhetoric: Language and Culture in Contemporary Egypt* as well as a contributor to various edited collections and journals.

Comics in Contemporary Arab Culture

Politics, Language and Resistance

Jacob Høigilt

I.B. TAURIS

LONDON • NEW YORK • OXFORD • NEW DELHI • SYDNEY

I.B. TAURIS
Bloomsbury Publishing Plc
50 Bedford Square, London, WC1B 3DP, UK
1385 Broadway, New York, NY 10018, USA
29 Earlsfort Terrace, Dublin 2, Ireland

BLOOMSBURY, I.B. TAURIS and the I.B. Tauris logo
are trademarks of Bloomsbury Publishing Plc

First published in Great Britain 2019
This paperback edition published 2022

A catalogue record for this book is available from the British Library.

A full CIP record is available from the Library of Congress

ISBN: HB: 978-1-7845-3985-6
PB: 978-0-7556-4907-5
ePDF: 978-1-7867-3548-5
eBook: 978-1-7867-2548-6

Typeset by OKS Prepress Services, Chennai, India

To find out more about our authors and books visit
www.bloomsbury.com and sign up for our newsletters.

Contents

List of Figures and Plates

Figures

Plates

Acknowledgements

I could never have written this book without the help and generosity of a lot of people. First and foremost, I would like to thank three individuals whose contributions were crucial to the research project. In Egypt, Muhammad Shennawy, co-founder of *Tuk-Tuk* magazine, the *al-Fann al-Tasi'* organization and the Cairocomix festival, introduced me to the world of Egyptian comics and patiently endured my many naïve questions. He also kindly let me use one of his wonderful cartoons as the cover image of this book. In Lebanon, Lena Merhej and Lina Ghaibeh went out of their way to help me understand the history and development of Lebanese and Arabic comics and graphic art. They both gave their time generously and put me in touch with several comic creators. As co-founder of *Samandal* magazine, Lena was my gateway into the Lebanese comics scene. As the director of the Mahmoud Kahil Award and associate professor of graphic design at the American University of Beirut, Lina kindly invited me to AUB twice for the annual comics symposium in connection with the award – I cannot thank her enough for that. Many others willingly gave their time and expertise. In Egypt, I want to thank Rania Amin, Muhammad Andeel, Hanan al-Karargi, Makhlouf, Magdi al-Shafi'i and Ahmad Shawqash. In Lebanon, George Khoury JAD showed me unparalleled generosity, sharing freely his knowledge as well as his extensive production of comics. Mazen Kerbaj and Fouad Mezher willingly took the time to answer my questions about their work. I am greatly indebted to all of these people, as well as to the many others who are not mentioned here but who allowed me to use their comics as illustrations in this book.

Most of the writing took place at the Peace Research Institute Oslo (PRIO) in Norway. I am very grateful to the PRIO administration and my many kind colleagues for providing a stimulating and warm academic home, and not least for giving me an extra grant that allowed me to complete the manuscript on time. During fieldwork in Cairo, the Netherlands-Flemish Institute in Cairo (NVIC) was my home. This institute is a gem because of its staff and its facilities. I cannot thank them enough for their hospitality. Special thanks go to Adel Abdel Moneim: teacher, friend and a model of intellectual enthusiasm and generosity.

Several colleagues read parts of what was eventually to become the book manuscript; I am particularly grateful to Kristin Bergtora Sandvik at PRIO and Gunvor Mejdell at the Department of Culture Studies and Oriental Languages at the University of Oslo. Other colleagues and students at the University also offered valuable comments and criticism during presentations of parts of the book. Two anonymous reviewers read the whole draft. I have seldom received

Acknowledgements

more valuable and constructive criticism, and I revised the manuscript considerably as a result – thank you very much.

Sophie Rudland at I.B.Tauris is the ideal editor: she has been immensely helpful, flexible and cheerful throughout the publishing process. Sebastian Manley's competent editing made the manuscript highly readable instead of just barely passable.

Bits and pieces of already published material have found their way into this manuscript. Parts of my article 'Egyptian Comics and the Challenge to Patriarchal Authoritarianism' (*International Journal of Middle East Studies*, 49, 2017) are scattered, in modified form, among chapters 3, 4, 5 and 6. Sections of chapters 6 and 7 are based on my book chapter 'Dialect with an Attitude,' in Jacob Høigilt and Gunvor Mejdell (eds): *The Politics of Written Arabic: Writing Change* (Leiden: Brill 2017), as well as on my chapter 'Everybody Can Write!' in Nora S. Eggen and Rana Issa (eds): *Philologists in the World: Festschrift in Honour of Gunvor Mejdell* (Oslo: Novus 2017). Thanks to all the publishers for allowing me to rework these publications and include them in this book.

A Note on Transliteration

This is not primarily a philological or linguistic work, so I have kept transliteration to a minimum to enhance readability. I have transliterated ʿayn and *hamza*, but I have not employed diacritics, on the assumption that those who read Arabic will be able to understand which Arabic letters are intended while those who do not will not benefit from seeing dots and lines under and over the letters. Furthermore, when transliterating the names of comics creators I have conformed to the way they themselves write their names in Latin script. Several of these creators are referred to in English and French publications, and this way of transliterating their names makes it easier for the reader to look them up. Long quotes in Arabic are written in Arabic and translated into English, as are the titles of the comics and magazines in the list of primary sources. Since Arabic is read from right to left, I have arranged pages from right to left in those cases where illustrations cover two pages.

1

Introduction

One of the most conspicuous features of the 2016 Cairo International Book Fair were the lavish lounges of the Ministries of Defence and the Interior. Situated side by side right after the entrance to the main exhibition hall, they easily outdid all the other stalls and lounges, including those of the Ministry of Culture and the General Egyptian Book Organization. One might think it strange that the Ministries of Defence and the Interior are represented at all at a book fair, but in Egypt anno 2016 this was only a logical consequence of the political development in the country. These two ministries, representatives of the main coercive forces in the country (the military and the internal security agencies), so completely dominate Egyptian society that it is not strange at all that their lounges were given pride of place during the main annual cultural event in the country.

However, just as conspicuous was the fact that both lounges were empty of people, and only a few books were on display. This was in stark contrast to the outdoor stall of start-up publisher Dar Tuya, where trade was brisk and a queue formed outside. The main attraction of the stall was the second volume of *al-Waraqa* ([notebook] paper), a collection of crudely drawn comics and cartoons by Islam Gawish. The hugely popular comics were originally published on Gawish's Facebook page, which was followed by 1.6 million people at the time. Adding to the hype was the fact that Gawish had been arrested and detained briefly a couple of days before. No less than ten police officers had stormed his workplace to arrest him on charges of possessing pirated software. It was well known that Gawish had recently published some rather irreverent cartoons of President Abd al-Fattah al-Sisi. Gawish's run-in with the police did nothing to lessen people's interest in his work; his two books and coffee mugs with cartoons on them as well as other spin-off items sold very well at the fair.

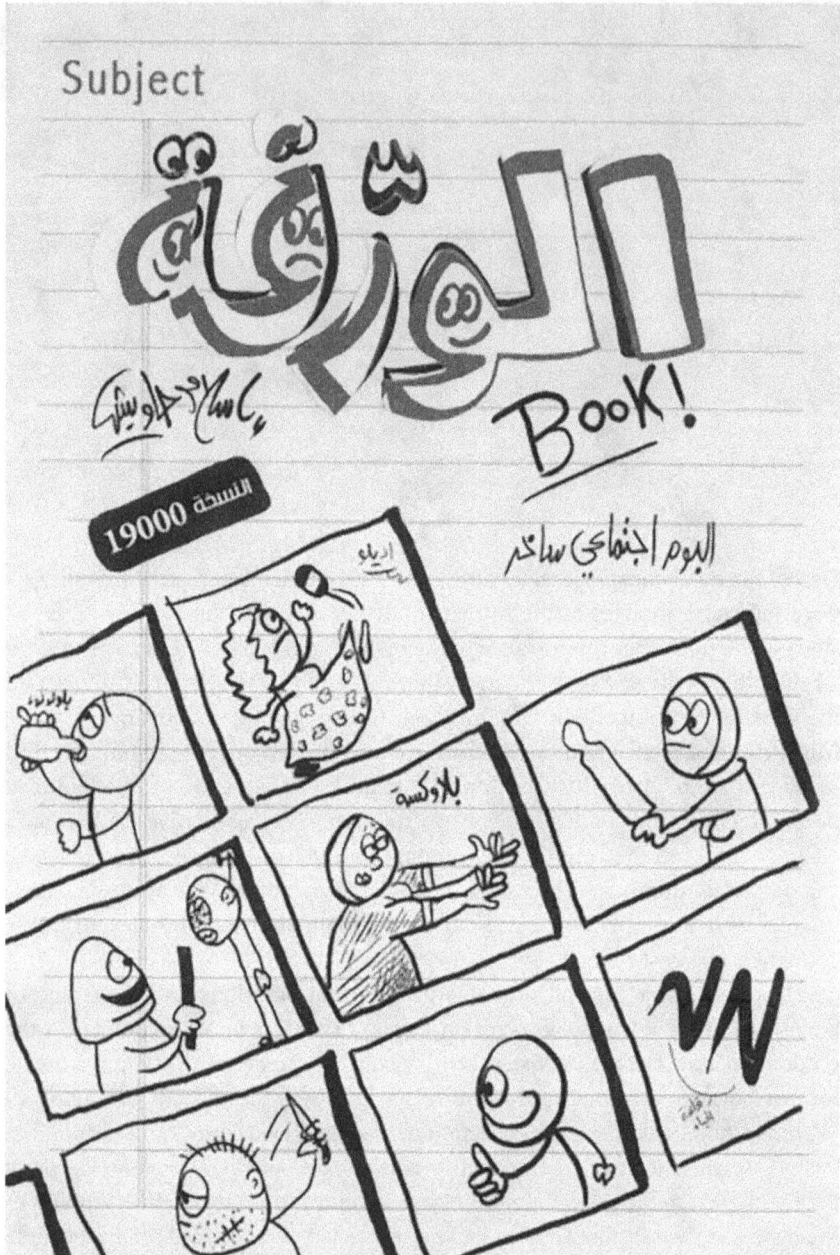

Figure 1.1 Cover page of Islam Gawish's *al-Waraqa*.

The contrasts of the Cairo International Book Fair illustrate the central concern in the pages that follow. This book is about subversive culture in the Arab world. More specifically, it is about the content and language of Arab comics for adults, a cultural product that has evolved rapidly since the mid-2000s.

Adult comics *from* the Middle East are something else than comics *about* the Middle East. The latter are well-known already. Joe Sacco, Marjane Satrapi, Guy Delisle and Riad Sattouf are all highly acclaimed comic creators who have published books about the region.[1] New works keep appearing, such as Jean-Pierre Filiu and David B.'s comics history of the relations between the United States and the Middle East.[2] Although some of these works are made by people who grew up in the area, they are typically written in English or French, published by European or US publishing houses and consumed by a Western audience. In contrast to such comics, the works we deal with in this book are comics written *in* the Arab world, by Arabs, in Arabic (for the most part), and published in the Arab world, notably Egypt and Lebanon. A whole new comics-for-adults environment has appeared in a number of Arab countries during the last ten years. Starting with the establishment of the comic/graphic art magazine *Samandal* in Lebanon in 2007, other initiatives and countries soon followed suit. Today, Egypt probably boasts the biggest scene (see Plate 1).

Already, this is a cultural product that has expanded beyond magazines. The annual festival Cairocomix in Egypt has gathered comic creators from Algeria to Iraq since 2015, and over the last few years several smaller comics workshops and events have taken place in Cairo and elsewhere in Egypt. In Lebanon, which was the first country to produce Arab adult comics, the American University of Beirut (AUB) hosts the annual Mahmud Kahil comics award and, uniquely in the Arab world, the AUB has faculty dedicated to the study of comics and graphic art and a special library section for this subject. Recently, the well-established francophone Festival International de la Bande Dessinée d'Alger (FIBDA) decided to have an Arabic section among its exhibitions; new, independent adult comic ventures continue to pop up all over the Arab world, from Morocco and Tunisia via Jordan to Kuwait.[3]

In other words, adult comics are by now a notable cultural phenomenon in many Arab countries. But why write a book about them? There is of course no lack of cultural products – films, photography, music, novels, poetry – that criticize and challenge various aspects of Arab society and politics, historically and presently. Furthermore, adult comics do not have much impact on Arab societies. Their audience is limited, their influence probably minuscule. Why, then, do they deserve a book? Adult comics are interesting in part simply because they are a new medium that has flourished in the last ten years. However, the medium is also intriguing in and of itself. The combination of images and text unique to comics makes them a powerful visual medium, but it also allows for whimsical playfulness. It invites intense immersion, but also easy reads: comics are an extremely versatile medium. Furthermore, adult comics in the Arab world are made by mostly young people writing in a youthful idiom, and they are made mostly for young people – those Arabs who participated or watched, exhilarated, as the 2011 uprisings expressed *their* desires and ambitions, *their* way of communicating and socializing. Many of these comics represent, in concentrated form, the spirit that animated the so-called Arab Spring, and unlike that breath-taking moment, they continue to flourish today. In short, Arab adult comics are interesting not for what they do, but for what they *are*: consistent attempts to depict and think life and society in new ways in countries where the ruling elite keeps recycling the same old oppressive patterns (patriarchy, authoritarianism, violent conflict and widespread censorship). These comics are colourful expressions of young people's views on politics, society and gender relations. In addition, since they are crafted by a combination of linguistic and visual codes, they provide an opportunity for studying how language and political criticism are connected. Finally, comics are connected to other cultural expressions and socio-political trends. Therefore, they are a good lens through which to observe how young Arabs employ cultural expressions as a means of carving out their own space and criticizing the current ideological order. This is what concerns me here. My aim in this book is to use comics as a window onto contemporary Arab society as seen by large sections of young Arabs. It is a cultural analysis in which the visual and textual codes of comics convey politically salient meanings.

The social and political relevance of comics is well established in research literature, with examples ranging from Dorfman and Mattelart's Marxist critique of the Disney comic universe, via connections between comics and war propaganda to comic interventions in social issues such as post-colonialism.[4] However, there is very little documentation or analysis of Arab comics. Douglas and Malti-Douglas's valuable volume *Arab Comic Strips: Politics of an Emerging Mass Culture* from 1994 remains the only book-length treatment of the topic.[5] At the time, there were extremely few Arabic adult comic works in existence, so the book focused mostly on children's comics, investigating the way comic creators inserted ideologically charged messages into their ostensibly innocent, humorous stories. The present book is an attempt to build on their work and expand the analysis. First, I focus only on comics for grown-ups. Secondly, the analysis reflects advances in comics theory since the publication of *Arab Comic Strips*. Insightful works about how comics 'work' and the development of the medium have been produced in France as well as the United States in this period.[6] Thirdly, the analysis in this book puts emphasis on two themes that emerge as important at the current cultural and political juncture in the Arab world: the connection between comics, other forms of popular art and the political ferment that led to the Arab uprisings in 2011 and beyond; and the social and political implications of the fact that these comics treat serious issues in a vernacular language and an informal style.

While there is only one book-length study on Arabic comics, a new and wonderful source of information and analysis emerged at the time when I started researching this topic. Jonathan Guyer's blog *Oum Cartoon* and his many articles on comics, cartoons and graphic art in the Arab world have made it much easier to navigate the landscape, get acquainted with new works and authors and put the source material into context.[7] While the analysis in this book is mostly confined to Egypt and Lebanon, Guyer's blog and articles have a wider scope and take in developments within the comic scene in the entire Arab world.[8] As the content of *Oum Cartoon* proves, Arab comics are a dynamic and expanding field, and hopefully the present book will only be part of a future chain of works on the topic.

A central contention in this book is that the new Arab adult comics are vehicles for ideology. Ideology is one of the core concerns of research into comics, and it is not difficult to understand why: the power of combining images and texts in the way comics can do is obvious.[9] Comics encourage stereotypes, at the same time as the combinations of images and text allow for ambiguity and multiple readings; and children and adults alike become engrossed in them. Such properties of comics were recognized by the US authorities early on, and consequently they put comics to use in propaganda, especially related to war efforts. In World War II and the Korean and Vietnam wars, the United States military used comics actively as a propaganda tool, and the big comics corporations cooperated, churning out superhero or war stories with Americans as heroes.[10] The pattern has been replicated elsewhere, and the Arab world is no exception in this regard. Arab children's comics have been used to pedagogical ends as well as to support the policies of ruling regimes; Mickey Mouse and the beloved comics character Samir have appeared on cover pages in military uniform more than once since the 1960s. There is also a unique example of comics hagiography in the Arab world, namely the political biography of Egyptian president Nasser, published by the African Journalists' Collective in 1973.[11]

However, comics have also lent themselves to anti-establishment messages. From the late 1960s, American and British comic creators crafted their own, often subversive stories, consciously trying to break every taboo in the book. These comix, as they became known, were self-published or published by small, independent printing houses. They challenged formal conventions of the medium and commented on social and political questions of the day, often with a solid dose of surreal humour. Though they are not as explicit as the 1970s comix, the new Arab comics stand in this tradition in several respects. They experiment with style as well as content, they are published and distributed independently, they exhibit a penchant for the surreal and funny – and most importantly, they comment on themes of great importance to contemporary Arab societies: authoritarianism, women's rights, social inertia, corruption and crime. It is probably no coincidence that the current wave of adult comics to some extent coincided with the Arab uprisings from late 2010 onwards. The Arab Spring saw the emergence of a home-grown liberalism among young people especially. Youthfulness and the struggle against patriarchal authoritarianism were notable features of the upheavals. Comics are part of a youthful, eclectic and open-minded trend in Arab cultural life that we would do well to remember now that the popular protests have been overtaken by violent struggles between autocrats, Islamists and various warmongers across the region.

Scope and themes

This book is not intended to be a comprehensive survey of all aspects of Arab adult comics.[12] I focus on the Egyptian and Lebanese comics environments first and foremost, simply because they are the two central countries in the production of adult comics. Thematically, I deal with four topics that appear time and again in Arab adult comics: authoritarianism, gender relations, the politics of youthfulness and the social and political implications of language use. These are important themes in the political dynamics and official discourse of contemporary Arab societies. The first two issues are well-known parts of the oppressive order of most Arab regimes. Whether in the guise of republics (e.g. Egypt) or what Clifford Geertz termed 'reconstructed traditionalism' (the Arab monarchies),[13] the post-colonial regimes in the Arab world have proven to be among the world's most resilient authoritarian states. Access to rent in the form of oil or aid, lavish spending on security services, support from powerful third countries like the United States, neopatrimonialism and crony capitalism all play a role in propping up these regimes. In this book I am less concerned with what explains authoritarian persistence than the consequences it has in the public sphere and public discourse, and how it is resisted in adult comics.[14] Coercion goes hand in hand with a public discourse that naturalizes a repressive and most often conservative social order: obedience is a central value, and social relations are strictly vertical.[15] The central role of the military has led to a corporatist view of society, where the values of discipline, unity and order take precedence over pluralism and spontaneity.[16] There are of course differences between Lebanese and Egyptian authoritarianism that we will look at in more detail in chapters 3 and 5; here I will just note that at different junctures since 2011, both the Egyptian and the Lebanese states have unleashed their coercive apparatus on young people who dare challenge the powers that be. Arrests, torture and murders of young dissenters have been the permanent reality of Egypt since the military coup in 2013, while in Lebanon, the sectarian elites cracked down on young demonstrators who railed against the elites' ineptness in late summer 2015. Such physical repression is accompanied by a combination of paternalistic discourse where citizens are often referred to as sons and daughters of the ruling elite on the one hand, and nationalist propaganda that labels critics 'enemies of the people' on the other.

The new adult comics confront the values of order, discipline and obedience head-on. At times they do so in very funny ways, while at others their criticism is harsh and the atmosphere of their stories dark. In both Lebanon and Egypt, young comic creators build on the work of an earlier generation, going beyond the heritage of criticism and experimentalism of such earlier artists to create their own idioms. The content of their stories as well as the graphic styles they have developed speak to their own generation, its experiences and concerns. Their stories address issues such as war, torture, emigration and a feeling of frustration and despair that became apparent for the entire world to see during the 2010–11 uprisings in the Arab world. Not entirely by coincidence, the comics scene virtually exploded at the time of these uprisings, and the political process following the Arab Spring also became a theme on which they commented. Particularly in Egypt, comic creators continued to poke fun at and criticize the authorities even as the space for free speech narrowed and eventually all but disappeared under the al-Sisi regime from 2013. Comic artists cleverly used humour and the rhetorical tools of comic storytelling to blunt the edge of their criticism, and perhaps it is this fact, together with the marginality of comics as a mass medium, that has largely spared comics from the intervention of state censors and legal persecution.

The second theme I address in the book is gender relations. The authoritarian preference for order and corporatism has produced ruling elites made up in large part by ageing men, whether they are royals, members of the presidential inner circle or (in Lebanon) the sectarian elites. The combination of an ageing, male elite and a neopatrimonial system supports and is in turn supported by patriarchal structures in the public and private spheres. The dominance of the father figure on all levels of society is and has long been a prominent feature of many modern Arab countries,[17] and it is convenient for many authoritarian elites, including those of Egypt and Lebanon, to pander to the conservative forces that restrict the freedom of women. The state colludes with religious conservatives in making women symbols of national honour – and hence subject to strict systems of control and discipline.[18] As Shereen Abouelnaga writes of pre-revolutionary Egypt,

> the dominant paradigm governing women's agency and subjectivity before 2011 was generated by a set of modern patriarchal values [...] that reduced female identity to the corporeal body by which abuse, mutilation, isolation and harassment were justified culturally.[19]

The subjection of women is engineered by the state through various means. One is the legal system. Inheritance and other personal laws severely restrict the freedom of women. In Lebanon, for example, the electoral law is blatantly gendered. Not only must Lebanese vote in the municipality from which their paternal forebears once hailed, but a married woman must vote in the same municipality as her husband – a kind of double discrimination. Another means of control is physical abuse. Both the Egyptian regime and the Lebanese sectarian elites have employed thugs to assault and harass women who participate in demonstrations or other oppositional activities. In Egypt, 99 per cent of the women surveyed reported having been the victim of sexual harassment of a verbal or physical sort in 2013.[20]

However, patriarchy is a dominant, but not hegemonic, paradigm, and resistance to the subjection of women has long roots in the Arab world as elsewhere. The contemporary young Arab comic creators have taken up this tradition and expressed it in their own idiom. They have made gender issues a core concern, and exemplify well a defiant spirit that has been on display at various occasions in both Egypt and Lebanon before and after the revolutionary moment in 2011. Egypt and Lebanon boast a strong presence of female comic creators, compared to early periods in key countries such as France and the United States. Whether through slapstick humour, wild exaggerations or strong visual symbolism, female and male comic artists express an ideology of gender equity and mutual respect. However, there is room for much more than ideological statements in these works. An irreverent attitude to both sexes and their social roles is on display, as is a deeply personal tone that probably strikes a chord with men and women everywhere, regardless of geographic and cultural distance.

The third theme addressed is the politics of youthfulness. Arab countries have failed to exploit the 'demographic gift' that a youth bulge normally represents, having let their huge youthful population sink into joblessness, relative poverty and disillusionment. Well before the Arab uprisings erupted in 2011, young people had started to question and challenge that state of affairs. Asef Bayat has captured this feature of Middle Eastern politics with the expressions 'reclaiming youthfulness' and 'the politics of fun'.[21] While there were certainly pockets of young and creative resistance before 2011, the Arab uprisings really broke the dam of youth exclusion, as young people emerged in droves to reject 'the meagre choices offered by sterile political, economic and social arenas', in the words of one UNDP report.[22] In the face of oppression, discrimination and marginalization, young people have risen to claim their dignity and rights, and they have done so partly by asserting their youthfulness. The new Arab comics criticize authoritarian and patriarchal policies and values, but at the same time they are one among several youthful cultural expressions that contribute to a 'politics of youth': an assertion of freedom, a creative counterforce to the authoritarianism and patriarchy they criticize. It is in their celebration of youthfulness that these comics most obviously relate to a whole wave of cultural expression that emerged during the 2000s in Egypt, in Lebanon and elsewhere in the Arab world. I try to show the intimate connections between comics and art forms such as graffiti and popular music, and how they all express a politicized youthfulness, expressed in vernacular Arabic. The combination of vernacular critique and popular cultural expressions gives young people a voice in Arab societies.

The question of voice brings us to the fourth and last theme of the book, which is the politics of language. Comics represent an increasingly visible tendency to write in the vernacular in several Arab countries.[23] This development is important because Arabic is a diglossic language, where the domain of writing is seen as the domain of the high (and prestigious) variety, *al-fusha*. It bears the stamp of officialdom and is elitist by default. Comics are one medium among several that make extensive use of written dialect, potentially contributing to fundamental changes in the Arabic language system and language ideology – essential parts of Arab identity. Arab adult comics are interesting in regard to language ideology, by which I mean particular ideas about language that influence language attitudes and usage.[24] The reason why adult comics are so interesting in this regard has to do with the phenomenon of *diglossia*, of which Arabic is often considered the paradigmatic case. According to Charles Ferguson's classic model, diglossic languages are divided into two varieties. The H(igh) variety (*al-fusha* in Arabic) diverges from the L(ow) variety (the dialects; *'ammiyya*, *darija*) in terms of syntax, morphology and lexicon, but they are clearly related varieties, not separate languages. The H variety is the vehicle of a large and respected body of literature and, importantly in the Arabic case, the sacred language of the Qur'an. It is nobody's mother tongue, but learnt at school, and is used for most written and many formal spoken purposes. The dialects are people's actual mother tongue and are used in all informal contexts, but they are typically not a written language and carry considerably less prestige. Today, however, this system of functional differentiation shows signs of strain. I argue that Arab adult comics are part of a trend towards writing the vernacular variety which has social implications and may also contribute to changing the whole language system in the long run.

I will have a lot more to say about the concept of diglossia and its definition in chapter 7. Here, I will only note that I view diglossia as a cultural product that has served the interests of specific social, religious and political groups to various degrees ever since the codification of classical Arabic in the eighth century. For our purposes, the crucial point of departure is the modern Arabic cultural renaissance, *al-nahda*, which resulted in a renewed focus on and prestige for *al-fusha*. First, I argue that the current reverence of this variety amounts to a standard language ideology, and that this ideology is in some ways (but not all!) connected to the marginalization of both the young and the poor in the Arab world. Secondly, I will argue that Arabic adult comics merit interest because they give us a particularly vivid picture of a hypothesized development: that written Arabic is becoming a property of the masses, and that one consequence of this is that there is more room for variation and informal styles in public written language.

One might object that it is selective to choose comics as an entry point to explore a hypothesis about informality, since comics are almost by definition an informal medium of entertainment. This is a claim that should and will be modified, but even if we were to accept it for the sake of argument, it would not detract from the attractiveness of comics as an object of linguistic analysis. The simple fact that the Arab world has seen a remarkable efflorescence of comics during the last ten years is by itself an indication of a tendency towards the informal in the cultural sphere, and seen in this light, comics provide a good vantage point from which to explore this tendency, by connecting it with other kinds of texts and asking whether traits found in comics are observable elsewhere, too.

The analysis of comics

I shall treat Arab adult comics as *discourse*, understood as 'all forms of meaningful semiotic human activity seen in connection with social, cultural and historical patterns and developments of use'.[25] Discourse is often viewed as simultaneously a place where asymmetric power relationships are produced and a place for renegotiating or challenging such relationships.[26] How to approach comics as discourse, then? It is important to recognize that whatever method is used, the analysis of a cultural product relies heavily on the interpretive effort of the analyst. Paul Ricoeur put it elegantly: 'Reading is like the performance of a musical score: it betokens the fulfilment, the actualization of the semantic virtualities of the text.'[27] Interpretation is necessarily subjective. But to arrive at a plausible and fruitful analysis it is necessary to have a good grasp of the context of the text in question as well as the technical and rhetorical means employed by the author. What may a comic writer/artist have intended by creating a story in one particular way? What may the comic in question tell us about the world-view of its creator and the society of which s/he is part?[28] The context of the new Arab comics is the subject of chapter 2, and I also provide contextual information in later chapters. As for the artistic and discursive strategies comic creators employ to get their messages across, I will outline my methodological approach here. How is meaning constructed in comics? The assumption behind asking such a question is that we can analyse (adult) comics as a specific symbolic form with its own set of conventions for meaning-making.

When comics invite immersion, it is because of the immediate and strong appeal of images as well as the fact that they require the reader to interact with the images to make the stories cohere. Most comics employ some sort of cartoons – pictorial icons – rather than realistic artistic renderings to represent characters. Comics are immersive partly because of this iconic form of representation. As Scott McCloud remarks, cartooning can be seen as a kind of amplification through simplification: by focusing on one or a few features of a character, process or object, the artist chooses to emphasize one or a few among its many possible meanings.[29] Comics also leave the reader to fill in the information that is omitted between the images. A simple example is found in a story by Ahmad 'Ukasha in the Egyptian comic magazine *Tuk-Tuk*, about a young man who has a motorbike accident. A series of inset panels depict him losing control over the vehicle on the road. On the next page the setting is completely changed, and the Grim Reaper appears: the reader is immediately able to infer that we have now entered the driver's head while he is lying unconscious on the ground, in a state between life and death (see Plate 2).

Not only do comic creators have, powerful meaning-making tools at their disposal. In addition, comics make meaning on several levels at once. There is an overt sequence of the images that make up the narrative; there is a system of connections between and within panels and whole pages; and lastly, there is the text, when it figures. All contribute to forming a coherent whole, hence the potential richness of meaning in comic stories and their attractiveness as windows onto contemporary culture and society in the Arab world.

French comic scholar Thierry Groensteen usefully distinguishes between three levels of comics analysis. First, the spatio-topical system of the comics page concerns the positioning of panels, their size and shape, and the rhythm that is established between them. These elements all contribute to the meaning of the images and the words in a graphic narrative, over and above the explicit surface content. A nice illustration of this feature is the Lebanese artist Mazen Kerbaj's comic 'Furr Furr Blues', which I analyse in chapter 5. When introducing the topic of women in the comic – the central theme of the story – Kerbaj suddenly shifts from several panels on the preceding page to one big panel featuring the head of a woman. The effect is not only to signal the entrance of the main subject, but also to interrupt the flow of the narrative and freeze it, as it were. The comic form leaves artists many possibilities to play with space, time and perspective, so these are aspects of comics that may carry meaning by themselves. Secondly, the narrative sequence is realized by the juxtaposition of images, normally with a space ('gutter') between them, which invite the reader to establish a temporal or aspectual relation between them. The reader's interpretation of an image will be conditioned by the images preceding it and those succeeding it. But comics storytelling necessarily involves an active interpretative effort by the reader to realize the narrative potential.

Lastly, the non-chronological meta-relations between panels in a narrative make for what Groensteen calls a 'braiding' effect: panels may be interlocked in a semantic sense, yet non-contiguous both spatially and temporally. Magdi al-Shafi'i's graphic novel *Metro*, which I present at some length in chapter 3, is a good example. The metro system of Cairo is a narrative glue in the story, and at various points in the novel the metro is represented either through drawings of actual stations or in the form of a line chart. Such non-contiguous cohesion adds another layer of meaning to comics that is independent of the sequential narrative and that is often used to significant effect by comic artists.

The power of the image of course runs through Groensteen's three levels. In a path-breaking study of the art of comics, Scott McCloud graphically shows how comics make one sense – sight – express all the others through the texture of the lines, the background, and the use of several conventionalized symbols, like the black spiral above a character's head to symbolize confusion or perplexity.[30] But although the images are the most striking feature of comics, the text is by no means trivial. The text may be part of the unfolding of events, when it appears in speech/thought balloons, or it may be part of a narrative that accompanies or perhaps serves as a counterpoint to the images. It may also enter the pictures as a graphic element, most obviously in onomatopoetic use, as when a jarring crash sound is symbolized by the word 'CRASH' in big, jagged letters across an image.[31] In such instances, as Charles Hatfield remarks, 'the written text can function like images, and images like written text'.[32] A good example of this in Arabic adult comics is the many instances where the Egyptian swear word أحا (approx. 'fuck') appears in huge letters, written in either Arabic or Latin script with capitals ('A7A'), as in Makhlouf's story 'The Magic Milk' in *Tuk-Tuk*.

There is clearly a pictorial element to the word, whose form gives it a function beyond the concrete, literal meaning: why choose Latin script instead of Arabic? In chapters 3 to 6, the very diverse array of visual effects employed by Arab comic creators (such as the use of lines, inking, colouring, backgrounds, and text) are investigated for their meaning-making potential.

Structure of the book

Before we delve into the analysis of comics we need to get a clear sense of what kind of phenomenon we are talking about. Chapter 2 is devoted to mapping the

Figure 1.2 Detail from Makhlouf's 'The Magic Milk' [al-Laban al-Sihri], *Tuk-Tuk* 5 (2012), p. 5.

scene of Arab adult comics. It focuses on Lebanon and Egypt, the two central case studies, but I also include a survey of developments in other countries. I believe this is valuable since the topic has not been treated comprehensively before. I provide an overview of the genres, form and content of the new Arab comics. I show which traditions these works draw on, and in what respects they represent something new in the Arab media context.

Jonathan Guyer pointedly asks if anything unites these comics other than the fact that they are written by Arabs. His answer is that '[o]ne common perspective that does unite this new wave of comics from the Middle East and beyond is a radical approach to politics'.[33] The main questions in chapters 3, 4 and 5 are how the new adult comics describe and criticize political and social structures, and how they represent new social and cultural trends that challenge the existing order. In chapter 3 I describe the repressive political systems in Egypt and Lebanon and show how adult comics criticized the authoritarian, patriarchal order of these societies before 2011. In chapter 4 I trace the comics' contributions to the revolutionary mood after the Arab uprisings, focusing on Egypt. Chapter 5 treats the gender dimension of adult comics. I argue that they combine direct criticism of the discrimination against and oppression of women with a celebration of the individual's integrity, regardless of sex. Everyday harassment of women, religiously legitimated patriarchy and structural oppression of women are all themes explored in this chapter.

The final content-related chapter addresses the issue of youthfulness and individualism. In societies that marginalize their youth and demand conformity to the system, cultural forms that celebrate youthfulness and take seriously young people's lifeworld have a subversive function. The comics under study often express a streetwise, urban sense of humour, feelings of alienation and loneliness, and a sense of individualism. I present a selection of comics that deal with the experience of being young in today's Egypt and Lebanon, with short detours to Morocco and Tunisia. The analysis of how comics treat these issues is connected to the recent literature on youthfulness in the Middle East and other kinds of cultural products in the Arab world that express the same spirit as the new adult comics. This chapter also provides an analytic bridge, moving from content towards form. In the last part I start looking at the combination of content and language variety. I widen the empirical scope and connect the language of comics and youth magazines to the large amount of dialectal writing that is now found in the new Egyptian literature, and the predominance of dialectal Arabic writing on social media.

In chapter 7 I concentrate on linguistic form more than content. First, I focus on how dialectal writing and code alternation are parts of situated communicative strategies. The informal and direct style that is embraced in comics, music and parts of the literary field stands in contrast to the stilted forms seen in official discourse, and it has the function of carving out a 'third space' that allows writers to criticize the norms of the mainstream culture without alienating themselves from it. In this discursive third space young people can find a voice to express themselves freely and authentically and to be heard by their peers. Secondly, I relate the linguistic form of comics to the language system and language ideology in the Arab world. The main argument is that comics are at the vanguard of a development which upsets the traditional model of Arabic diglossia and its attendant language ideology, which favours *fusha* for writing purposes. The standard language variety in the Arab world is connected to elitism and socio-political exclusion. At the same time, it is revered by most Arabs as the sacred language of Islam and it has often been used to subvert dominant ideologies in the Arab world. Thirdly, building on language debates in the Arab world and several examples of dialect and standard writing in contemporary Arab comics, my discussion criticizes the tendency among Arab cultural and political elites to view diglossia in terms of a zero-sum game, presenting dialectal writing as a resource in a changing language system. The conclusion summarizes the argument by drawing together the different areas treated by each chapter.

2

Mapping the scene

In 2013, Magdi al-Shafi'i's graphic crime novel *Metro* was included in an authoritative survey of international comic art, to illustrate the liberating and politically explosive potential of comics.[1] The example was well chosen. Published in 2008 (and promptly banned by the Egyptian authorities), *Metro* is among the works that inaugurated the current outburst of comic art in Egypt and elsewhere in the Arab world (see Plate 3). Its political criticism of the Mubarak regime is devastating and in thinly veiled terms it encourages its readers to beat the system by rebelling against it. *Metro* is an independent piece of art and storytelling, and it was published by one of Egypt's nascent alternative publishing houses at the time, Malamih (signs). al-Shafi'i has repeatedly noted that *Metro* was intended as a rallying cry, and that there are direct lines connecting the mindset it propagates and the outbreak of the 2011 uprising in Egypt. We shall return to this graphic novel in more detail later. My point here is that in five years, adult Arabic comics went from being virtually unknown even among culturally interested Arabs to receiving international recognition. What lies behind this remarkable trajectory? To properly situate Arab adult comics and their history we need to rewind a little.

Comics have a long history in the Arab world, starting with children's magazines in Egypt and Lebanon in the 1950s, like *Sindibad*, *'Ala al-Din* and *Samir*. The Egyptian adult comics environment owes much to a rich tradition of such children's comics as well as innovative cartoons and illustrations. It is not a coincidence that Muhiy al-Din al-Labbad (1940–2010) was honoured with a special exhibition at the first Cairocomix festival in 2015. al-Labbad was an accomplished book illustrator, creator of children's comics and prolific cartoonist: his drawings and cartoons were published in the four-volume collection *al-Naẓar* in the late 1980s. The originality and daring of his cartoons taught other artists 'how to think and not how to think like him. He gives you the tools for thinking, like why and how and who', according to one contemporary cartoonist working for the newspaper *al-Shuruq*.[2] Another prominent influence on today's comic writers is Ahmad Hijazi, the creator of al-Tanabila (the lazy boys), three cartoon characters that inhabited a number of popular comic strips from 1964 onwards in *Samir* magazine. Ostensibly created for children, the subtle political messages in Hijazi's stories earned him the epithet 'radical'.[3] Hijazi was a leftist, and supported such causes as anti-imperialism and heavy regulation of private business, but his political attitudes were far more radical than this; he extended his satire to encompass 'critique of nationalism and even patriotism, hostility to militarism, the state, and all modern forms of authority and hierarchy'.[4] In the stories of al-Tanabila, he satirically addressed issues such as corruption, exploitation and lack of social solidarity. The Tanabila characters were hugely popular in Egypt, as the stories were funny and appealed to children and adults alike, each age group reading different messages into the comics. Hijazi's influence on the current generation of Egyptian comic artists was acknowledged by the founders of *Tuk-Tuk*, who wrote a eulogizing text about the subversive nature of *al-Tanabila* and how the series taught them the craft of comic storytelling.[5]

al-Tanabila was a remarkable achievement, since it succeeded in telling stories that were entertaining and fun to read for children while at the same time commenting on contemporary Egyptian culture and society in a way only adults could grasp. And Hijazi was not alone. In Egypt as well as several other Arab countries there were talented and thoughtful comic artists who took their young audience seriously and inserted social and political messages in their work. Another comic that is mentioned by several of today's Egyptian comic creators as an important source of inspiration is *Flash*, a pocket-sized magazine that was published in the 1990s. This magazine (not to be confused with the American superhero comic of the same name), which seems to be largely forgotten today, was different from the mainstream children's comics at the time, like *Samir*, *'Ala' al-Din* and *Mickey*.[6] Its importance for us inheres in the fact that it depicted ordinary life and Egyptian characters in smart and funny ways, and that, unusually for a children's comic at the time, substantial sections were written largely in *'ammiyya*, the Egyptian dialect, rather than *fusha*.[7]

Some of today's adult comic creators have themselves played important roles in the children's comics segment. Rania Amin, who put together Egypt's first independent comics anthology for adults, *Kharij al-Saytara* (out of control, 2010), is the creator of the acclaimed illustrated children's book series *Farhana*. Magdi al-Shafi'i, who authored *Metro*, has worked for the *'Ala' al-Din* children's magazine.

For all their talent and skilfully crafted references to the world of adults, until recently comics remained a medium addressed to children in the Arab world, with two exceptions. The first, a quasi-Arab comic biography of Gamal Abdel Nasser, proved to be inconsequential. The work, entitled simply *Jamal 'Abd al-Nasir*, was written by one Muhammad Nu'man al-Dhakiri and drawn by Algerian-born

Figure 2.1 al-Tanabila: cover page of *Samīr* magazine, January 1967 (original in colour).

Jean-Marie Ruffieux, who went on to have a career in French-Belgian historical comics. It was published in 1971 by the Libyan Ministry of Information and Culture. Funded and perhaps even commissioned by the Qadhafi regime, this work is a good example of how comics may be a vehicle for ideology, in this case, the pan-Arab nationalism which was spearheaded by Nasser and to which Qadhafi subscribed (in his own, idiosyncratic way, it should perhaps be added). The story is a political biography of Nasser, eulogizing his rule while ignoring his personal life, the other personalities of the nationalist regime and its internal dynamics. However, it was skilfully designed and drawn, and not least, it was published in Arabic and intended for a mature audience. But it seems to have been largely forgotten among Arab comic artists until Makhlouf, a co-founder of *Tuk-Tuk*, rediscovered it and wrote an article about it in the Egyptian comics newsletter *al-Fann al-Tasi'* (the ninth art). At that time, the new comics for adults had already established themselves, and Makhlouf pointedly asks: 'Why didn't more comics like this appear again later? And why have comics not been used as a media weapon and documentary tool in an age in which the image has become the protagonist?'[8] Good questions indeed – but it should be kept in mind here that when the Nasser biography was published, adult comics were still an underground phenomenon in a country like the United States. In any case, the Nasser biography did not spark any interest in adult comics among Arabs.

The second exception is not a single work, but rather a person and the environment that formed around him. In 1980, the Lebanese graphic artist George Khoury (JAD) published *Carnaval*, a metaphoric graphic novel about his experience of the Lebanese civil war (this comic is analysed in chapter 3). Together with Lina and May Ghaibeh, Edgar Aho and others, Khoury went on to establish the JAD workshop, which produced adult comics until 1989.[9] Nothing similar happened in other Arab countries, however, and in the 1990s and early 2000s comics for adults seem to have disappeared from the scene altogether.

It took a group of young Lebanese to reinvent the experiment, and this time other Arab countries followed suit. In 2007 the first issue of the Lebanese magazine *Samandal* (salamander) was published. *Samandal* inaugurated the new wave of comics for adults which I concentrate on in this book. I should mention in passing that comics are part of a wider phenomenon that is aptly termed an 'informal graphic movement' by one observer.[10] This movement comprises artists who work within and across the fields of comics, graffiti, graphic design and illustration, and there is a considerable degree of shared references and historical experiences. Most of the artists are in their twenties and thirties, were raised in the media globalization of the late 1990s and early 2000s, and experienced the watershed Arab uprisings from 2011 onwards. Geographically, the movement is concentrated around two centres of gravity: Beirut (the environment around the magazine *Samandal*) and Cairo (several artists and initiatives of which *Tuk-Tuk* is the first). At the major comic events in these two countries – the Cairocomix festival and the Mahmud Kahil comics award in Beirut – artists and enthusiasts from all over the Arab world meet and network.[11]

Where in the comics landscape do the works we consider here belong? Adult comics can be many things, from underground splatter violence via autobiographies to pornographic works. Borrowing a term from American comics research, the new wave of adult graphic art in the Arab world may be termed *alternative* comics.[12] It has little to do with the mainstream children's comics or the superhero comics market. Instead, it aims to depict ordinary lives either realistically or by metaphor, and it serves as a vehicle for artistic visions or ironic slapstick humour. It explores the limits of both content and form.

Let us survey the scene in Egypt first. In June 2015 the monthly magazine *Ibda'* (innovation), which is published by the General Egyptian Book Association, devoted a double issue to Egyptian adult comics. This publication marked the establishment of comics as a topic for serious cultural analysis in Egypt – a 'consecration' by an important part of the establishment, to use Bourdieu's term.[13] *Ibda'* is a magazine that is professionally produced and printed on high-quality paper. This particular issue ran to almost 200 pages and included comic stories from many of the most well-known young comic creators, including short introductions to each writer/artist. That same year in October, the Cairocomix festival was held for the first time, gathering artists, journalists and an interested audience from several Arab countries and abroad. The festival included exhibitions, a well-stocked comics fair and several panel discussions on the artistic and socio-political aspects of comics. It was a resounding success, not least in terms of providing links between comic artists in different Arab countries and between artists and publishers. Although adult comics are still in their infancy, as noted by one of the contributors to *Ibda'*, 2015 was the year when they became part of mainstream culture.[14] But what is the background for their emergence in Egypt?

Until 2011 there were few comics specifically intended for an older audience. al-Shafi'i's graphic novel *Metro* was banned and confiscated upon publication in 2008, probably because of its criticism of the political system and its depiction of corruption in the police. Apart from this work the only comics I am aware of that did not cater to children were those of the short-lived venture AK Comics, which produced a series of superhero stories with a clear Muslim and Arab identity in the mid-2000s. The company soon went bankrupt, however, and the stories did not catch on, possibly because of the wide availability of American superhero comics in English and in translation at the time, as well as the similar (but much more professionally produced) Kuwaiti superhero series *The 99*, which appeared at approximately the same time.

The emergence of the new adult comics had nothing to do with such superhero tales. It is driven by a small, but seemingly growing, number of young and enterprising artists and writers outside of the established publishing houses and cultural institutions in Egypt. The most significant project is the comic magazine *Tuk-Tuk*, the first issue of which was published on 24 January 2011, the day before the Egyptian uprising started. A collective of prominent young graphic artists and cartoonists established this magazine: Muhammad Shennawy, Muhammad Andeel, Tawfiq, Hicham Rahma and Makhlouf. Shennawy, the *primus inter pares* of the group, explained the idea behind the magazine and why it is named after the small tricycle that drives passengers and goods through Cairo's overpopulated streets:

> Our magazine is like this tricycle: efficient but annoying thanks to its ironic tone. [...] Laughing and satire are characteristic traits of the Egyptian spirit – they let us get across what we're trying to say.[15]

The *Tuk-Tuk* team skilfully employ social media to advertise and organize their activities and create platforms for sharing. The communications possibilities inherent in the World Wide Web are extremely important for the Arab comics scene. Information about the recent Cairocomix festival was mainly spread via Facebook, and in 2015 the Egyptian comics enthusiast Ahmad ʿAbduh set up the portal *Comics Gate* as an information hub for Arab and translated comics.[16] Self-publishing technology has made adult comics available to a wider audience at a low price, sometimes even for free. The website *Kutubna*, which offers on-screen reading for a small fee, has made it possible for comic creators to sell their work without intermediaries, and it also carries digital versions of back issues of *Tuk-Tuk* and other magazines.[17] Digital technology makes comics easier and cheaper to produce, and some ventures, like *Tuk-Tuk*, have received EU funding for a limited period of time.[18] Other productions are financed by the writers and artists themselves.

As evidenced by the outpouring of adult comics around the time of the Egyptian revolution (25 January to 11 February 2011), a development towards creating comics for adults was already in motion before that watershed event; the revolution was an important catalyst for a creative urge that already existed. Before the revolution, political oppression made artists afraid to do what they really wanted (see the example of Magdi al-Shafiʿi's *Metro*), and it was difficult to get licences for new publishing houses. After the revolution the controls were loosened and comics blossomed. It seems that the adult comics are part of a wider cultural and pop-literary efflorescence that occurred in the late 1990s and 2000s. One notable trend was the publication in book form of blogs written in an informal style, often with a heavy dose of dialect, *ʿammiyya*, instead of the standard literary variety *fusha*. This development coincided with a new bookstore culture and the rise to prominence of cultural centres like Townhouse and Sawi Cultural Wheel in Cairo and the new library in Alexandria that drew young crowds to experimental as well as mainstream expressions of art, theatre, literature and music. Muhammad Shennawy places the emergence of the new comics within this context:

All the people who were born during the last regime – me, for example, I am 30 years old – grew up in a society with its own form. And although the press was freer in Egypt than in many other Arab countries, it did not offer youth a proper venue for expressing themselves. And so people started making their own underground and independent projects, not least because sources of funding became available. And they started discovering that there was a market for this – independent books by new authors sold pretty well, for example. The same happened on the music and theatre scene.[19]

The recent political setbacks clearly have not stemmed this tide of new comics for adults. The self-publishing website *Kutubna* listed 46 comic titles in March 2016. The oldest of these was published in 2011, and the majority appeared after the military coup in June 2013. Looking at the dramatic increase in publications for teenagers and adults does not really provide the whole picture, however, since a lively subculture has developed around these publications. The *Tuk-Tuk* collective and individuals associated with it have organized several comic workshops that have been amply documented. And in 2013, the organization MAZG was established. Its aim is to nurture a comic culture in the smaller cities and villages of Egypt to help them 'interact with the social and artistic revolution that is in fact taking place in Egypt', as a report puts it.[20] Since 2013, MAZG has organized workshops to introduce young people to the art of comics in several Egyptian provinces: Alexandria, Mansura and Asyut. It also published a collection of comic stories entitled *Express.*

Given all these developments it is probably justified to speak of a 'comics movement', as the online news outlet *Mada Masr* did when reporting on the 2015 Cairocomix festival.[21]

The consecration by *Ibda'* magazine I described above suggests that adult comics are recognized as a literary product. As such they intervene in a field with characteristics that are socially, politically and linguistically salient. Literature is viewed as a noble and edifying art in Egypt, and authors tend to see themselves as the 'conscience of the nation', in Richard Jacquemond's apt phrase.[22] This self-conscious attitude to their work goes hand in hand with a blunt elitism and a tolerance for censorship on moral and political grounds. Historically, writers have not necessarily objected to censorship as such, but to who should perform it (they think they are best suited themselves) and on what criteria (they have agreed to censorship of products that harm the 'fundamental values' of the country). The entire Egyptian intellectual elite also exhibits an 'over-evaluation of the written word', having made literature into 'the most important expression of the national imaginary'.[23] The literary ideology that informs Egyptian education is related to this elitist view of literature, and it has sociolinguistic consequences. In Egyptian schools, traditional poetry is presented as being the ultimate form of literature. Students are presented with a syllabus that consists mainly of poetry with an obvious moral and/or nationalist message, presented in a purist form of Arabic. As Jacquemond comments,

> [T]he education system has acted to broaden the gap between the elitist and traditionalist linguistic and literary ideology for which it is the bastion, and the real social uses made of the language and of written materials, uses that are massively out of step with this ideology.

This literary and linguistic ideology is the background against which we must assess the impact of adult comics in the linguistic and the cultural field, which will be our concern in chapters 7 and 8.

We turn now to Lebanon. The comic magazine *Samandal* was established by a team of six young Lebanese in 2007. Carrying stories in Arabic, English and French by Lebanese, Arab and foreign artists, it is an arena for experimenting with form and content. As with *Tuk-Tuk*, the name is not randomly chosen. The salamander (*samandal*) lives between land and water, and the magazine is similarly intended to cover different worlds: text and image, fine art and popular art. *Samandal*'s subtitle is 'stories from here and elsewhere', which underlines its hybrid character.[24] *Samandal* is a unique experiment in Lebanon. Although the country has produced some very fine and sophisticated comics, there was never a big environment for it, and around the beginning of the twenty-first century what environment there was had largely disappeared as the artists were dispersed. Consequently, *Samandal* started from scratch, as emerging young Lebanese graphic artists realized they had nowhere to turn to publish their work.

> Most of the collective are Lebanese, or they have some kind of connection to Lebanon. But we also wanted to print people from abroad. We started with a very small pool, it was hard to find people, nobody was experienced, nobody was published. This was a place that we wanted to create for people to print their comics.[25]

The founders all had different tastes and interests – Lena Merhej spent two formative years in the United States reading alternative comics in the American tradition, while others would point to European influences – and they perceived this to be a strength, as they were able to include a wide variety of styles and ideas in the pages of the magazine from the very beginning.

Unlike *Tuk-Tuk*, which is written exclusively in Arabic, has a distinctly Egyptian flavour and often depicts ordinary life, however absurd the stories might be, *Samandal* is extremely eclectic in terms of themes, style, genre and language. It is partly a sandbox for trying out ideas, and a number of the stories are meta-comics or unorthodox collages of photographs, newspaper clippings, text and drawings. Some of the stories seem to be mostly art for art's sake: rich in graphic imagination but with little narrative content. There is less focus on humour and more on exploring the depths of the human psyche and imagination. The editors have since the beginning sought to include inventive contributions that use the medium of comics in new and unexpected ways.

Less than half of the stories are written in Arabic. Several of the Lebanese contributors write in either French or English, and there are frequent appearances of comic artists from non-Arab countries. At the same time, the editing team remained the same from the start in 2009 until 2015, and this makes for a certain continuity as well as considerable self-referencing. Some of the most interesting and well-developed stories have been serialized, such as 'Salon Tariq al-Khurafi' by 'Umar al-Khuri, 'The Educator' by Fouad Mezher and 'Murabba wa-Laban' (jam and yoghurt) by Lena Merhej (the latter was later published as a comic book). In later issues of *Samandal* stories appear that refer to other stories published earlier in the magazine. This is probably a reflection of the small size of Lebanon's graphic arts communities (after all, it is a small country) and the centrality of a handful of people to the vitality of this environment.

The above short survey of contemporary Egyptian and Lebanese adult comics is not exhaustive – far from it. My aim has been to sketch a trajectory and describe the most visible environments on the comics scene. However, this brief description does not do justice to the burgeoning comics environment in the Arab world. I will introduce some of the recent and interesting initiatives in later chapters, but some should at least be mentioned here to suggest how rich and vibrant this art form is. First, *Tuk-Tuk* has inspired numerous other magazines that act as mouthpieces for independent comic creators. In Egypt, *Garage* and *Pass by Us Tomorrow* are two promising ones. Similar magazines have shown themselves to be viable in Casablanca (*Skefkef*) and Tunis (*Lab619*), bringing a distinctly Maghrebi atmosphere to the independent comics community. Then there are artists whose work is admired and well known, but who pursue their projects outside the Arab world. Thus, the acclaimed Egyptian graffiti and comic artist Ganzeer has played an important part in the evolution of street and comic art in that country, but he now lives in the United States and produces comics in English, published online, that are not related to conditions in the Arab world.[26] In the same manner, Lebanese comic artist Zeina Abirached was educated in Lebanon, but lives in France and publishes her comics through European publishing houses – her most well-known graphic novel is the beautiful *A Game for Swallows*, a memoir about her childhood in wartime Lebanon.[27]

Arab comic creators go abroad, and naturally, influences from other countries have made their mark on comics produced in the Arab world. With its long-standing tradition of mostly French-language comics, Algeria has been important for the development of Egyptian comics, not least through the annual Festival International de la Bande Dessinée d'Alger, which gathers comic creators from all over the world. Several comic creators in Egypt that I have met say the European tradition is important for them, but central figures from the American underground scene of the 1960s and 70s, like Robert Crumb, are also mentioned.[28] The driving force behind *Tuk-Tuk*, Muhammad Shennawy, acknowledges his debt to fanzine comics and other independent expressions of the ninth art. One of the most active Egyptian comic artists, Hanan al-Kararji, is heavily influenced by the Japanese manga style and aesthetics on the one hand, and the Disney universe on the other.[29]

There are some striking similarities between the emerging adult comics in Cairo and Beirut and the evolution of underground 'comix', and later alternative comics, in the United States and the United Kingdom. While the lack of institutional support makes the economic basis for adult comics rather shaky, it also means that the creators are free to pursue their own interests and ideas to a greater degree than if they were hired workers. This is a feature of the emerging field of adult comics in Egypt that recalls the underground comix tradition in the United States and the UK during the 1960s and 1970s. Free from institutional constraints and printed on cheap paper using simple technology, these comics defied the industry's self-imposed Comics Code Authority in the US and radically criticized the predominant values and ways of life in Western countries.[30] Underground comix gained steam with the hippie counter-culture. The artists adopted the format of established, industrialized mainstream comics and exploited it to create subversive, highly personal and often bizarre characters and stories. The foremost of the underground writers in the US, Robert Crumb, wrote stories based on his LSD trips, and the breaking of sexual taboos – visually and verbally – was a characteristic feature of many comix works. Sex and drugs are two central themes that characterized these comics, and the autobiography was an important genre that paved the way for alternative comics and the graphic novel form. As one observer put it: 'The first thing [the reader] notices is that these comics deal with "taboo" subjects: drugs, sex (including accurate drawings of penises, vaginas, and other necessary evils), shit, religion, snot, politics, etc.'[31]

It was not until the introduction of women's comics and gay comics, which came on the heels of the underground, that sex and social politics received serious treatment. The environment up until that point had been male and to some extent even misogynist. There were also elements of criticism in the works, however. As Charles Hatfield notes, the parodies of mainstream comics were often 'deliberately freighted with broader social concerns, turning spoof into a vehicle for cultural argument'.[32]

Similar to the American and British underground comics, the new Arab adult comics are self-financed and sold directly on the market. They are not as sexually explicit as their American and British counterparts were, but they are daring enough to warrant a 'for adults' sticker on the cover page, and they deal with issues like drugs, sex and politics in forthright and irreverent ways. There is no lack of bizarre stories in them. Consider, for example, the over-the-top parody of superheroes in the story 'The Magic Milk', which I mentioned briefly in the previous chapter.

Figure 2.2 Makhlouf, 'The Magic Milk,' *Tuk-Tuk* 5, 12.

In this story, the ridiculous and pathetic figure 'Super Mach' fights it out with Santa Claus, who has, inexplicably, landed his sleigh in Cairo and turned to harassing young women. The story is utterly surreal. At the same time, it is impossible not to read it in light of the uproar caused by unprecedented sexual harassment in public places in Egypt at the time the magazine was published. None of the men in the story are left with much dignity. The gender question highlights a difference between Arab and American/British underground comics: the Arabs skipped the infantile phase of their American and British counterparts and have instead confronted the problem of gender inequality and sexual harassment head-on, as we shall see in chapter 5.

The comparison between Euro-American comix and Arab adult comics can be taken one step further. The alternative comics that appeared in the West from the early 1980s were less outrageous than the underground comix, less concerned to break taboos. They explored artistic frontiers instead, experimenting with genres, learning from comics traditions in other cultures, addressing personal and political themes boldly and in depth. The pioneering pair of alternative comic magazines that appeared in the US in the 1980s were *Raw* and *Weirdo*. They were different in that '*Weirdo*'s perspective always came closer to recognizing where comics were coming from than did *Raw*'s, which was more interested in finding out where comics were going. [...] [M]ore than competing, the two titles complemented each other.'[33]

This difference between *Raw* and *Weirdo* is almost replicated when looking at the two main adult comic magazines in the Arab world today, *Samandal* and *Tuk-Tuk*. From the very start, *Samandal* was intensely personal and self-consciously focused on graphic art, similar to *Raw*. There is no shortage of stories, or even serialized narratives, but a striking feature of *Samandal* is the graphically experimental pieces that push the boundaries of what is commonly understood as 'comics'. Some contributions get close to art, while others are manipulated photo-stories rather than drawn stories. Many of the pieces are not particularly narrative-based, but instead attempt to catch a mood, a feeling, an aspect of a situation or a fragment of a dream. By contrast, *Tuk-Tuk* features straightforward comic stories in styles that tend towards the iconic rather than the realistic and down-to-earth, streetwise humour rather than the dreamy and fantastical (although there are plenty of surreal stories in Egyptian comics).

Having briefly compared Arab adult comics to trends elsewhere, we must in conclusion situate them in the cultural field of the contemporary Arab world. Relatively few Arab adults read for pleasure, and those that do seldom turn to comics. According to a survey based on interviews with some 2,500 literate Cairenes in 2013, only 2 per cent of Greater Cairo's population had even heard of *Tuk-Tuk*, and fewer than 1 per cent had read it.[34] It should be mentioned here that the figures for book reading in Egypt and elsewhere in the Arab world are dismally low: in the same survey, only 6 per cent of those asked had heard of the blog-cum-novel *'Ayza Atgawwiz* (I want to marry), which is one of the Arab world's bestselling books in recent years. In fact, *Tuk-Tuk*'s sales figures are remarkably good when compared to sales figures for books. However, they are dwarfed by the print runs of the children's magazines that people normally associate with comics.

Comics probably have negligible effect socially and culturally: *Samandal* started printing 2,500 copies but later reduced the print run to half of that amount.[35] The first issues of *Tuk-Tuk* were, surprisingly to the editors, ripped away at release parties, but the dedicated audience is still small: for the first issues the print run was 1,500.[36] In other words, Arabic adult comics are very much an avant-garde phenomenon. But they are an interesting cultural product because they employ a new form in creative ways to convey messages that are socially and politically relevant. Like modern Arab literature, which is also a small field, adult comics are interesting because of their literary and artistic features as well as their social and political critique. They give a glimpse into a way of viewing modern Arab life and a way of thinking that is, judging from the Arab uprisings in 2011, shared by many. The comic creators are among those who have the ability to voice and make legible their ideas, hopes and anger. Therefore, it is valuable for us to get acquainted with adult comics in the Arab world today. If Walter Armbrust's *Mass Culture and Modernism in Egypt* sees popular movies and music as a broken mirror of modernism, full of ambiguities and contradictions,[37] the adult comics are windows into a self-conscious, youthful cultural environment that is critical of social and political realities but that has not hammered out its own coherent alternative. Comics are not necessarily 'mass culture', although the industrially produced American superhero comics or children's comic magazines in the Arab world may be given that label. Adult comics often express themselves in popular ways, as in the cartoon-like comics of many Egyptian and some Lebanese artists, but they may also be experimental and difficult to consume. And the audience is not the masses, but people who take a special interest in graphic culture. On the other hand, comics are not the place for the lofty ideals and pretension found in the literary environment described by Richard Jacquemond in his analysis of the literary field in modern Egypt.[38] Adult comics are in-between.

Perhaps a good parallel to today's independent Arab comics is found in the work of multi-talented Lebanese artist Ziad Rahbani. At the height of his creativity in the 1970s and 1980s he was attracted to the spontaneous language and expressions of ordinary people and aspired to give them voice through his music, plays and radio programmes.[39] Neither Rahbani nor the comic creators we study here are *sha'bi* artists in the sense of popular folk artists, since their references are often far from folk culture. Yet they feel attachment to and sympathy with the ordinary and with street culture. Like Rahbani and so many other Arab artists, the young comic creators of today are sharp political commentators. For example, two of the co-founders of *Tuk-Tuk*, Makhlouf and Andeel, are also well-known cartoonists, drawing political cartoons in independent newspapers before and after the 2011 uprising. Makhlouf is a cartoonist in the widely read *al-Misri al-Yawm*. Andeel started working for the boldly oppositional newspaper *al-Dustur* in 2005, then went on to *al-Misri al-Yawm* and now draws for *Mada Masr*, currently one of the few truly independent news outlets in Egypt.[40] He was the first cartoonist to draw caricatures of President 'Abd al-Fattah al-Sisi, but there is much more to his approach to cartoons and comics than breaking political taboos. Notably, Andeel worked with Basim Yusuf on the latter's famous satirical talk-show *al-Barnamig* (which was shut down by Egyptian authorities in 2014). He also contributed emotional, dark animations depicting political oppression to an American documentary movie about Yusuf, *Tickling Giants*.[41] In a recent interview, Andeel nicely sums up his view of critical art, which fits with the whole boundary-breaking idiom of contemporary Arab comics for adults: 'Critical art to me is art that opens possibilities.'[42] In the next five chapters we shall see what kinds of possibilities the new adult comics contribute to opening.

3

Resistance against authoritarianism and war: Adult comics before 2011

I am addressing all of you from the heart, a speech from the father to his sons and daughters . . .

> – Husni Mubarak[1]

Patriarchal authoritarianism is an important feature of Egyptian and Lebanese society, albeit in different guises. In both countries, independent adult comics clashed with the system and were taken to court. The episodes serve as good introductions to the critical potential of comics in both countries, so we will treat them in turn, starting with Egypt.

The political and social order that was instituted by the Mubarak regime, and which President Sisi set out to reanimate in 2013, has been called 'post-populist authoritarianism' and 'liberalized autocracy'.[2] It is characterized by crony capitalism, a selective rule of law where political rights are *not* safeguarded, severely restricted press freedom, a limited scope of action for civil society actors like NGOs, and marginalization of large social groups such as the middle class and the young.[3] In Egypt under Mubarak, this illiberal political order was increasingly combined with economic neoliberalism. The regime imposed economic reforms from the early 1990s in accordance with demands by the World Bank and the International Monetary Fund. While the reforms made these institutions happy, they spelt disaster for ordinary Egyptians. Unemployment increased, and a general trend of impoverishment was in evidence throughout the 1990s; social inequality grew to monstrous proportions.[4] As part of its neoliberal agenda, the Mubarak regime introduced limited and superficial trappings of democracy such as elections and limited press freedom, to make it seem that Egypt conformed to the global neoliberal order. However, the wide powers enjoyed by the executive meant that under Mubarak, Egyptians were 'nationals of their country, rather than citizens in the full sense of the term'.[5] It is noteworthy that Western countries supported the authoritarian policies of the Egyptian regime by turning a blind eye to its repression of political dissenters and injecting massive amounts of aid into the state apparatus in return for Egypt's continuing adherence to its peace treaty with Israel.[6]

In liberalized autocracies elites are built around a strong, personalist leader who employs trust based on class, kinship, sect or region to link the elite and the security sector. Patronage based on rent (oil or aid) is used to lubricate the networks of trust and dependence within the state apparatus. In this way, modern state structures are interwoven with clientelist practices. It is an exclusionary system that leaves the majority, notably the young, disenfranchised, but they are nevertheless expected to show obedience to the state and its leader.[7] The Mubarak regime perfected this system.

It is of course buttressed by coercion pure and simple. However, coercion is seldom sufficient. The authoritarian regimes must also justify their existence and conduct by way of discourse, and this is where the Mubarak quote above comes into the picture. The reference to himself as father and ordinary Egyptians as his sons and daughters expresses an ideology of patriarchal authoritarianism. One of the effects of this order and its discourse is to thoroughly marginalize the voices of women and young people, the latter of whom make up most of the Arab world's population. The Arab authoritarian systems are deeply conservative and male-oriented, and social relations are strictly vertical, in accordance with the structure of clientelism. A system of unilateral respect for the strong leader, based on fear and submission, informs the social and political realm, producing subjects who favour the status quo. There is no true social contract in such a system: 'Crime is not distinguished from sacrilege or rebellion; and punishment is intended not to reform but to restore the sanctity of the law and to safeguard existing social relations.'[8]

It is a deeply conservative system that goes well with conservative visions of religion: both abhor cultural production and public utterances that seek to liberate people's minds and widen their horizons. Salwa Ismail has captured how this dynamic shaped Egypt's religious and cultural fields with her term 'conservative Islamism'. Its propagators work within the established order rather than in opposition to it, promoting hierarchical and patriarchal values reinforcing the status quo. Conservative Islamism relies on a discourse of cultural confrontation that displaces the social and national struggle, sustaining the dominant relations of power. This dynamic has a profound effect on cultural life:

> A gradual process of Islamisation of state institutions and the public space has ensued, with the cultural arena located at the centre. In propagating its own brand of Islam, the government has sponsored religious newspapers and television programmes and has expanded al-Azhar's powers to censor artistic and intellectual productions.[9]

Thus, in the 1990s, when the revolutionaries of 2011 grew up, conservative and liberal forces were locked in 'culture wars' that were largely won by the conservatives to whom Mubarak's regime pandered.[10] These conflicts served as useful distractions from very real economic problems. The regime nurtured a conservative, nationalist discourse that cast both radical Islamists and freedom-seeking liberals as threats against the Egyptian nation and its Islamic identity.

Eventually, however, no amount of discursive cover-up could hide the reality of the regime from the masses of discontented Egyptians. A number of factors combined to show the true face of the regime. The internal threat from radical Islamism subsided – one of the main excuses the regime used to perpetuate a state of emergency that set aside the rule of law. The second intifada and its aftermath showed the Egyptian regime to be an ally of Israel rather than the Palestinians. Lastly, it became increasingly clear that Mubarak groomed his son Gamal to take over power.[11] Gamal surrounded himself with a business elite that symbolized the economic and political dispossession of ordinary Egyptians. At this time, around 2005, a protest movement started that would provide inspiration for the revolutionaries six years later.

Enter the Arab world's first independent graphic novel. Magdi al-Shafi'i's *Metro* was published by the publishing house Malamih in 2008, and it was a landmark achievement in the development of Arab comics. Having previously created comics for children, al-Shafi'i turned to adult themes and contemporary Cairo in this pioneering Arabic graphic novel. The narrative revolves around Shihab, a young computer programmer. He possesses good computer skills, he has developed useful software and he has a viable business idea, but in the corrupt world of crony capitalism it is impossible to start a business or even get a loan. Shihab is forced to borrow money on the black market and is threatened with being killed when he cannot repay the debt on time. In desperation, he decides to rob a bank owned by a particularly corrupt businessman. His logic is simple: the bank is basically a criminal venture and so it is not immoral to steal from it when one has exhausted all the possibilities for honest work there are. Shihab hatches a plan and executes it with the help of his buddy and assistant Mustafa. They get away with the crime, but become entangled in a murder case while escaping, and their own safety gets ever more threatened by a web of corrupt police, business and media. In the end the men manage to disentangle themselves from the murder, but for Shihab the story does not end well: his buddy Mustafa takes the loot from the bank robbery and escapes the country alone, leaving Shihab with nothing.

Metro combines a haunting portrait of Cairo's darker sides, a crime noir plot, sympathetic portrayals of the people of the street, and scathing criticism of the corruption and violence experienced daily by so many young Egyptians. A central episode in the novel is a protest march against the regime in which Shihab's girlfriend Dina takes part. The regime's thugs close in on her and are about to assault her when Shihab comes to the rescue and beats them up: a scene that was repeated in real life some years later, when Cairo's lower-class urban males engaged in street fights with Mubarak's security forces and hired thugs during the uprising in 2011. In many ways, the novel mirrors Salwa Ismail's research on dispossessed young people in the popular districts of Cairo, whose life chances and even physical freedom are severely restricted by the state's grid of control, enforced by the police.[12] Shihab's violence against the regime's thugs would be repeated in real life in 2011, when Egyptians set fire to hundreds of police stations across the country. At the time of publication in 2008, however, Mubarak's government was very much in place, and shortly after the comic was released, police confiscated all the copies, banned the work and briefly arrested Muhammad al-Sharqawi, the owner of Malamih, its publishing house. He and al-Shafi'i were later issued fines of EGP 5,000, allegedly for having violated public morals. There is admittedly a short sex scene containing mild nudity in the story. However, as anyone familiar with the offerings of Cairo's pavement bookstalls knows, racy literature is not hard to come by. Most observers took it for granted that the real reason for the ban was al-Shafi'i's straightforward and harsh criticism of the Egyptian regime. Using a metaphor from the computing world, Shihab explains his view of the political system: 'When the program has too many bugs, you throw it out and start over. And our program doesn't just have bugs; it's basically a virus.'

Neither the arrest nor the fine did anything to diminish the standing of the work in the eyes of independent-minded literati and art lovers – not to mention foreign observers. *Metro* got much more international attention than it probably would have were it not for the ban and fine. It was translated into English, German and Italian. In his 2013 survey of comics as an art form, the British comics authority Paul Gravett placed *Metro* squarely within the tradition of underground comics in the US, comparing its liberating, critical message to that of the legendary *Mad* magazine.[13]

Metro was an original comic in terms of both its content and its target audience. Perhaps equally important, it inaugurated a trend of stylistic experiments and streetwise authenticity in subsequent Egyptian comics. al-Shafi'i's drawings vividly convey the pulse and atmosphere of Cairo's busy streets and dark alleys. Some of that effect is achieved by discarding the cartoonish style that typifies children's comics and newspaper cartoons, with relatively few and often thick, bold lines. In *Metro*, the characters are drawn in hurried, but realistic lines, and al-Shafi'i emphasizes the features that signal their socio-economic position. Shihab, the protagonist, always carries a modern shoulder bag containing business documents and his computer, and his lean figure, tight jeans and close-cropped hair are features that invoke the ambitious, struggling young males who populate the streets of Cairo, trying (and too often failing) to market their university-earned skills in the city. Shihab's elderly and nearly blind friend, a shoe-shiner, is the archetype of the old, broken men in *gallabiyyas* who should have been able to enjoy the autumn years of their life but are instead working for small change to make ends meet somehow. The focus is on the characters, easily recognizable ideal types in the Cairene cityscape, while the city itself is a constant, cluttered background, drawn in a somewhat sketchy style. Nothing here is clear, orderly or cheerful: it is all gritty, chaotic and dark. The authenticity of the drawings is reflected in the language. *Metro* was written not just in the Egyptian dialect, but in a sometimes coarse register that reflects the direct language of the street. al-Shafi'i's answer to my question about his choice of language is a good description also of his graphic approach:

> I want to reach out to ordinary people. And I work in contrast to the official way of doing comics. When I worked on *'Ala al-Din* [a children's comic magazine], for example, that's a degrading of language, topics and thought [...] I learnt during that time what the problem of comics was – they employed a language that is not truthful [*ghayr sadiqa*], for comics are a popular [*sha'bi*] art form, so you need to employ the language that is used in the street.[14]

In *Tuk-Tuk* and other Egyptian comic magazines that appeared some years after the publication of *Metro*, one can see the same desire for authenticity and affection for street life and popular culture. The cityscapes and urban scenes that appear in *Tuk-Tuk* and magazines like *Garage* have made some in the Arabic comics environment speak of an 'Egyptian school' in comic art.

Figure 3.1   Magdi el-Shafee, *Metro*, 96–7.

Returning to the content of *Metro*, it proved to be a harbinger of the Egyptian revolution. If the protagonist's metaphor about the virus-infected programme was a clear indictment of the Egyptian regime, the ending turned out to be positively prophetic. Shihab and his girlfriend arrive at the metro station then called Mubarak (the name was changed after the 2011 revolution), where Shihab's friend and partner in crime Mustafa calls him. He has taken all the loot from the bank robbery for himself and is leaving the country, telling Shihab that in Egypt, one must look after oneself first and foremost to survive. Devastated, Shihab reflects on the futility of any and all projects to realize one's dreams in a country like Egypt, and in a reference to his life situation comments 'we missed the train' as the couple arrive at the platform. They stand there, looking at each other hand in hand, and Shihab tells Dina: 'Let's get out of this tunnel.' That was exactly what millions of Egyptians decided to do in January–February 2011. The work has lost none of its relevance and urgency in today's Egypt, where the space of freedom is even more restricted than it was under Mubarak.

The second case of comics' encounters with an authoritarian state is from Lebanon, where *Samandal* magazine had a very different kind of run-in with the authorities in 2010. In order to understand this incident, we need to describe the Lebanese political system in some detail. In Lebanon, patriarchal authoritarianism appears in a different form than in Egypt, but it is no less visible. Lebanon's state is a relatively weak and fragile creature bandied around by the country's sectarian elites and their foreign sponsors. Since its establishment in 1943, the Lebanese state system has led a precarious existence as a compromise solution between the major power brokers among the country's officially recognized religious sects. Lebanon is a so-called 'consociational democracy' arranged according to faith communities, and no less than 18 different confessions make up the country's religious map. Of these, the most important ones politically speaking are the Shia, the Sunnis, the Maronites, the Greek Orthodox and the Druze – an offspring of the Ismaili branch of Shia Islam.[15]

When Lebanon achieved its independence from France in 1943 and became a republic, an unwritten national covenant was agreed upon which stipulated that the president should be a Maronite, the speaker of parliament a Shia Muslim, and the premier a Sunni Muslim. This is not the place to enter into details about the unequal power relations that marred the system from the beginning. Suffice to say that the arrangement was very much one between sectarian elites, and it ensured that political life was organized around prestigious families and patriarchs within the different faith communities. Therefore, votes were cast according to clan membership and religious belonging instead of political persuasion. The Lebanese civil war was of course closely related to this system, although there were several other factors at play, too. Be that as it may, the important fact is that the Taif agreement which ended the war built on the sectarian principles of the National Pact from 1943 adapted to new demographic and political realities, even though its stated aim was to end sectarianism. Various reforms in the administration and army were designed to facilitate sectarian equality, but the main point remains that all these changes merely served to perpetuate the sectarian system in a modified form.[16] Thus, already in the early 1990s scholars noted that administrative appointments had become an arena for sectarian struggles, something which paralyses political life and prevents efficiency and competence in the administration.[17] This is still very much the case in Lebanon today.

Equally important is that the Taif agreement did nothing to end the clan-based elitism of Lebanese politics. Writing shortly after the first elections since the Taif accord, Farid Khazen noted that the elections were the most divisive ever since independence, that the gap between the elites and the grassroots had widened dramatically, and that politics in the regular sense of the word was crippled, because both the government and the opposition were impotent.[18] The reason for the latter situation was of course the Pax Syriana that lasted from 1991 until 2005, the year Syria was forced to withdraw its troops from Lebanon after the assassination of Prime Minister Rafiq Hariri. Since then, Lebanese politics has been characterized by a series of conflicts and stand-offs between the various sectarian groups, now with a strong Shia component in the form of Hizbullah: as a result of a particularly paralysing conflict between the elite groups, Lebanon was without president and a functioning parliament for more than two years, between April 2014 and October 2016. In the Lebanese context, where the state is weak, and the sectarian communities are the prime political actors, Hisham Sharabi's notion of *factionalism* is useful to understand how patriarchal authoritarianism works in this country.

> A person is lost when cut off from the family, the clan, or the religious group. The state cannot replace these protective primary structures. Indeed, the state is an alien force that oppresses one, as is equally civil society, a jungle where only the rich and powerful are respected and recognized. In one's actual practice one conducts oneself morally only within the primary structures (family-clan-sect)[.][19]

Although weak and fragmented when compared with the other Arab republican states, the Lebanese state also operates along authoritarian lines, complementing the patriarchy inherent in the sectarian system. The state's intolerance of peaceful dissent was put on display in the summer and autumn of 2015, when Lebanese protesters of many political colours took to the streets to protest the state's failure to secure proper rubbish handling. As a result of political stalemate and flawed policies, the contract with a private rubbish collector expired in the summer of 2015 without anyone managing to find a replacement or renegotiate the contract. Inevitably, stinking heaps of rubbish piled up in the streets of Beirut and Mount Lebanon in the summer of 2015. A grassroots protest movement called 'You Stink' appeared, and in a short while thousands of people were galvanized to take part in a peaceful protest against the incompetent authorities. Unable to answer the criticism, the government simply chose to try to repress it, and scenes familiar from so many Arab countries ensued: protesters were hit with batons and fired at with rubber bullets; the security used sound grenades; peaceful demonstrators were arrested and held incommunicado for 24 hours. Sectarian elites contributed, too, by forbidding party members to participate in the protests and using the private TV networks to discredit the protest movement.[20] The episode illustrates the neo-patriarchal combination of impotence and repression: while the dysfunctional state cannot get even the simplest logistical tasks like rubbish disposal right, the sectarian elites stand together when the system is threatened by the people – and they have an iron grip on power. The Lebanese authors of a 2009 UNDP report put the matter simply: 'Violence is the fabric of the Lebanese system, and it is always threatening to get out of hand.'[21]

As argued in a recent volume on postwar Lebanon,

> Most men and women suffer from the sectarian system's disciplinary techniques, women far more extensively and violently than men, however. To start with, the disciplinary logic of the sectarian system denies Lebanese their existence as citizens with inalienable political and social rights, reducing them instead to unequal members of state-recognized sectarian communities regulated by extended patriarchal kinship groups and clientelist networks.[22]

Salloukh et al. describe how sectarianism is used to justify a lawlessness whereby everything, including the judiciary, is politicized. Lena Merhej, a Lebanese comic creator, argues that Lebanon has moved from an 'epoch of the militia' to a 'present era of the mafia, where neither state nor non-state armed factions can be trusted'.[23] She should know. Merhej is among the founding editors of *Samandal* magazine. When she published a story in that magazine which included an innocent caricature of Muslim and Christian religious leaders, *Samandal* was prosecuted and, some years later, convicted of blasphemy in the Lebanese court system. Nobody knows exactly how *Samandal* got referred to the court system or why, but the Lebanese comic artists and their lawyer have made some educated guesses. A member of the Christian political elite apparently wanted to make his influence felt and complained about the comics to the Ministry of Culture, which dutifully brought the complaint to the Ministry of Justice. The state prosecutor then opened a case against the comics collective, claiming that they incited sectarian strife, denigrated religion, and spread false reporting and slander. The case against them was paper thin on all accounts, but in a political system where the judiciary is subject to the interests of the sectarian elites, they were found guilty in 2015 and ordered to pay a hefty fine or face two years in prison.[24]

The *Samandal* collective had not in fact intended to criticize the regime at all. Their case shows how arbitrary authoritarian repression can be and also shines a stark light on the dysfunctional sectarian political system in Lebanon. *Samandal's* sin was to have published two comics involving religion and religious symbols, and the editors were dragged to court for having offended religious values. The 2009 issue where the two stories were published was entitled *Revanche/Intiqam* (revenge), made in collaboration with the Belgian independent publisher L'Employé du Moi. Ironically, in light of the court case, the issue was partly funded by the Lebanese Ministry of Culture through the Beirut World Book Capital 2009 initiative. One of the offending stories was written by Lena Merhej. Entitled 'Lebanese Recipes for Revenge', it humorously translated some common Lebanese profanities into illustrated recipes to show how violent and absurd folk expressions may be. One of them was the commonly used *yihriq dinak* (lit.: 'may your religion burn'), and Merhej illustrated it by having a giant, evil woman setting a Christian priest and a Muslim woman on fire (see Plate 4).[25] The other comic to which the authorities took exception was written by French artist Valfret. It was a comic about homosexuality and shame, and it contained an image of a Roman centurion standing in front of the crucified Christ, muttering to him, 'You're the faggot [not I].'[26] While Valfret's story was certainly provocative, it could hardly be construed as defamatory of Christianity, since the Roman centurion was a homosexual who tried to relieve his shame at his sexual orientation by killing innocent civilians, with Jesus being a representative of the latter. Adding to the surreal quality of the case, the man who initiated the process against *Samandal*, former minister of information Tarek Mitri, was later unable to remember why he had done so in the first place and expressed regret over the whole affair. Although the case had no merit, the defendants did not have any political connections, making them a soft target, and the judge appears to have sentenced them just to avoid trouble with whoever raised the issue to begin with. *Samandal* was issued a fine of USD 20,000, which nearly broke the magazine's back.[27]

The two cases of *Metro* and *Samandal* had different but related implications. Magdi al-Shafi'i showed that the medium of comics could be a serious and powerful vehicle for political criticism and a liberating message. The legal persecution of *Samandal* perfectly illustrated how little the principle of freedom of expression is worth when the judiciary is a tool in the hands of powerful elites. By producing art that did not take sectarian concerns into consideration, and by choosing to rely on the theoretically independent legal system, the editors of *Samandal* were doomed.

A tradition of political critique: War comics in Lebanon

Metro and *Samandal* are two recent and well-known examples of the political contentiousness of adult comics in the Arab world. However, the critical edge of Arab adult comics was apparent earlier, and in a specific genre of works: Lebanese war comics.

War comics are a well-established genre. Historically, mainstream war comics in the US and Europe featured spectacular stories about heroic deeds on the battlefield, and they were often part of war propaganda. Later, more critical narratives emerged, whether in the Anglo-American tradition or in the Francophone tradition. A particularly well-known example is *The Trench Wars* by Jacques Tardi, which tells the terrible story of World War I's trench warfare through the eyes of ordinary soldiers.

These comic creators tell the stories of others. At best in terms of authenticity, s/he does it like a journalist or historian, like Jacques Tardi or Garth Ennis. At worst, the depictions are pure fantasy, which is the case in the majority of mainstream war comics through the decades. In either case, the stories revolve around soldiers and battle, and they remain second-hand accounts of something the comic artist must try to imagine. Everything in these accounts is extreme: the suffering, the heroism, the moral choices, the contrasts between battle and short periods of rest.

Lebanese war comics were pioneered by George Khoury JAD in 1980, and they turn the war comics genre on its head. The works of JAD and later Lebanese war comic creators – Zeina Abirached, Mazen Kerbaj and Lena Merhej – must also be termed war comics because war is what they are about. But they do not focus on soldiers or battle, and they do not tell second-hand stories of others. Instead, they are personal, first-hand accounts of how war affects the lives of ordinary people.

It is not strange that Lebanon should provide such a rich field for this kind of comic. The Lebanese have experienced more than their share of war and destruction. From 1975 to 1990 the country was ravaged by a civil war where Syria was heavily involved on one side. During that war Israel invaded the country twice, in 1978 and 1982, with devastating results. About 120,000 people were killed and 1 million Lebanese fled their country during the civil war, and untold numbers of people were displaced. Sixteen years after the war ended Israel bombed and invaded Lebanon again, responding to a cross-border raid by Hizbullah in which eight Israeli soldiers were killed and two captured. In the 2006 war, more than 1,000 Lebanese were killed and 1 million were displaced. The civil war and the 2006 war are the topics of four highly original and very different Lebanese comics. In one way or another, they all answer the same question: what was it like to be an ordinary Lebanese during these wars?

George Khoury JAD's *Carnaval* was a pioneering effort in Lebanon – a graphic novel in three parts about the civil war made as early as 1980. This comic is an intensely personal exploration of how absurd the war felt. It has the form of a dream, in which the protagonist dreams that he participates in a carnival – with references to the hedonistic reputation Beirut had before the outbreak of the civil war in 1975 as the Paris of the Middle East. JAD takes a swipe at the intense pleasure-seeking and the hollow sense of collectivity that is based only on consumerism; notice the Coke bottle here. But the mood soon turns sinister as

Figure 3.2 George Khoury JAD, *Carnaval*, 12, 17, 44, 47–8. From JAD's personal archive, reproduced with permission.

armed and aggressive participants start appearing, and the revellers then take on frightening forms, as you can see here. The carnival ends in a bloodbath. Then follows a section where the protagonist wakes up from this bad dream or transitions to another, even worse one. Here, he is in the most Kafkaesque manner arrested, tried, convicted and executed in a mock court for a crime that is never even referred to. However, it turns out that the whole procedure is merely a play at

the circus, and he gets up and walks away from the arena. Here starts the third part of the story, a wordless part where language has apparently broken down and the protagonist literally gets caught up in panels that depict warfare through the ages. He tries to escape the story while the wordless, devastating warfare takes place around him. This is a particularly striking illustration of the claustrophobic feeling of being caught in a war you do not participate in: the protagonist is not an integral part of the panels, but still they persecute him; they do not let him get away from their reality.

Eventually, he breaks down when he arrives at his own home, which is reduced to rubble by war. He goes to sit by the sea, and there the story ends. JAD uses the page layout and the panels to convey a sense of desolation towards the end. The panels get steadily narrower, and on the last page there is a lot of empty space. The ending communicates emptiness and loneliness – a feeling of being all alone in a world gone mad. JAD's depiction of Lebanon in the 1970s is a perverted carnival that ends in tragedy and loss – and for the protagonist as well as the reader the whole experience remains as inexplicable as it is inescapable.

While *Carnaval* was written in French, JAD later turned to dialectal Arabic in his comic strip *Abu Shanab*. He explains this choice as part of his need to assert his identity as a Lebanese and to communicate in an idiom that felt more 'right' for him (issues we will return to in chapter 7). *Abu Shanab* ran for several years in the newspaper *al-Nahar* and featured sarcastic comments on Lebanon's political process and the games of the sectarian elites. JAD's strips promoted tolerance and resisted the elites' conflict-mongering, as can be seen in Figure 3.3. In this strip, published in the middle of Lebanon's civil war in 1983, he depicts ordinary

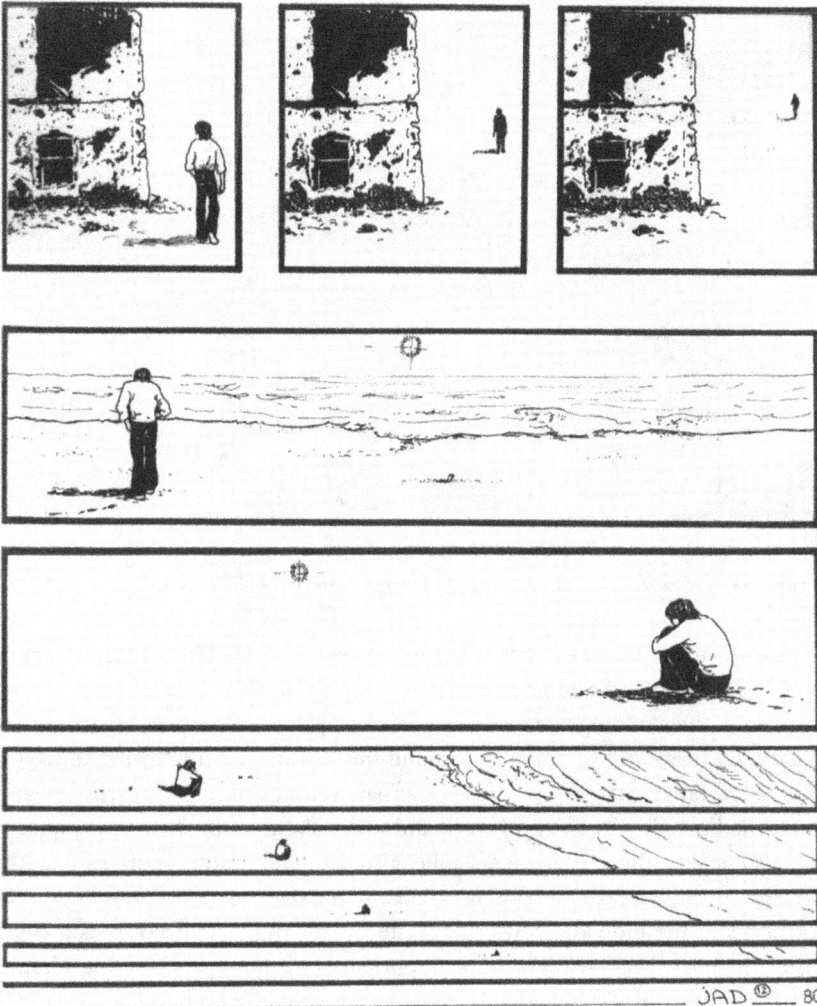

Lebanese as helpless, mute pawns in a sectarian power game, unable to make their own voices heard in the din of propaganda coming from the various factions of the civil war.

The second Lebanese comic to treat the civil war is Zeina Abirached's graphic novel *A Game for Swallows: To Die, To Leave, To Return.* (Here we will make a small exception to the principle of treating comics written in Arabic and published in the Arab world; Abirached's novel was originally written in French and published in France.) Abirached was born in Beirut in 1981, six years after the Lebanese civil war started. Her comic, published in 2007, is a childhood

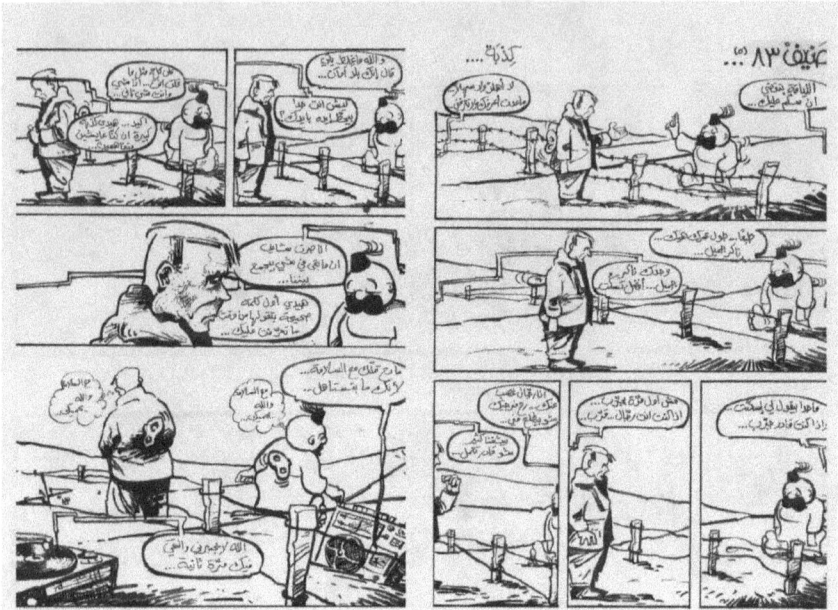

Figure 3.3 'Abu Shanab,' comic strip by George Khoury JAD.

memoir focusing on one night when her parents fail to return from a visit to Zeina's grandmother. She and her little brother are taken care of by the other tenants in the building, and all wait nervously for the parents, fearing they might have been shot by a sniper. Around this anxious waiting scene Abirached spins a narrative that shows how the urban warfare in 1980s Beirut severely constricted people's freedom to work and move about – not only in the streets, but also inside their apartments. She also paints beautiful portraits of the tenderness and solidarity among civilians trapped in a war zone in her portrayals of the individuals who populate the building she lived in as a child. Lastly, the novel bears witness to the importance of belonging, of having a home, and the sadness of leaving: after a grenade shell hits the house, Zeina's parents decide they cannot live there any more, and the family eventually leaves Lebanon altogether.

Abirached's style is two-dimensional, with clear, bold lines and black-and-white contrasts without shades of grey. It makes for highly stylized images where all the details are clearly visible. She uses this style to pronounced effect in several ways. First, the two-dimensional style lends itself to depictions of Beirut as well as the apartment Zeina lives in as maps that show how the war constricts and diminishes the space people can move in, outside and inside. Figure 3.4 shows a map of Zeina's family's apartment, which as the war proceeds gradually gets reduced from a spacious home to only one safe room: the foyer.

Figure 3.4 Zeina Abirached, *A Game for Swallows: To Die, To Leave, To Return*, 34–7.

The two-dimensional drawings also facilitate a kind of stacking effect where elements of an image are put on top of each other, sometimes resulting in cluttered images. In this way, the stacking serves to underline the claustrophobic feeling of being stuck inside a very small space, and at the

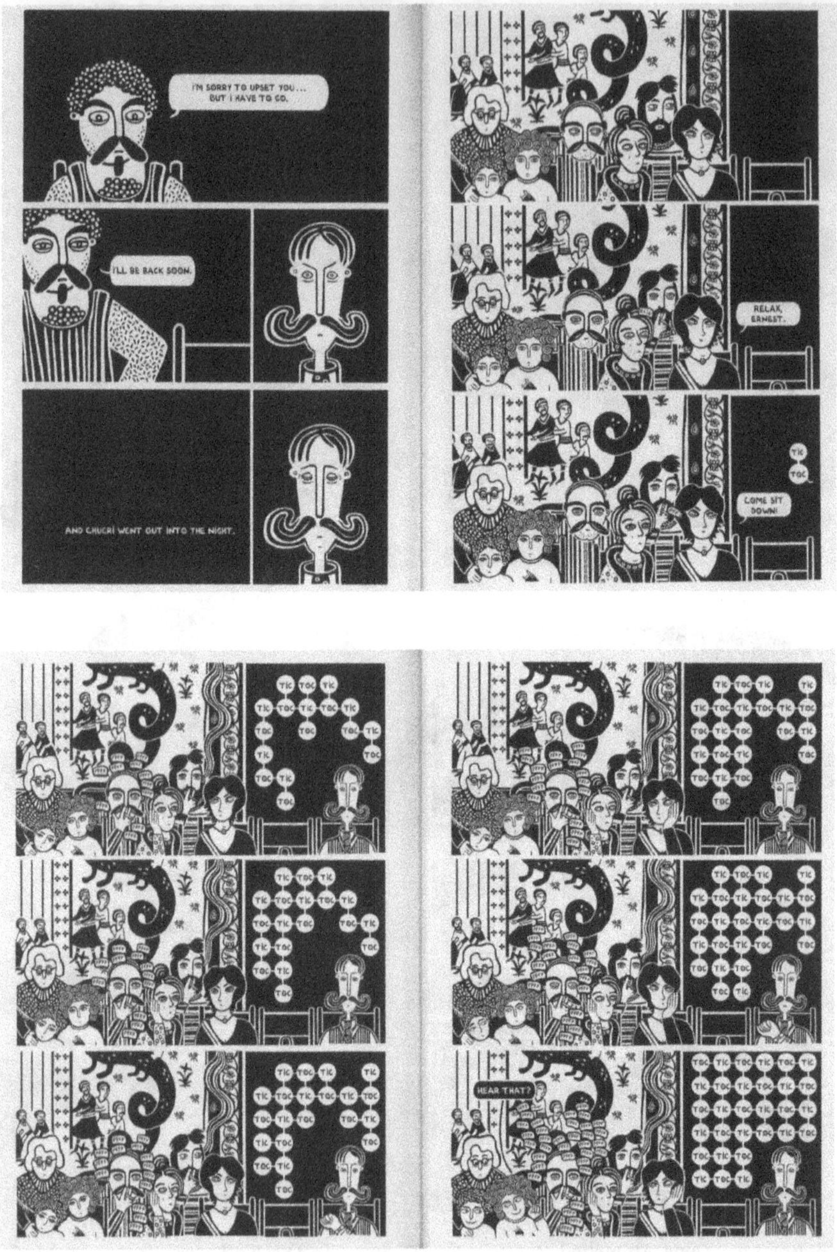

Figure 3.5 The waiting sequence in *A Game for Swallows*, 148–53.

same time it is a great storytelling device. The tableau-like sequence reproduced in Figure 3.5 is a good example of this. Very little happens, yet the panels show increasing tension and nervousness. The children and their neighbours are anxiously waiting for Zeina's parents. The parents are by now very delayed and

Choukri, a young, kind and fearless man who lives in one of the other apartments in the building, has gone out to search for them. The rest of the building's tenants now have three persons to worry about, and feigned cheerfulness at last gives way to a long and anxious silence that is dominated more and more by the tick-tocks of the large clock. Notice also the steadily increasing smoking of one of the tenants in the building. One little sentence at the end – 'did you hear that, children?' – breaks up the tableau and the next page is full of movement as the parents arrive and embrace Zeina and her brother.

At about the same time as Abirached's memoir was published two other Lebanese comics dealing with the 2006 Israeli aggression on Lebanon appeared. These were made by Lena Merhej and Mazen Kerbaj, two central figures on the current Lebanese comics scene. Their works are raw, unpolished attempts to convey personal experiences more than they are narratives in the regular sense of the word.

Lena Merhej's comic *I Think We Will Be Calm During the Next War* was published in Beirut in 2007. It is a simple account of the author's daily life and thoughts covering the start of the war and how daily life was affected for the roughly 40 days of bombardment and war between Israel and Hizbullah. Merhej's comic focuses on the effects of war on mundane activities, like eating, socializing and keeping clean, and the feelings and thoughts that run through people who are caught in a situation in which they have very little control. For example, she describes how the lack of water to shower leaves her hair sweaty and oily in the heat, and she humorously speculates about the positive effects of the veil in this situation – it conceals all the grime and protects the hair from dust. Then, just a couple of pages afterwards, she describes her rollercoaster of feelings, and juxtaposes her abrupt bouts of grief and almost hysterical mirth with images of dead children in plastic bags and refugee children playing happily in the streets. In this way Merhej shows the stark contrasts between mundane concerns that do not let a war get in their way and the extraordinary, heart-breaking suffering she also witnesses every day. These contrasts lead to strain and emotional conflict within herself.

Merhej ends the story by contrasting the violent feelings she and her siblings experience to the behaviour of her parents, who lived through the 15-year-long Lebanese civil war. They display a mixture of calm, protective care and resigned sadness – nothing like the extreme ups and downs Lena and her generation are given to. Her speculation that she and her friends will react in that same calm manner when the next war breaks out is a pessimistic comment on what war does to you. The natural, blunt reactions to the fear and the violence are transformed into stoic resignation, a recognition of how fruitless it is to speculate and think too much and that the only thing one can do is care for one's friends and family and quietly hope for the best.

Figure 3.6 Lena Merhej, *I Think We Will Be Calm During the Next War* (unpaginated).

Merhej's style is an important part of the story. It may perhaps be described as studiously naive. It is simple and cartoonish, with few ornaments or details. The clear lines of the drawings match the simple, straightforward text. In a way, it renders adults as children, focusing on the power of simple, down-to-earth

48

observations and thoughts that run through people's heads as they try to lead normal lives in abnormal situations. Yet at the same time there is ambiguity and emotional richness because Merhej juxtaposes disparate but equally strong feelings.

The comic reads as a kind of memento of the war experience, not least because of the ending, where she recounts some of the wry jokes that circulated among

Lebanese during the war. It is as if it was created to share with other Lebanese feelings that were apparently widespread among ordinary people, at least in the writer's environment, forging solidarity among the helpless victims of the war, something to say: 'We lived through this together, we shared this experience.' At the same time, there is a certain fatalistic sadness in the reactions her parents

Figure 3.7 Mazen Kerbaj *Beirut Won't Cry* [Bayrut lan tabka].

show: they do not bother being full of feelings, because they have lived through it once already and whatever they did made no difference either way.

The last war comic we will look at is Mazen Kerbaj's *Beirut Won't Cry*. Although it strains the definition of a comic, it is fitting to include it in a survey of Lebanese war comics because of the importance of the images and also because

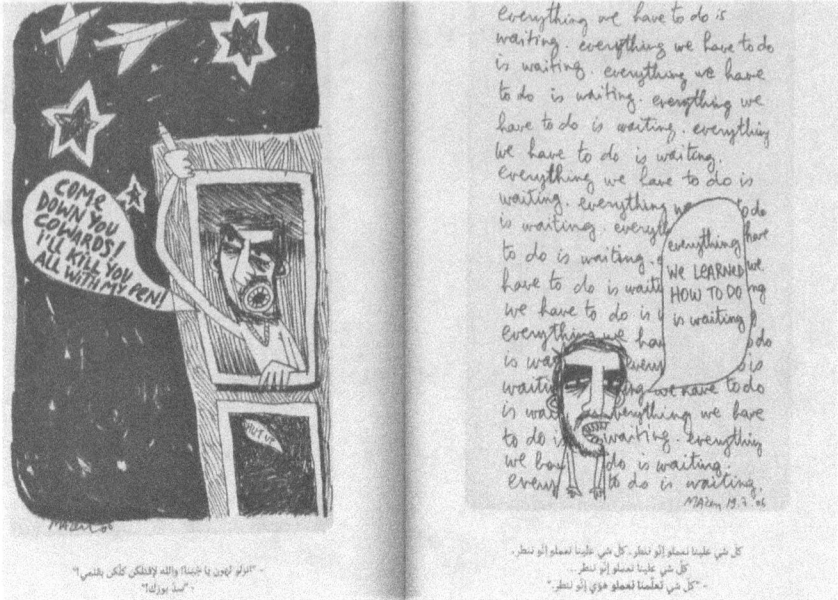

Kerbaj is one of Lebanon's most original comic artists. This work was originally a diary from the 2006 war, published in the form of a blog that rapidly attracted much attention at the time. Kerbaj's wife left Beirut with their son because of the danger of staying. Kerbaj stayed, refusing to let the Israeli war machine drive him away from his home. An accomplished trumpeter, he became famous for standing on his balcony, playing the trumpet defiantly as the nightly Israeli air raids went on. On his blog he posted artwork and text every day, and then later published the whole blog in a book entitled *Beirut Won't Cry*.

Of the four war comics we look at here, this is the most immediate and unpolished documentation of how war affects ordinary people. It is a rich work, situated on the borderline between comic, diary and art, which is typical of Kerbaj's production. He is an artist who challenges conventions and pushes boundaries. I shall highlight two of the emotions and thoughts he shares with the readers. First is the heightened sense of fragmentation when the war isolates family members from each other, and the anxiousness one feels when separated from loved ones in a dangerous situation, the raw pain of loss. Kerbaj shows this by drawing a family tree, where two of the branches are cut off: the one to his girlfriend and the lowest one to the family in the south, who were buried under the rubble of their bombed house. Secondly, he depicts feelings of impotence and despair. Figure 3.8 is an angry criticism of how young Lebanese have been brought up by the establishment to tolerate unsustainable conditions and just passively wait for things to get better. The following page is a self-portrait where he rages against the Israeli bombers, daring them to come down and fight him: 'I will kill you with my pen!' The weary 'shut up' from the apartment below underlines how pathetic his challenge sounds, how powerless he is against the brute force of the Israeli war machine.

What is the significance of these war comics taken as a whole? First, it is important to remind ourselves that they are all authentic works of non-fiction. They provide us with personal accounts of the war experience. Obviously, they cannot be used as empirical data in the normal sense. They are works of art that aspire to represent how the civilians experience a war. I think they may be read as moral, political works preaching an anti-war message. This is so not only because they show how devastating war is, but also because they turn the destructive phenomenon of war into something creative, and they give evidence of the human will to love and solidarity, uprightness, in extreme conditions. As non-fiction they give voice to a moral message. Secondly, they are also something more than the stories of ordinary people caught in war. They are works of art: refined, carefully crafted and edited works of non-fiction, rich in metaphors and evocative images. They are already representations of experience that we again interrogate and reinterpret, in the classic hermeneutic process outlined by Paul Ricoeur. And the point of doing so is that we hope that as works of art, they have something profound to say about the experience of war, that they may somehow formulate or get at emotions and experiences that are hard to express in ordinary discourse, as in a research interview.

Critique of authoritarianism in *Samandal* magazine

After 2006, Lebanon got its own adult comic magazine: *Samandal*, which we encountered earlier in the chapter. It is extremely varied in content and style, but in certain important respects it picked up from where earlier comic creators left off in terms of political criticism. From the very first issue of *Samandal* in 2007, two serialized comics addressed issues of authoritarianism, repression and mind control: 'The Educator', by Fouad Mezher, and 'Salon Tariq al-Khurafi', by Omar Khouri. 'The Educator' (Figure 3.8) revolves around a male student who is trying to make it to the top in a totalitarian society where fear and insecurity keep the population quiet. A small ruling elite monopolizes power and has orchestrated an artificial threat to society whereby sinister 'nihilists' employed by the regime spread fear among the populace with gas that makes people go crazy. Only the government has the antidote. This game of duping the populace is not far removed from the antics of the Lebanese sectarian elites, who are apparently enemies unto death, but who unite against the people when their privileges are threatened (as during the 'You Stink' campaign) and enter into alliances with supposed enemies without hesitation if they can profit from it. Mezher's drawing style is expressive and leaves little room for ambiguities: clean and simple lines, clearly bounded panels, cartoonish figures and only a limited amount of detail. The simplicity draws attention to the large eyes of the protagonists, which are used to convey moods and feelings. It also highlights Mezher's reliance on *chiaroscuro*

– expressive contrasts between black and white for dramatic effect. The story is at once a criticism of Lebanese society and a tribute to influential superhero comics, obvious from several visual references throughout the story. Mezher himself summarizes the personal, artistic and political impulses that went into creating the story:

> I first thought of 'The Educator' when I tried on my graduation gown in the last year of high school. It felt like something a superhero might wear[...] I was asked to submit something for the test issue of *Samandal* a couple of years later so that's when I made the first chapter. A lot of that first chapter rips off ideas from *V for Vendetta* [by Alan Moore and David Lloyd] and *Sin City* [by Frank Miller] but what I think still holds up about it is that it reflected how people felt about the bombings and political assassinations taking place in Lebanon around that time [2007[]...] My earlier works like 'The Educator' were a little too preoccupied with the sort of tropes that have become popular in young adult fiction these days (young people pitted against a dystopian society) but considering the political climate at the time they were made, I think they reflected a sense of nihilism that comes from living somewhere an explosion went off every other week.[28]

As a story 'The Educator' is not nihilistic; the sympathy clearly lies with the young students struggling against an evil political system. But there is certainly ironic comment, from the choice of superhero outfit (academic gown and hat) to the lack of reverence displayed by the young protagonist John Fawkes towards the Master, the Educator himself. Mezher was a student at the time he wrote the comic, and he was fed up with the way some of his classmates looked up to this or that sectarian leader as a hero that would change politics and society for the better. To Mezher, all these leaders were playing the same violent game, and ordinary people were invariably the victims.

'The Educator' seems to have remained an experiment, because the ending, in *Samandal* issue six, was an open one. The Master had been killed and students had proven their mettle, so the stage was set for a bigger story of confrontation with the whole system, not merely the headmaster of the school and his henchmen. However, the story ended up seeming like a prelude to an epic struggle between free-thinkers and an authoritarian system, and 'The Educator' never moved beyond the rather limited universe of the academy where the protagonist is a student. Nevertheless, it was an early example of Lebanese comic artists' orientation simultaneously inward (an unstable political situation and very real authoritarianism) and outward (the references to contemporary superhero comics).

Omar Khouri's 'Salon Tariq al-Khurafi' (Tariq's mythical barbershop), which ran parallel with 'The Educator' in the first issues of *Samandal*, is based on a similar idea, although the style is very different. Where 'The Educator' takes place in an undefined location, 'Salon Tariq al-Khurafi' is set in Beirut. The difference

Figure 3.8 Fouad Mezher, 'The Educator,' *Samandal* 4, 154–5.

shows not least in the linguistic aspect of the two comics. 'The Educator' is written in English, although its creator is a Lebanese who lives in Lebanon, and this adds to the sense that the story could be taking place anywhere. In contrast, 'Salon Tariq al-Khurafi' is written in Lebanese Arabic. While the state in 'The Educator' drugs the people to keep them compliant, the authorities in 'Salon Tariq al-Khurafi' deny the people sensory stimuli. Public displays of religion have been banned and the state discourages the use of the imagination. Images other than state television broadcasts are forbidden, and police and other state officials wear masks showing only a symbol to inform people of their function (a question mark for the thought police and a quotation mark for the news anchors). There are small groups of dissidents who do not comply with the ban on either public religion or images, and the story revolves around three young persons who fight for the freedom to create images and use their imagination. The storyline develops in a magical direction, apparitions of a huge Buddha-like statue appearing in the streets. Just as the plot thickened the story was abruptly discontinued after the fifth issue of *Samandal*.

Khouri created 'Salon Tariq al-Khurafi' shortly after returning to Beirut from studies in the United States. He found a country in crisis after the Israeli war on Lebanon in 2006, and the spectre of a new civil war loomed on the horizon. Having grown up during Lebanon's long civil war from 1975 to 1990, he had avoided politics in his work until this point, but just like Fouad Mezher he realized that not dealing with politics was a political statement in itself in the realities

Figure 3.9 Omar Khouri, 'Salon Tariq al-Khurafi,' *Samandal* 1, 70–1.

Lebanon was facing. He decided to confront the thorny religio-political realities of Lebanon head-on:

> The first of my art that was consciously political was also my first comics story entitled *Salon Tareq el Khurafi* (or 'Tareq's Mythical Barbershop') dealing with censorship and the separation of religion from the state, which began publication in 2007 in *Samandal* Comics Magazine issue Zero. Since then, even though politics is not the main focus of my work, I have stopped shying away from it and I deal with it in my work whenever the need arises.[29]

Since 'Salon Tariq al-Khurafi' is explicitly set in Beirut, the political references may be interpreted as comments on the Lebanese predicament. They offer an interesting thought experiment: Khouri imagines a post-sectarian society where an absolutist, monolithic state has taken the place of Lebanon's real-life sectarian elites. In the real Lebanon politics is shaped by the power rivalries between leaders of the different religious communities, but in Khouri's universe, any sign of religion has been banned from public space. However, this has not led to more freedom for the Lebanese, since now they must contend with an intrusive state that violently suppresses any other mindsets than its own, impersonal and technocratic one. This state's sinister, mechanical mode of operation is illustrated by a sequence of panels in which a faceless police officer readies his investigation kit: a suitcase that is designed to work as a mobile forensic tool, complete with mechanical arms and hands. Khouri's vision of Lebanon after sectarianism is bleak and thought-provoking: how may Lebanese politics be redesigned in a way that precludes the political exploitation of religion and at the same time preserves Lebanon's pluralism? He does not answer this question, pointing instead to one possible pitfall: a totalitarian, anti-religious state.

***

Independent adult comics were not an entirely new phenomenon when the Arab uprisings suddenly engendered a remarkable outburst of popular culture, including comics. Their history goes back at least to 1980 and George Khoury JAD's reflections on the Lebanese civil war. There was a hiatus in the 1990s and early 2000s, but then started the stirrings of the adult comics movement we see today in the Arab world. *Samandal* magazine, established in 2007, was a pioneering magazine effort, and *Metro* remains a milestone achievement as the first full-blown graphic novel written in Arabic. In several of these comics the political and the personal go hand in hand, as I have tried to show in the case of the Lebanese war comics. Political criticism was expressed by the use of metaphor, however thinly veiled: *Metro*, 'The Educator' and 'Salon Tariq al-Khurafi' are all adventures that comment on the political and social state of Egypt and Lebanon in the 2000s.

The Arab uprisings coincided with a veritable explosion of graphic creativity in Egypt, and the comics that came out of this efflorescence had a distinct style combining sometimes surreal humour with an explicit critique of political and social conditions. Self-consciously designed as popular cultural products, these comics are linked to urban youth culture in Egypt and quickly inspired similar ventures in countries like Tunisia and Morocco. We turn now to Egyptian revolutionary comics.

4

Comics in revolutionary and
post-revolutionary Egypt

Don't listen to anyone but me. I am speaking in all seriousness, don't listen
to anyone but me.

Egyptian president 'Abd al-Fattah al-Sisi, 24 February 2016[1]

This statement, so wonderfully blunt and simple, was part of a televised speech in
which the Egyptian president elaborated on his grand scheme for development,
dubbed 'Egypt 2030'. The wall behind the stage from which he spoke was
decorated by a banner proclaiming 2016 to be 'the year of Egyptian youth'.[2] It is
hard to think of a better illustration of the Orwellian order in Egypt today, where a
rhetoric of democracy and youth empowerment is combined with authoritarian
discourse and policies that have completely marginalized the youth movement
which was the driving force behind the 2011 revolution.

President al-Sisi has assumed the same condescending rhetoric towards
ordinary Egyptians as Mubarak did: he seems to regard them as subjects rather
than citizens.[3] He has resorted to explicit displays of paternalism and
authoritarianism several times to hinder any critical voices from being heard.
The quote at the beginning of this chapter is one example. Another is a remark he
made during a televised roundtable in April 2016 including politicians and
journalists. al-Sisi spoke for two hours about his policies. When a politician tried
to ask a question after his speech, the president simply stated: 'I did not give
permission for anyone to speak.'[4]

The Sisi regime continues to resort to conservative and patriarchal values to
discredit any and all opposition and bolster its own legitimacy. This mode of
discourse was apparent even before al-Sisi became president. When asked to
defend the military's practice of forcing young female demonstrators in Tahrir

Square to undergo 'virginity tests' after the 2011 revolution, al-Sisi, who was head of military intelligence at the time, justified the practice with the comment that these girls were 'not like your daughter or mine', suggesting they were immoral and deserved the treatment they got.[5] Patriarchy and illiberal conservatism are apparent in the legal apparatus as well as in specific regime policies. The government and the parliament it controls have done nothing to change an old, idiosyncratic law that allows private citizens to press charges against others for offending public morals. This law was used recently to drag author Ahmad Naji to court in 2016 for his morally and politically subversive novel *The Use of Life*.[6] Even politically innocent cultural initiatives are thwarted by the regime as part of its struggle to eradicate all opposition. The Karama libraries, run by a charity and catering to children in some of Egypt's under-privileged areas, were abruptly shut down by the authorities without explanation in December 2016.[7] It was probably no coincidence that they had been established by Gamal Eid, director of the Arabic Network for Human Rights Information (ANHRI) and one of Egypt's most courageous human rights activists.

Indeed, most Egyptian NGOs which the regime considers bothersome, whether Islamist, feminist, human-rights-orientated or liberal in any way, have been intimidated, legally persecuted or forced to close entirely. These crackdowns often take place without legal justification, but the regime has also invented laws to allow for such repression to be considered legal. Thus, in December 2014 al-Sisi decreed a new law that put strict limits on the work of Egyptian NGOs and associations. The law made it risky for NGOs to receive funding from abroad, stipulating up to life sentence for 'harming the national unity' when such activities were funded from abroad.[8] Later, a new and even stricter law was added. 'Law 70 of 2017 on Associations and Other Foundations Working in the Field of Civil Work' required all civil society associations to register and comply with its strictures, which included a ban on activities that might in any way be interpreted as 'political'. One international rights organization described it as 'one of the most draconian civil society laws adopted in the Middle East if not worldwide'.[9] Together with a very liberal definition of 'terrorism', such laws are strangling civil society in Egypt, as attested to by several reports that have been published after the military coup in 2013.[10] At the time of writing, the so-called 'Case 173' is still in progress in Egypt. Initiated in 2011, the court case targets 43 individuals – many from the most important civil, human and women's rights NGOs in Egypt – for having received funding from abroad. As the NGO Egyptian Initiative for Personal Rights succinctly wrote on its website, commenting on the case:

> The independent human rights community in Egypt is at unprecedented risk. The recent imposition of travel bans, asset freezes as well as the interrogation of NGO staff by investigative judges illustrate a clear plan to prosecute the entire independent human rights movement.[11]

At the same time as it cracks down on civil society, the state ensures that the media play the right tune. Almost all Egyptian media outlets, whether public or private, now toe the regime's line, barring a few issues where they are allowed some leeway. Those that do not face prosecution and shut-downs. In 2015, only China had imprisoned more journalists than Egypt – in absolute numbers. This is the background against which the Egyptian revolutionary comics emerged and developed.

Drawing a revolution

I documented the revolution in drawings.

Hanan al-Karargi[12]

Speaking in 2015, after the military had largely succeeded in neutralizing the Egyptian uprising of 2011, comic artist Hanan al-Karargi made a crucial point: works of art, created in a moment of intense turmoil and hope, may preserve essential truths that tend to get lost in the political fog that descends after the first heady days of mass mobilization. Comics are not authentic documentary images. They are expressions of interpretations of social reality, incorporating the artist's feelings and impressions of the events s/he depicts. This is exactly what makes them powerful and compelling narratives of that reality – consider, for example, comic journalist Joe Sacco's celebrated reports from Palestine and the Balkans, or Guy de Lisle's comic-book account of his family's stay in Jerusalem.[13] The narratives of comics are powerful also because they give the reader a lot of freedom. The reader is sometimes said to participate in creating a comic story. Unlike in movies, where the director determines much of the viewing experience (since a movie starts at A and ends at Z without pause), comics do not force the reader to move along at a predetermined pace, or even in only one direction. S/he can jump back and forth between the panels or linger on one for as long as s/he likes, in effect manipulating time. In addition, the space between the panels (the gutter) automatically encourages the reader to imagine what happens between one panel and the next; people have been known to remember comic images that were not in fact included in the story they read, but emerged from their own imagination as they read the comic.[14] All this may of course be relevant to comic depictions of the Egyptian and any other mass uprising or revolution. For example, comic narratives may combine with people's memories to create vivid images of the heady days of the uprising, helping people remember the high spirits and the values of defiance, friendship and dignity that prevailed in public spaces.

How then is the revolutionary process mirrored in Egyptian comics? The uprising of 2011 was a watershed for cultural production, not least for comic art. It provided material for comic artists to comment on, make fun of, describe and criticize. The atmosphere of freedom and boldness that prevailed for a time after

Mubarak's fall in February 2011 also encouraged comic creators to criticize authoritarian and patriarchal power structures. More than that, these artists kept the flame of liberty burning when the post-uprising political climate turned sour, ending in country-wide polarization and a military coup that brought to power the most repressive Egyptian regime since the days of Nasser. Let us look at some examples.

There are two comic books that simply tell the story of the Egyptian revolution from the perspective of the activists: *18 Days* (2011) and *Ta'thir al-Jarada* (the locust effect, 2014). The scriptwriters are different, but their theme and messages are closely related and both were drawn in the same style by the above-mentioned Hanan al-Karargi, so we will discuss them together. Although they were rather slim volumes, both books were marketed as 'graphic novels', possibly to grant them a literary aura; they were published by the start-up Comics Publishing, which is a sister company of al-Riwaq, a well-established publishing house specializing in young authors and market-friendly novels and essay collections. While shorter and less complex than works normally categorized under the label of 'graphic novel', these two comic books nevertheless added to the flora of Egyptian comics, which at the time was dominated by magazines with a focus on short episodes or gags. Written by Muhammad Hisham 'Ubay, *18 Days* gives a chronological account of the uprising, ending with the ouster of Husni Mubarak on 8 February. The main characters are a group of young activists – instigators of the uprising – but the perspective shifts between them, regime figures and an omniscient narrator. The story is a mix of panels and long stretches of narrative text where the narrator describes the emotions and tactics of the revolutionaries and imagines the calculations of Mubarak and his son Gamal as they watched the uprising unfold. Shifting between textual narrative and action-packed comic narrative, the story includes most of the iconic moments of the uprising: the first huge gatherings at Tahrir Square, the so-called 'Battle of the Camel' (when thugs hired by the regime attacked demonstrators on camels and on horseback), the human chain defending the Egyptian Museum from the arson attacks of thugs, the army's appearance in the streets, and so on. It is a celebration of the youth activists and their spirit, including young Copts and Islamists who disobeyed their elderly leaders' instructions and actively took part in the events.

The Locust Effect is notable for being the first Egyptian comic story where a graphic artist cooperated with an established novelist. For this story, Hanan al-Karargi cooperated with Khalid Ahmad Tawfiq, who is a well-known author in the genres of youth, fantasy and horror literature, with dozens of books to his name. The story seeks to illustrate the claim that the revolution was inevitable because of the oppressiveness and arrogance of the regime. The plot is simple. In post-revolutionary Egypt, a corrupt scientist has invented a time machine. He approaches Husni Mubarak and his son Gamal, who are under house arrest, and offers to go back in time and change the course of events so that the revolution

Figure 4.1 Muhammad Hisham 'Ubayd and Hanan al-Karargi, *18 Days*, 14.

does not occur, charging 500 million Egyptian pounds for the service. The rest of the story revolves around his many attempts to change the past at critical junctures. He tries to get the police to arrest prominent activists and intellectuals pre-emptively; dissuade Mohammad al-Baradei from going back to Egypt; and alert Khalid Saʿid to the danger he is in so that he will not die and become a martyr for the revolutionaries. All these attempts fail, either because the authorities are too arrogant to heed his warnings, or because of the sheer brutality and bloodlust of the security forces and their thugs. In the end, the protagonist ends up getting beaten to death together with Khalid Saʿid.

The course of events depicted in these two books is well known for any Egyptian. How does al-Karargi employ the toolbox of comics to make these stories come alive? By her own account her style can be described as 'Arab manga', wherein easily recognizable aspects of Japanese manga style (large eyes, cartoonish drawings) are combined with a distinctly Egyptian atmosphere. Three aspects of this style are particularly interesting with regard to the subject matter of popular revolution against tyranny. First is the well-known tendency in manga to dwell on dramatic scenes and capture different aspects of the same scene by the use of many images. Often several panels depict the same scene from different angles and distances, including panoramic overviews of a situation and close-ups focusing on details in the image. al-Karargi relies on this technique when depicting the dramatic events between 25 January and 11 February 2011. The illustrations I have included from *18 Days* are two examples of such visual rhetoric, depicting a dramatic scene of struggle with thugs in Tahrir Square (Figure 4.1) and the forming of a human chain to protect the Egyptian Museum (Figure 4.2). Figure 4.1 shows how al-Karargi conveys a sense of action-packed drama by zooming in on a wide-open eye, dividing up the panels at sharp angles and making it hard for the reader to decide which path to follow through the panels. Figure 4.2, on the other hand, shows a still picture that depicts a moment during the defence of the Egyptian Museum. It is divided into four panels. The uppermost panel covers the width of the page and provides an overview of the facade, guarded by a human chain. The panels then progressively zoom in on two of the protagonists, ending with the bottom panel, which also covers the width of the page. It is a close-up of the intertwined hands of the female protagonist and her friend, clearly showing the cross on the wrist of the girl, which marks her as a Copt. The man is presumably Muslim; *18 Days* highlights the solidarity between Muslims (even Islamists) and Copts during the revolution.

Secondly, al-Karargi lets a few of the images 'bleed' beyond the frame of the panel to achieve a sense of drama; this is also a well-known feature of manga style that has been adopted in other kinds of comics. At one point in *The Locust Effect*, for example, Gamal Mubarak gets angry and shouts while he thrusts out his arm to point at the protagonist. His hand protrudes beyond the frame of the panel, creating the illusion of him thrusting his pointing finger in the face of the reader. Thirdly, al-Karargi draws on manga style's predilection for iconic representations rather than realistic ones. This feature allows the artist to make use of stereotypes and caricature in her depictions of people. Some of the characters are easily

Figure 4.2 *18 Days*, p. 42.

recognizable (Husni Mubarak, his sons, and Minister of the Interior Habib al-ʿAdli), and at the same time she employs the latitude for exaggeration and caricature to depict these persons in an unflattering way. Mubarak has a disdainful, heavy face, while his son Gamal is portrayed with a permanent scowl. In contrast, the revolutionary demonstrators are energetic and have open but angry faces. The security officers and thugs are depicted as mean-looking, while the regime supporters look tired, their features drawn, even as they are demonstrating.

The net effect of al-Karargi's style is to create a simple and action-filled graphic universe that complements the narrative by describing graphically the two sides in the conflict and the dramatic battles they fought. The result is appealing, easy-to-read comic books that offer quick recapitulations of why and how the Egyptian revolution happened, seen from a regime critic's point of view.

***

In chapter 2 I situated the new Egyptian independent comics as building on the legacy of Ahmad Hijazi's art, especially his Tanabila characters. Tellingly, the first issue of *Tuk-Tuk* included an essay about the Tanabila, written by Shennawy and Makhlouf. In it they praise Hijazi's craftsmanship, but they also emphasize his critical attitude:

> From the first pages of the first adventure... there are topics such as revolution; police control over the people's opinions; the banning of opposing views; [...] the defamation [*tashwih*] of any opponent, no matter how right he is; and also the tendency of the masses to rally behind rumours, even when they oppose their own interests![15]

Shennawy's and Makhlouf's affection for and appreciation of the critical edge of the Tanabila in the first issue of *Tuk-Tuk* suggest that they consciously take up the mantle of creating streetwise, subversive comics by launching their new magazine. A thematic line runs from the 1960s to the 2000s in Egypt. As if to underline this affinity, that first issue of *Tuk-Tuk* magazine was released on 24 January, the day before the demonstrations in Cairo started. The magazine quickly went on to become something of an institution on the Egyptian and even Arab comics scene. While its first issue had been produced before the uprising, its second, third and fourth issues were obviously influenced by the ongoing turmoil in 2011. The *Tuk-Tuk* collective were in fact unintentionally entangled in the mass demonstration in Cairo on 25 January. They had just been to Alexandria to release the very first issue of *Tuk-Tuk*, and were on their way to Townhouse gallery in downtown Cairo, boxes of *Tuk-Tuk* in hand, when they got caught up in confrontations between protesters and security forces. Fleeing tear gas and the police's batons, they took an alternative route by the old opera house in Abdin Square, but were surprised by military troops who were stationed in that area. The officer in charge demanded to see the contents of the cardboard boxes. He was not at all pacified by the *Tuk-Tuk* collective's feeble assertions that they were merely comic artists, and the cover page of the magazine (a cartoon of a police officer) probably did not help. He seemed to have made up his mind to arrest the team and confiscate the copies of the magazine when he suddenly received an order to withdraw the troops from all public spaces – and in an instant, the *Tuk-Tuk* team were left all alone in the square, miraculously saved by the Egyptian generals' decision not to involve the army in the demonstrations.

The dramatic turn of events naturally had its effect on the next issues of *Tuk-Tuk*. The cover of the second issue set the tone of the magazine's engagement with the revolution: irreverent, humorous and streetwise. The cover image depicts a local Egyptian 'axis of evil' against which the revolutionaries fought: a business executive, a police officer, a thug (*baltagi*) hired by the regime, a conscript in the central security forces, and an evil-looking TV set, presumably representing the state-controlled media. The image leaves no doubt about the *Tuk-Tuk* collective's view of the Mubarak regime, and at the same time it is a humorous caricature, not least considering the exaggeration embodied by the red-eyed crow sitting on the conscript's helmet and the oversized gun barrels sticking out behind the police officer (see Plate 5).

Inside that issue, Hicham Rahma contributes a story about two graffiti artists who are tired of hearing everybody referring to the powers that be by saying 'they tell you, you know...' (*bi-yi'ullak*). They spray-paint the sentence 'No more bye2011ak' (no more 'they tell you') on a wall, cleverly using a combination of letters, numerals and the 'Franco' script in which the letter ق is represented by the digit '2', so the message acquires a second sense – 'Bye 2011' – meaning goodbye to the Mubarak regime that always tells people what to do and think. Suddenly a terrible monster appears, yelling the words 'They tell you' until one of the boys starts vomiting (incidentally or not, this scene is strikingly reminiscent of King Arthur's encounter with the Knights Who Say 'Nih' in *Monty Python's Search for the Holy Grail*). However, the other boy is immune to the monster because he is listening to music through his smartphone earphones. He tells the monster to listen to his music, takes out the earphones, and a famous love song by Egyptian crooner and national symbol 'Abd al-Halim Hafiz streams out of the mobile phone: 'Tell him, tell him the truth.' The monster cannot withstand the lyrics, especially the word 'truth', and is instantly reduced to a pool of slime. In this comic, popular Egyptian culture in its contemporary (graffiti) and classic ('Abd al-Halim Hafiz) garbs defeats the bullying regime.

Members of the *Tuk-Tuk* collective also documented the activism in and around Tahrir Square during the revolutionary process in the form of drawings and cartoons. *Tuk-Tuk* 2 included drawings of the uprising made by Shennawy and Makhlouf and commissioned by the French satire magazine *Charlie Hebdo*.

Figure 4.3 Hicham Rahma, 'They Tell You…,' *Tuk-Tuk* 2, (reproduced from p. 101 in the first *Tuk-Tuk* collectors' book).

The drawings capture the remarkable solidarity of the square by depicting Coptic priests and Islamists demonstrating together, and they also document ordinary Egyptians going about their business without heeding the tanks that were stationed around Cairo.

The sympathy for ordinary people and street life, often mingled with affectionate sarcasm, is a defining characteristic of the *Tuk-Tuk* collective. They refer to themselves in the same manner. In *Tuk-Tuk* 2 Andeel tells the story I recounted above of how the very first issue was nearly confiscated by the military, in a little piece entitled 'The Incident of the Cardboard Boxes'. Andeel focuses on how the mundane task of transporting a stack of comic magazines becomes entangled in a historic, revolutionary drama: the absurdity of everyday affairs and momentous events taking place in parallel. The absurd sequence of events is underlined by the ending, when the comic artists find themselves all alone on a quiet, deserted plaza, miraculously saved by the military leadership's decision to immediately withdraw all troops from the streets. Small lives, big events: if there were a slogan for the *Tuk-Tuk* team during the revolutionary ferment in 2011, that must have been it.

In the next two issues of *Tuk-Tuk* many of the comics continued to comment on the revolutionary process with light-hearted sarcasm. Makhlouf made fun of Egyptians with his story 'The Smurfs Are Bewildered' in *Tuk-Tuk* 3.[16] He borrows directly from Belgian artist Peyo's famous *Les Schtroumpfs* stories which were serialized in the comic magazine *Spiro* from 1958, but he draws the Smurfs in his own characteristic, thick line, a combination that underlines the intentional ludicrousness of the story. Baba Smurf (i.e. Mubarak) has just stepped down, and the Smurfs are dismayed by this news. They do not know what to do, since Baba Smurf had run the country all by himself, literally making the Smurfs throw away their brains. Many Smurf characters are considered as new candidates for the position of king, but they all have shortcomings that make them unsuitable. Finally, one of the Smurfs suggests that they should just go ahead without a leader. 'But what if somebody attacks and occupies us?' the others ask. 'That's just what we want! Then *they* will have to take care of our affairs and rule us, and we spare ourselves the worry.' After having reached this conclusion, he goes off to eat some fly amanita, a poisonous mushroom well known for causing hallucinations. The story obviously mocks the post-revolutionary handwringing many Egyptians engaged in over the new and chaotic state of affairs.

For Makhlouf, wittiness and political satire rather than elegant artwork seem to be paramount. This story is rich in text (written entirely in the Egyptian dialect), and the drawings are made with clear, bold lines. The choice of the Smurfs for his political parody is particularly interesting, since *Les Schtroumpfs* has been interpreted as a parody of authoritarian socialism or even fascism. The Smurfs are collectivist and conformist, their king is all-powerful and they are obsessed with purity.[17] Regardless of whether Makhlouf's choice is informed by these interpretations or not, the simplicity of the Smurf concept makes it amenable to allegorical tales; one can pick the Smurf character that suits one's purpose or simply invent new ones, like Makhlouf does.

Short gags were also used to comment on the revolutionary processes in Egypt and elsewhere. In *Tuk-Tuk* 4, a comic creator writing under the pseudonym

Abdallah contributed three strips that treated politics and corruption in the Arab world.[18] The longest one features a king perched on his oversized throne, wielding a stick and shouting '*bet bet, zanga zanga*', an unmistakable reference to Mu'ammar al-Qadhdhafi's notorious speech shortly before he was ousted, where he vowed to hunt down revolutionaries 'house by house' (*bet*) and 'alley by alley' (*zanga*). The king is overpowered by a protester who soon discovers that the deposed sovereign has a tail! It turns out that the king is connected to another, identical king who shouts the exact same phrase. The short strip pointedly states that the various autocratic Arab regimes are identical in nature.

Revolutionary criticism and humour in Egyptian comics

While the uprising that toppled Mubarak provided inspiration for many comics, a critical impulse was apparent in Egypt even before January 2011, and after that date comic creators have continued to take satirical aim at politics and society, while the space for criticism has steadily narrowed.

An early, no-nonsense satirical contribution is a short comic story entitled 'The Prison', written and drawn by Hicham Rahma. Rahma is one of the co-founders of *Tuk-Tuk*, but this story appeared in the anthology *Out of Control*, which was produced before the 2011 uprising and released in January that year. Depicting a generic Arab country (presumably Egypt) as a prison located on a small isolated island, Rahma tells a Kafkaesque tale of a youngster who, like his fellow inmates, does not understand why he is behind bars. He tries to get out via formal channels by meeting with the prison director and applying to leave, but his stated reason for wanting to get out – that there are no jobs in the prison – is met with ridicule and scorn. When outside authorities reject his application to leave (probably a reference to European immigration authorities), the prison management just laugh and tell him they agree with the rejection. He is then approached by a suspicious-looking character who offers to smuggle him out. In a clear reference to today's refugee crisis in the Mediterranean region, the protagonist is instructed to jump into the ocean and swim to a waiting boat that will take him to the mainland. The story ends abruptly when the boat sinks and the protagonist is depicted as food for fish.

Rahma's dependence on *chiaroscuro* and his sinister-looking characters make for a claustrophobic and surreal feel to the story that perhaps reflects the emotions of the many young and poor Egyptians who are stuck in a country that offers them no prospects. Scott McCloud has noted that comics tend to represent concepts rather than reality.[19] The drawings in Rahma's story express the metaphor of Egypt as a prison: a massive, cone-shaped form that is reminiscent of a beehive, though lifeless on the outside and, as the reader learns later in the story, suffocating on the inside. Lest there be any doubt about the nature of social relations within the prison, Rahma depicts a pirate banner

Figure 4.4 Hicham Rahma, 'The Prison,' *Out of Control* [Kharij al-Saytara], 25, 27. Comics in Arabic are arranged right-left, as they are read.

ربما دخول الحمام
مش زي خروجه ولكن
الحمام حاجة والسجن
ده حاجة تانية خالص.
ناس كثيرة بتبص على
السجن ده على إنه
أحسن من غيره..
ملناش غيره...
سهل قوي إنك
تتخلق جوه السجن
لكن صعب إنك
تخرج منه

زي ماكل حاجه وليها
رئيس ... كمان السجن
ليه رئيس ... قاعد فوق،
وإحنا كنا ملناش علاقة
بالرئيس اللي فوق...

71

fluttering on top of the structure. The accompanying text is worth reproducing in full:

ربما دخول الحمام مش زي خروجه ولكن الحمام حاجة والسجن ده حاجة ثانية خالص.
ناس كتيرة بتبص على السجن ده على إنه أحسن من غيره، وملناش غيره... سهل قوي
إنك تتخلق جوه السجن لكن صعب إنك تخرج منه

زي ما كل حاجة وليها ريّس... كمان السجن ليه ريّس... قاعد فوق، وإحنا تحت ملناش
علاقة بالريّس إللي فوق...

> Entering the hammam may not be the same as leaving it,[20] but the hammam is one thing, while the prison – that's something completely different. Many people regard the prison as being better than other things, and [say that anyway] we don't have anything else ... It's very easy to adapt to the prison, but very hard to get out of it.
>
> As with everything that has a boss, the prison has one, too. He sits at the top, and we are down below, without any connection between us and the boss who's at the top ...

The statement that the 'boss' (al-rayyis in Egyptian dialect) lives at the very top, with no connection to 'us' down below, is a reference to the Egyptian reality so thinly veiled that Rahma might as well have dropped the pretence of metaphor. The use of the first person here is telling, since the narrator is someone other than the protagonist: it is easy to think that it must be Rahma himself addressing his words to fellow Egyptians. The category 'us' can be interpreted to include the reader to whom the text is addressed, and that reader is likely to be a young Egyptian. The graphics and the narrative convey scathing criticism of a top-down political system that literally kills its youth.

Andeel, another co-founder of Tuk-Tuk, comments on the oppressiveness of patriarchal authoritarianism in even more explicit terms. His story 'The Boy Who Cried Wolf'[21] is about a brutal officer in the secret police who routinely tortures his victims to death, leaving his assistant to clean up the mess afterwards (see the right-hand frame in Figure 4.5). During one interrogation, the officer's young male victim, unable to endure more verbal abuse, jumps out of the window to his death on the pavement below. Appalled that his manner of speaking alone could induce another to kill himself the officer becomes a broken man, a symbol of a failed and evil political system.

The story's drawings and language contribute to its message. The officer's eyes – the mirror of the soul – are almost invisible to the reader until the turning point of the story, where Andeel devotes a whole panel to the wide-open eyes of the officer, who is shocked by the sight of the young man leaping to his death. Similarly, Andeel has the officer utter the profanity 'aha' (أحا) on realizing that his intimidation caused the young man to kill himself. This word, roughly equivalent to the English word 'fuck', took on particular significance in Egypt after the uprising, with many using it privately and some artists publicly to characterize the deterioration of the country's political arena (see chapter 6 for a more thorough explanation).[22] From the lips of the security officer, the word can be read on one level as an expression of dismay, and on another as Andeel's commentary on a brutal security establishment that has re-emerged with a vengeance. For Andeel, the struggle against patriarchy is central, and no less so after the military coup in 2013 which installed former general 'Abd al-Fattah al-Sisi as president:

> I think it is everywhere – I think patriarchy is what shapes our world right now [...] The whole world is designed by the mentality of the father looking after his children [...] The problem is that in countries like Egypt you can see it on a very primitive level [...] You can see how al-Sisi goes on TV and calls the Egyptian people his 'children' [...] I believe that the patriarchal design exists in Egypt, but also on a global scale.[23]

al-Sisi's references to Egyptians as his 'children' are the benign face of patriarchy; the coercive policies of his regime are the less friendly one, and it is this violent manifestation of patriarchy that Andeel's story critiques. The immediate political context is relevant to this story. It appeared just after the Egyptian Supreme Council of the Armed Forces oversaw a massacre of largely Coptic demonstrators in Cairo (the so-called Maspero incident) as well as a brutal crackdown on revolutionaries during the 'Muhammad Mahmud' clashes (in October and November 2011, respectively).

The *Tuk-Tuk* collective continued to address political developments after the uprising and displayed a critical attitude not only to the authorities, but also to society as a whole. The comic creator Migo serialized a dystopic vision of Egypt in the near future, entitled 'Yagug and Magug' (*Tuk-Tuk* nos. 7–11). Even though it is an Egyptian comic published in *Tuk-Tuk*, it is not typical for the magazine. 'Yagug and Magug' is a horror story revolving around a Cairene man, his mistress and his daughter, and their attempt at escaping the scourge of Yagug and Magug, a race of human-like monsters that appears in Islamic apocalyptic lore. They come to the earth to wreak havoc, killing and eating all humans in their path.

The story may be read as a dystopic fantasy, an allegory of the brutalization and lack of solidarity among modern, urban Egyptians confronted with a collective menace. The populace is seemingly helpless, unable to organize and stand together against the monsters that attack Cairo. Families and individuals are left to fend for themselves; the police or the state in general is nowhere to be seen. However, the story may also be read as a more direct indictment of the Egyptian upper middle class, to which the main characters belong. The grotesque and unreal monsters that infest Cairo are in some ways no more than a backdrop to the central story of how Egyptians react to the threat. This story centres on the

Figure 4.5 Andeel, 'The Boy Who Cried Wolf,' *Tuk-Tuk* 5, 22–3.

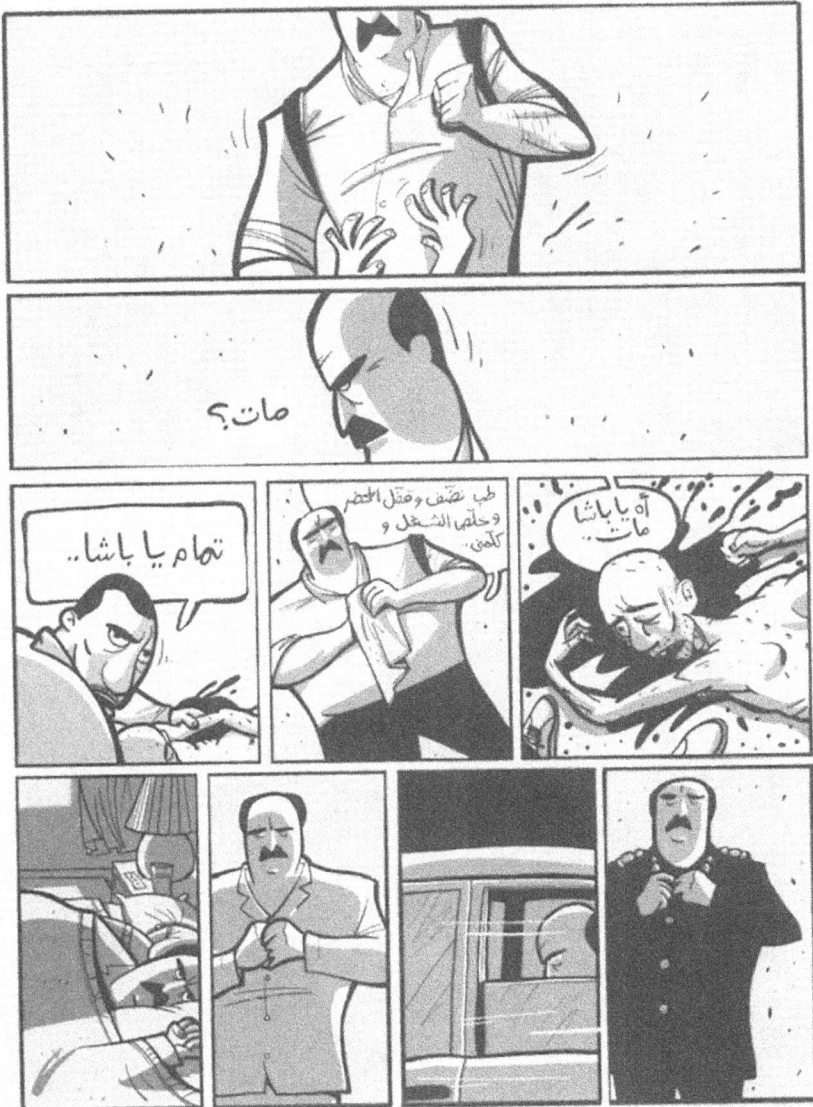

immorality of the two adult protagonists, Hisham and his mistress Rim. Both are shockingly egotistic. Hisham murders his wife to start a new life with Rim just as the monsters descend on Cairo. When the pair accidentally run into Hisham's daughter while escaping from the monster-infested city, Rim intends to knife her so that she and Hisham may enjoy life together without distractions. Hisham is not willing to go that far, however, and the three of them flee Cairo together, the two adults grumblingly taking responsibility for Hisham's daughter. On their way

Figure 4.6 Migo, 'Ya'gug wa-Ma'gug,' *Tuk-Tuk* 7, 46–7.

out of the city, Hisham does not hesitate to run over other desperate people who cry for help. His daughter cries out in dismay and shock – the only member of the trio to show human compassion – but the two adults are just annoyed. As the first part of the series ends, the caption in the lower left-hand corner of the last panel reads: 'And life continues in the world of Yagug and Magug.'

The frame layout is conventional, with framed panels and gutters that leave the reader to fill in the small periods of time that separate the images. The two pages depicted above are from the ending of the first part of the series, and Migo lets the panels indicate a cadence towards the end, going from two panels to one, and then at last zooming out to one large image. In the beginning of the story, the frame layout suggests that the grown-up pair are the central characters in the story, since the first panels in the story that cover the length of the page depict Hisham and Rim in close-ups. Throughout the story, the monsters remain part of the background: a counterpoint to the main theme, which is the juxtaposition of morally corrupt adults and the little group of good people who are dependent on them for their survival. The pair of Hisham and Rim may be viewed as human mirrors of Yagug and Magug, the devilish figures of Islamic lore that will threaten humankind towards the end of time and eventually be defeated by the *Mahdi*, the godsent saviour. A story of upper-middle-class Egyptians as cynical egotists who abandon and even betray their compatriots in the midst of a national crisis, and that invokes a well-known Islamic myth, would be hard to read as merely a cultural pastime in the summer of 2012, when it was published.

Far from all new comics have explicit political or social agendas; many may be read mostly or only for pleasure. However, those creators that do think in terms of social and political criticism are very clear about their goals. Magdi al-Shafiʻi, who produced the graphic novel *Metro*, went on to collaborate with the Hisham Mubarak Law Center to publish a comic album about the new constitution and human rights in 2011–12, entitled *Dushma* (ammunition depot). His comments about the project during an interview in late 2012 leave no doubt about his political intentions:

> We want to change society. There are real democratic signs, but the revolution made democracy's deficits clear in its first year! [...] You want to teach people that the will is free, and that the President ought to serve them. But things don't work like that now, and we need to strive to make that a reality. That's my political vision. [...] We have something that the people who restrict free thought don't have: imagination – because imagination is connected to freedom. And they fear this. And so we decided to express the problems with the constitution in the form of comics.[24]

al-Shafiʻi spoke at a time when Egypt had an Islamist president and the Muslim Brothers and Salafis dominated Parliament. His comments about the connection between freedom and imagination should be read in that context; the 'culture wars' in Egypt during the 1990s and early 2000s pitted Islamists against cultural workers and intellectuals. However, his words are no less relevant after the military coup that ousted President Muhammad Mursi in 2013. If anything, their relevance increased as the al-Sisi regime engaged in the most comprehensive crackdown on civil society (including the cultural sector) since Nasser's time. Given the political climate in Egypt after 2013, it is quite remarkable that these writers and artists still dare and are still able to publish critical comics.

Perhaps a key to understanding their successful navigation in the post-2011 politics of Egypt is their often-implicit critique and disarming humour. In *Tuk-Tuk* 8, released in November 2012, four of the stories treat the issue of freedom and dignity in diverse ways, none of which appear to be particularly politicized on the surface. But the editorial team themselves draw attention to the political implications of these stories in the preface to the issue, which reads:

هتوحشينا!

في العدد اللي مش مخططله ده..

تلات أرباع القصص حوالين

حاجة واحدة كدة!

اللي واضح إن الحاجة دي

هتوحشينا قريّب أوي!

We'll miss it!

In this unplanned issue... Three quarters of the stories are about this one thing! What is clear is that we're going to miss this thing very soon![25]

The four stories are all about personal freedom in one way or the other, whether it is the freedom to live as you wish or the freedom to complain about poor public services and pollution in Cairo. This issue of *Tuk-Tuk* was released at a time when the socially conservative Muslim Brothers and the ultraconservative Salafi movement were at the height of their power, and media discourse had started vilifying people and organizations that displayed a 'negative' attitude to Egypt's political and social trajectory. Ordinary people were expected to endure their many troubles silently for the good of the nation, and the space for public critique was shrinking. By their oblique reference to freedom which – when heeded – connects four seemingly innocuous stories to the deteriorating political climate in Egypt, the *Tuk-Tuk* collective ensured that only those who take the time to read the magazine properly catch the message.

Another rhetorical strategy when dealing with social and political issues is joking and ambiguity. Shennawy has a special knack for commenting on serious issues that are on people's minds in a light-hearted way. A staple of *Tuk-Tuk* is Shennawy's signature character, a valet who has internalized his job to the extent that nearly all situations, public or private, awaken in him the valet persona. At one point, during the tense period where the military's role in Egypt's transition was unclear, Shennawy drew a cartoon in *Tuk-Tuk* where the valet guides an army tank to a free parking spot somewhere in central Cairo as if it were

Figure 4.7 Muhammad Shennawy, 'Valet and tank' *Tuk-Tuk* 11, inside cover (original in colour).

a private car (Figure 4.7). At one level the cartoon is simply an innocent comment on how strange it feels to have tanks in the streets. However, it may also be construed as telling the military they are no different from any ordinary Egyptian as far as the average citizen is concerned.

Figure 4.8 Muhammad Shennawy, 'Domestic Disintegration' *Tuk-Tuk* 10, 18 (original in colour).

It is no coincidence that Shennawy's signature character is a valet, a simple man toiling away in a humble position. The world of ordinary, urban Egyptians pervades most of Shennawy's comics. He displays a consistent interest in and sympathy for 'the little man', and his affectionately sarcastic depictions of the ordinary also allow him to voice criticism without appearing to stand aloof.

Nowhere is Shennawy's deft combination of criticism and humour clearer than in his story 'Tafakkuk usari' (domestic disintegration) in *Tuk-Tuk* 10, which was released in March 2014. The story was originally written for the French liberal daily *Libération* and treats the issue of the constitutional referendum. The referendum took place in Egypt on 14–15 January 2014, six months after the military coup and amidst strong polarization in Egyptian society between those who favoured the new president al-Sisi and those who were critical of the military. In particular, it pitted the young revolutionaries against the parent generation. The former were deeply disappointed that none of their demands since 2011 had been met, while the latter were disillusioned with the whole idea of the revolution and a new social order. On the first page of the comic, Shennawy presents the various groups and their stance in those crucial days in an endearing way while at the same time signalling his own critical stance. Shennawy draws in a realistic style, and all the characters in these panels are instantly recognizable types. The first panel shows angry students having a discussion at a downtown café, but one of them cares more about his *shisha* than the referendum. In the second panel, some young IT professionals express their dismay at the way people are coerced into voting 'yes' to al-Sisi's proposed changes to the constitution – but one of them serenely (and quite unrealistically) predicts that Mursi will soon be back and all will end well. Shennawy then moves to the parent generation and wonderfully captures the mood among those who viewed al-Sisi as the knight in shining armour coming to save the country, complete with a radio blaring a nationalist song. Finally, he mocks the media: a journalist stands in front of the camera and talks about the fateful decision Egyptians will make the next day, while in the background there are huge billboards saying 'Yes [to the constitution]'. The story ends, predictably, with everybody voting yes, some voluntarily and others involuntarily. (In an elegant reference to his own cartoon universe, Shennawy has his likable valet stand in the voting queue behind a student who agonizes over what to vote, telling him good-naturedly: 'Get on with it, son – just write "yes" so we can go home again!') Without vilifying anybody, Shennawy succeeds in showing how Egyptians felt compelled to support the new constitution, or at least keep silent about their misgivings, after a campaign where 'no' supporters were arrested and participating in the referendum was described as a national and patriotic duty.

Shennawy's rhetorical strategy, Hicham Rahma's 'The Prison' and Migo's 'Yagug and Magug' call to mind James Scott's concept of 'hidden transcripts'.[26] When open criticism of the system is not accepted, and when those who are dominated lack the means to openly challenge the powerful, then people devise more circumspect ways of expressing their discontent and undermining power. They devise what Scott calls hidden transcripts. The hidden transcripts stand in contrast to public transcripts. For Scott, the public transcript is the 'open interaction between subordinates and those who dominate'. Here, the dominated must talk and behave as is expected of them as underlings. In contrast to this discourse of obedience, the hidden transcript is 'discourse that takes place "offstage," beyond direct observation by powerholders'. It consists of quiet nonconformism, jokes about the power-holders, gossip, poems or fairy tales and other cultural expressions that resist, ridicule and criticize the system. Hidden transcripts are part of almost all societies. In the Arabic context, a famous literary example is the story of the sultan from *A Thousand and One Nights* who disguises himself and walks the streets at night to hear what his subjects really talk about. The point here is that nobody would tell him what they really thought if they knew that they were speaking to the sultan – because he has the power to punish them.

In the contemporary Arab world, hidden transcripts in the form of coarse jokes, malign gossip or stories of injustice are very numerous. One particularly juicy example from Egypt is a joke about Husni Mubarak recounted by Samer Shehata. The joke is set in the 1970s and plays on the perceived sexual promiscuity of Anwar Sadat's wife Jihan.

> Once, when Sadat was leaving Egypt to go to America, he became afraid of what could happen to Jihan in his absence. He decided to put a chastity belt on her which was constructed in such a way that whatever would go into it would immediately be cut off. Sadat then left and went to America. When he returned to Egypt he called all his ministers into a room and made them take their pants off. Every one of them had his dick cut off except Husni Mubarek. Sadat went to Mubarek and said to him, 'You are a very good man Husni, I knew I could count on you.' Mubarek said, [speaking in a mumble], 'Thank you very much Mr. President.' *The joke teller utters Mubarek's last line in such a way as to indicate to the audience that Mubarek's tongue had been cut off by the chastity belt!*[27]

There are many such jokes about the hated elite in Egypt and other Arab countries, and of course their purpose is to express contempt for the power-holders and to create solidarity among the oppressed.

The concept of hidden transcripts is well suited to understanding popular culture in the Arab world. In her insightful study of Syria under Hafiz al-Asad, Lisa Wedeen has commented on how public and hidden transcripts together constitute a political culture of pretending. The Syrian regime nurtured a veritable cult of personality around the president, who was presented as almost superhuman and praised everywhere, all the time. Political criticism or even debate was anathema. Referring to Scott's hidden transcripts, Wedeen writes that 'the absence of open discussions of political issues under authoritarian regimes leads people to create "private enclaves of publicity."' In the privacy of Syrian homes, among people who trust each other, 'criticism can and does thrive, often in the form of stories, sheer speculation, rumors, and jokes'.[28] These hidden transcripts exist exactly because people are afraid to speak their mind to those with power, and so they signify a very circumscribed resistance with clear limits. They are not less interesting for that, especially when they are brought into the public sphere in more or less disguised form. This is exactly what happens in the stories by Shennawy, Rahma and Migo. Shennawy's cartoon of the valet finding a parking spot for a tank does not incriminate him, and it is not even visibly derogatory. At the same time, it would not have been funny without the existence of private discourses in which the military authorities are laughed at or criticized. It takes for granted certain hidden transcripts that circulate in private conversations. Similarly, the story 'Tafakkuk Usari' does not mention the existence of oppressive and predatory military authorities; instead it shows the effects these authorities have on ordinary people's lives by wittily illustrating frustrating experiences and encounters people can recognize from daily life.

Unlike jokes and rumours that are spread orally, these comics voice criticism in a durable manner. At the same time, their limited distribution and position at the fringe of the cultural field apparently allow them a somewhat wider space of freedom than other cultural products. Their message is often expressed in an indirect, oblique or encoded way, but if we decipher these codes, they provide an interesting window to analyse political and social dynamics in a region in political turmoil.

5

Gender relations

أنا اخترت إني أخرج برا القالب ده وقررت أبقى رسامة.. ويمكن لحسن حظي إني
كنت بنت فأهلي مضغطوش ا قوي علي إني أخش كلية الطب زي ما عملوا مع إخواتي
الولاد.. عشان أنا في الاخر بالنسبه لهم مصيري أتجوز وأخلف زي كل البنات.. يمكن
الناس مابتعتبرش تخصصي في الفن حاجة مهمة زي الطب.. بس الأهم بالنسبة لي إني
بعمل الحاجة اللي بحبها وفخورة بنفسى.

I chose to break the mould and decided to be a graphic artist. Perhaps I am
lucky to be a girl, for my family did not pressure me to enter the faculty of
medicine, as they had done with all my brothers. As far as they were
concerned, my destiny was to marry and have babies like all girls. Perhaps
people don't regard my specialization in art as being as important as
medicine, but for me the most important thing is that I do what I love and
that I can be proud of myself.

Dina Muhammad[1]

The Arab uprisings were replete with strong young women who led protests.
Female activists such as the Yemeni Nobel Peace Prize laureate Tawakkul Karman
and the Egyptian Asma Mahfuẓ were instrumental in getting protesters onto the
street and fearlessly spoke the truth to the authorities. Unfortunately, such cases
stand out as lighthouses in a sea of discrimination and violence against women.
In a recent report on Egypt, Amnesty International writes that '[t]oday,
discriminatory laws trap women in abusive marriages, the judicial authorities fail
to bring perpetrators of sexual and gender-based violence to justice, and security
forces subject women in detention to torture and ill-treatment'.[2] Public and
domestic violence against women is widespread. Egyptian human rights
organizations reportedly documented 500 cases of gang rape and sexual assault
between June 2012 and June 2014; and 'over 47 per cent of respondents among

married, divorced, separated or widowed women stated that they had experienced some form of physical domestic violence at least once after reaching their 15th birthday'.[3] Such figures are uncertain because of the lack of reliable statistical data, but they indicate a serious situation.

The state actively nurtures the oppression of women in Egyptian and Arab society. The Egyptian legal framework is not well designed to deal with domestic violence, and sexual assaults in the public sphere tend to go unpunished.[4] The state is in fact actively involved in furthering sexualized violence against women for political purposes. The same pattern is of course seen elsewhere, too: as Sylvia Walby writes, rape and battering is a form of social control of women everywhere, and often the state is 'implicated in the perpetuation of this violence'.[5] However, during and after the Egyptian uprising public harassment and assaults on women reached unprecedented heights. An infamous and highly mediatized incident occurred in late 2011, when soldiers dragged a female protester along the street so that her tummy and bra were exposed in a public space. They proceeded to step on her while she was lying in the street.[6] A recent report documents how the state before and after the fall of Mubarak employs sexual violence as a tool to discourage women from getting involved in activism, and describes the widespread harassment of women as a 'systemic' problem in Egypt.[7] One particularly grotesque example is the so-called 'virginity tests' carried out on young, unmarried female demonstrators during the sit-in at Tahrir Square after the ouster of Mubarak. The women were led into the cellars of the Egyptian Museum or to military prisons, where they were subjected to humiliating 'medical investigations' of their genitals by medical staff who did not bother to shield them from the soldiers' gaze. As mentioned in chapter 4, then General al-Sisi defended this practice by casting doubt on the respectability of the women, who were 'not like your daughter or mine'.

al-Sisi's statement fits nicely into patriarchal notions of respectability and obedience. These values have been used to keep women dependent on and subservient to men despite their entry into the labour market in the 1970s and 1980s. Commenting on the crisis of traditional patriarchy that was brought about by women joining the workforce in large numbers, Deniz Kandiyoti argues that women donned the veil from the 1970s and 1980s as a 'traditional modesty marker'. By wearing it, they signal that even if they are now 'exposed' to the public view they are still worthy of 'protection', that central value of classic patriarchy.[8] In other words, women are expected to adhere to the same set of ideas and values even if times and the social structures change. Kandiyoti saw this practice as part of a transitory stage in the crisis or perhaps even dismantling of classic patriarchy brought about by modernization. However, the ruling elite in Egypt has halted that transition by perpetuating an association between respectability, conservative social mores, Islam and obedience to the system,[9] and it used this value system – which has considerable power in important parts of the Egyptian public – to discredit rebellious, nonconforming young women – before 2011, during the revolution and after it. They were able to get away with the most egregious assaults. In the case of the 'blue bra' woman who was dragged along the street and stepped on by soldiers, even women from Cairo's poor neighbourhoods did not necessarily support her:

> Many questioned her moral standing and why she was in the street in the first place. She was even criticized for not wearing more clothes under her outer garment as a precaution against potential exposure. Through these accounts, the soldiers were viewed as victims of the woman's aggression and incitement and, rather than focusing on the physical violence and violation the woman was subjected to, the attention quickly shifted to affirming the virtue of the soldier who covered the chest of the woman after she was repeatedly trampled by the other soldiers.[10]

Egyptian authorities have consistently appropriated and distorted the international women's rights discourse to further their repressive policies. State authorities acknowledged in the 2000s that there was a problem of sexual harassment and assaults in Egypt, but they detached this problem from state repression (despite the fact that numerous cases of sexualized violence by police officers have been documented since the 1990s) and conveniently inscribed it in a discourse of culture. In this discourse, men, especially lower-class men, pose a sexual threat because of their uncivilized culture, and the state must protect 'respectable' women from this threat. In this narrative, sexual harassment and violence against women is a phenomenon that is alien to Egyptian society and has 'intruded' on it from somewhere else, having nothing to do with the 'true values and morals of the Egyptian street', despite the fact that 99 per cent of Egyptian women report having been sexually harassed.[11] Women who are not respectable (e.g., sex workers or the young demonstrators who camped in Tahrir Square in tents) are not worthy of the state's protection, and by positing themselves as the protectors of respectability and the security of respectable Egyptians, the authorities attempt to evade charges of sexualized violence.[12]

A much-used rhetorical weapon against the protesters in Tahrir Square in 2011 (and the Lebanese protesters in Martyrs' Square in 2015) was the claim that they had sex with each other and that they used drugs. This narrative was meant to discredit them by drawing on middle-class valorization of respectability.[13] The division of the populace into respectable citizens on the one hand and morally dubious dissenters on the other is a classic way of propping up an ideology by unification and fragmentation. The state unifies the supposedly loyal group by constructing an in-group that is morally superior, and at the same time it fragments the populace by different strategies of 'othering' against those who oppose the regime.[14] Thus, feminist organizations that criticize state policies are accused of propagating 'foreign' agendas hostile to Egypt, while government officials blame such villains as teachers, religious discourse and Egyptian TV dramas for presenting a negative image of Egyptian women that supposedly leads to harassment and violence against them.[15] It is a grim irony that the director of the widely respected feminist NGO Naẓra was issued a travel ban in the same month that the (female) minister for social solidarity extolled the Egyptian woman as the backbone of society.

The authorities are able to draw on the obedience-respectability-modesty nexus exactly because it has to a large extent been adopted by many Egyptians. For decades, the Egyptian security state and large parts of the Islamist environment have colluded in nurturing what Salwa Ismail calls a 'conservative Islamism', regardless of the ups and downs of Islamist–authorities relations. This collusion promotes 'hierarchical and patriarchal values reinforcing the status quo'.[16] It is entirely reasonable to draw a link between this promotion of a conservative religious discourse and polls which find that the vast majority of men and women in Egypt today think husbands are justified in beating their wives if they refuse to have sex or act 'disrespectfully'.[17]

In Lebanon, oppression and violence against women are not as visible as in Egypt, and Arab and foreign visitors to Beirut might be forgiven for thinking that Lebanon seems to be a liberal society that offers women more freedom than other Arab countries. There is little harassment to be seen, and girls and women of all ages partake visibly in Beirut's street and night life, whether with or without male company. Appearances are deceptive, however. Lebanese law still discriminates blatantly against women, despite the fact that Lebanon is a signatory (with reservations) to the Declaration of the Elimination of All Forms of Discrimination against Women (CEDAW). In their personal affairs, women and men are subject to different laws according to which religious community they belong to, and Christian women are not better off than their Muslim counterparts:

> Personal status laws have enshrined a patriarchal social structure that reinforces a culture of discrimination against women in their social roles and lifestyle. Personal status laws reinforce the traditional approach, ascribing gender roles to biological and physiological differences, thereby rendering discrimination permanent and unchangeable. Women are thus regarded as inferior and subordinate, while men monopolize authority, effectively reproducing the same patriarchal structure that generates and entrenches discrimination.[18]

Some concrete consequences of this state of affairs are that a woman is still regarded by the law as a commodity that is transferred from her father to her husband; marital rape is not covered by the law, leaving husbands free to rape their wives; and women cannot pass on their citizenship to their children – to mention some of the laws that discriminate against women. After reviewing the long list of legal discrimination against women, one scholar goes as far as saying that the Lebanese woman 'undergoes "civil death", in that her identity is covered by her husband, upon marriage, forfeiting thereby most of her rights and effectively losing control of her life'.[19] The fact that most Lebanese men love their wives and do not abuse their prerogatives hardly justifies perpetuation of the status quo. And moving from the well-to-do sections of society to the less privileged, one finds that quite a lot of men have few qualms about hitting or otherwise 'disciplining' their wives, daughters and sons, for reasons as trivial as having made a mistake or having been 'disobedient'.[20]

Lebanese women's second-class citizenship status is closely tied to the system of sectarianism, which we described briefly in chapter 3. In this system, women are tied in informal and formal ways to the religious community their father or husband belongs to. For women, the formal, bureaucratic aspect of sectarianism works as a double disempowerment. Lebanese citizens are registered not by a unique citizenship number, but instead by geographical and sectarian belonging. When a woman marries, her citizenship file is moved from the folder of her father's birthplace to that of her husband, and from then on, she must vote in the municipality where her husband was born, instead of where she grew up or currently lives. The absurd consequences were eloquently summarized on the website of Lebanese feminist organization Sawt Al Niswa (women's voice) on the eve of the Lebanese municipal elections in 2016:

> Suppose a woman from Nabatieh moves to Beirut for work and lives there for 10 years. She cannot vote for the Beirut municipality, where she pays her taxes and fights her daily battles, etc. This is the same for men and is a serious problem that needs to be changed so that people register and vote where they live. On top of this, say she marries a man who is originally from Baalbak but also lives in Beirut. Now, not only can she not vote in Beirut (where she lives) or in Nabatieh (where she's from) but she is expected to vote for the Municipality of Baalbak. And so, many women are double-detached from their municipalities' councils. When people complain that women follow their husbands' instructions on who to vote for, they forget that this electoral law is designed for women to follow their husbands' registry. How then are they not supposed to follow their husbands' political preferences?[21]

The women of Egypt and Lebanon face discrimination in different ways, but there is no doubt that they are being discriminated against. Social institutions, the legal system and state or elite policies all conspire to prop up a patriarchal, authoritarian order that leaves very little room for the voice of women. We may *a fortiori* assume that the situation for women in most of the Arab countries is as precarious as or worse than in Lebanon and Egypt.

How do adult comics contribute to the struggle for empowerment of women and more equitable gender relations, and how do they challenge the marginalization of femininity in the public sphere? First, let us look briefly at the role played by women in Arab adult comics production.

Women's participation in creating Arab adult comics is in fact quite remarkable when seen in comparison with the American, British and Franco-Belgian history. In Europe and the United States, women participated in comics production from the outset, but they were rarely given the opportunity to create comics, working instead anonymously as inkers, colourists, and so on. The content of the comics was often infused with male, sexist humour or (in the case of the superhero comics) male power fantasies. Comics intended for girls were largely limited to stereotypical 'girly' themes, such as horse stories. Even the underground comics, subversive though they were, were clearly male-dominated and in many cases even had a misogynistic streak. When the independent comics made by women appeared on the scene they were largely reactions to the male chauvinism evident in comics. It was not until the mid-1980s that general awareness among publishers and creators emerged about the representation of women and women as part of the audience for comics.[22] Female comic artists usually receive little attention in histories of the medium, although they have contributed greatly to it for a long time, as attested to by the works of Julie Doucet, Marjane Satrapi and Alison Bechdel, to mention just three well-known artists. The representation of women in mainstream comics has continued to be dominated by the male gaze, not least in the big, mainstream comics series published by Marvel and DC (although recent years have seen some improvement and the emergence of strong female characters, for example in *Bone*, created by Jeff Smith).

By comparison, the new adult comics in the Arab world have been characterized by a strong female presence and interesting representations of women from the start. This might be connected to the fact that there is no history of male-dominated superhero comics in the Arab world that could set the parameters for comic art, as was the case in the UK and the US. The pre-existing Arab comics were addressed to children, often with a pedagogical aim, and the aggressive masculinity that informed European and US comics for teenagers has no place in such children's comics. Arab writers and artists are in a sense freer to mould their own adult comics culture from scratch.

Women actively take part in this endeavour in Egypt and Lebanon alike. In Egypt, the notable presence of women on the comics scene is to a large degree connected to the spirit of the 2011 uprising. The gender question was an important part of the revolutionary process and continued to be so for a long time after the ouster of Mubarak, not least because the newfound sense of liberty among young women clashed with the military's and the Islamists' insistence on patriarchal values after the demise of Mubarak. Shereen Abouelnaga describes how the backlash against women after the 18 days of protesting led women to become warriors instead of victims. They started to challenge the state politically, ignoring dominant patriarchal values that equated women's bodies with the national honour.[23] The predicament of women was taken up by female graphic artists: Duʿa al-ʿAdl published (and still publishes) cartoons critical of patriarchal authoritarianism in the Egyptian independent daily *al-Misri al-Yawm*, and the artistic project WOW (Women on Walls) created graffiti pieces in Egyptian cities that challenged then President Muhammad Mursi and the Islamist movement's gender policies.[24] The first anthology of Egyptian adult comics, *Out of Control*, was edited by Rania Amin. Amin made a name for herself as author-illustrator of the children's book series *Farhana*; many of the stories in *Out of Control* contrast sharply with the happy, harmonious atmosphere of her children's books. One of Amin's own stories in the collection, 'The Glue Factory', depicts the miserable life of Egyptian street children and the sexual and physical abuse they are subjected to by older men and police officers (Figure 5.1).

Other young female comic creators soon appeared on the scene. Hanan al-Karargi and Shirin Hana'i collaborated on comics inspired by the manga aesthetic, including the comic album *18 Days* (Figures 4.1 and 4.2) and the horror comic *Death Another Day*. These are just two examples; many more have appeared in recent years, not least thanks to the feminist comics initiative developed by the feminist NGO Naẓra and its publication *Shakmagiya*, on which more below.

The presence of women in Egyptian adult comics is matched in the Lebanese adult comics scene, where female graphic artists made their mark before adult comics even appeared in Egypt. Lina Ghaibeh is among the pioneers who collaborated in the JAD workshop in the 1980s, and she is currently director of the newly established Mu'tazz and Rada Sawwaf Arabic Comics Initiative at the American University of Beirut. The JAD workshop environment (see chapter 2) inspired a new generation of comic artists who went on to publish *Samandal* magazine from 2007 onwards; here, Lena Merhej is a driving force and author of a comic biography about her German mother, *Jam and Yoghurt, or: How My Mother Became Lebanese*. She and fellow graphic artist Jana Traboulsi have contributed in large measure to *Samandal*'s artistic success. The next generation of female comic artists is already appearing: Raphaëlle Macaron has represented Lebanese comics at the annual Angouleme international comics festival and produces original and interesting work in Arabic, French and English. Two other Lebanese comic creators should also be mentioned here, although they write in English and French, respectively: Leila Abdul Razzaq, who produced *Baddawi*, a memoir of life in a Palestinian refugee camp in northern Lebanon; and Zeina Abirached, who lives in France and writes in French, and has won accolades for her graphic novel *A Game for Swallows* about the Lebanese civil war (see chapter 3).

Just how successful female comic creators are in the Arab world was brought out by the fact that most of the prize winners at the 2015 Cairocomix festival were women. Hanan al-Karargi won the award for best graphic novel with her book *The Locust Effect* (story written by Ahmad Khalid Tawfiq). The 2015 Mahmoud Kahil Awards granted by AUB's Arab comics initiative mostly went to male

Figure 5.1 Rania Amin, 'The Glue Factory,' *Out of Control*, 104.

creators, it is true – but there were many female finalists, and Syrian illustrator and art director Lujayna al-Asil won the honorary award for her lifetime service to the art of comics and illustration. At the 2016 Cairocomix festival only one female artist won a prize, but at the same time the number of female artists participating in the festival was high enough to occasion admiring remarks from Paul Gravett, an internationally renowned comics scholar who was invited to speak at the festival.[25]

Taking a genre and geographic detour, progressive gender ideas are apparent also in superhero comics. The successful Kuwaiti comics series *The 99* (which was made into an animation series) is a superhero comic for tweens inspired by Islamic and humanistic values in which strong women play a central role. The creator of the series, Naif Muttawa, explicitly states that he wanted to avoid the 'tough men, merciful women' trope, and the only character who fights with their fists in the series is female.[26] Muttawa's celebration of strong women is reflected in the Arab readership of the superhero and manga genres. At the 2016 Egycon festival (described in more detail in chapter 6), only the gaming area was dominated by boys and men. The cosplay sections and the main stage were full of women. Many had dressed up in hilarious and elaborate superhero costumes, and others sang on stage. It was a memorable experience for me, a European male not well acquainted with the Japanese comics tradition, to see Egyptian middle-class girls mount the stage and perform sing-along versions of their favourite Japanese anime theme songs – in *Japanese*, mind you – to the acclaim of hundreds of Egyptian youths.

In other words, the Arab comics environment is far from being a male-only preserve. But what about the gender-related *content* of comics? How do adult comics relate to the marginalization of women, sexual harassment and women's rights in general? Let us first explore what kinds of stories are told about women in Egyptian and Lebanese comics. Then we will delve into how and to what effect the symbolic tools of comics are put to use in these stories. I shall intentionally employ a rather wide range of examples in order to illustrate that gender issues occupy an important place in the new adult comics.

Gender relations: a core issue

In contrast to descriptions of the pioneering American underground comics of the 1960s and 1970s as male chauvinist and even misogynistic, Arab adult comics seem to have escaped the male domination syndrome that afflicted the rise of American and European alternative comics.[27] None of the Arab adult comics surveyed for this book can be said to be chauvinist. Unflattering stereotypical images of women do occur, but not to a greater degree than of men. What is remarkable is the space given to women's position in society, to women's experience in the social realm, and to the female point of view. Let us consider some examples.

Tuk-Tuk's seventh issue was dedicated to Egyptian girls and women and it contains several stories that revolve around the position of women in Egyptian society. As the editors write in the preface:

كان المقصود إن العدد ده يطلع "حريمي" علشان خاطر البنات والستات اللي بتقرا توك
توك! وبعدما زهقنا من كل القصص اللي فاتت اللي كلها بيدور في عالم الذكور المُقرف
ده! في الآخر.. العدد طلع زي ما إنتوا شايفين كدة

> The intention was for this issue to be a 'women's' issue, for the benefit of the girls and women who read *Tuk-Tuk*! We were fed up with the previous stories, all of which revolve around that putrid world of males! And in the end... the issue ended up looking like what you see here!

The issue features four stories that either take a female view of social relations or explicitly treat gender relations and the oppression of women. 'Miss Limma' is a satirical comment on the discrepancy between female fantasies of marriage and the ugly reality.[28] Featuring a lonely female landlady and her married male tenant, it is set in a lower-middle-class neighbourhood, and it revels in elements of folk culture, such as the belief in magic and verbal virtuosity, the latter being evident in elegant wordplays and rhymed narrative. Mr 'Abduh is a coarse man who abuses his wife verbally and physically. However, towards the landlady, Mahasin, he is all deference because he is always late with the rent. The landlady is a widow and dreams of having a man, children and a happy married life. She is also quite unscrupulous in her pursuit of happiness, so she goes to a sorcerer to make Mr 'Abduh's wife disappear so she can have the man for herself. Everything goes according to plan, but from the moment they are married, her new husband starts yelling at her and beating her whenever the *mulukhiyya* is not to his taste or the breakfast is not ready before he wakes up, or even when his tie is not ironed – despite the fact that he never wears a tie. In the end, the landlady makes the sorcerer reverse the magic, so that she is freed from the grip of the abuser. She then starts renting out to single females.

If 'Miss Limma' is typical of the funny, street-level tone of many Egyptian comics, the second story, 'A Private Affair' ('Usarri'), is very different. Here, the tone is realist, and the images are manipulated photographs, with text in speech balloons. They tell the story of a young man who can hear the next-door couple arguing and the husband starting to beat his wife. Too timid to intervene, the protagonist looks up the number for a hotline for women who are subject to domestic violence and slips a note under the door of his neighbours' apartment. This only makes things worse for the poor woman, since her husband finds the note, goes into a rage and starts hitting her again. Hearing the woman sob, the young man says to himself: 'Next time, God willing, I will do something.' The last image is rendered out of focus, as a visual comment on his lack of resolve and courage. It is a bleak story of male violence and cowardice. The next two stories in this issue of *Tuk-Tuk* will be treated in some more detail shortly. Here I shall only mention that 'Shawk' (thorn) is a wordless, allegorical comic that depicts women as fruits that are peeled and eaten by men, while 'What a Disgrace' (*al-'ar bi l-zayt al-harr*) combines the problem of sexual harassment with the issue of violence in southern Egypt, featuring a harasser who is killed by the family of the offended girl.

The *Tuk-Tuk* special issue was not just an exception to a rule of male domination in the new comics. The medium has in fact been put to use explicitly in the cause of women's empowerment. In 2014, the Egyptian women's rights organization Naẓra published the first issue of a comic magazine entitled *Shakmagiya* (a second issue was published online only on the website Kotobna.net in 2016). Naẓra describes itself as an organization that advocates the integration of young women and men in the public and political sphere and that supports women and human rights activists by providing legal, psychological and medical support. It places particular emphasis on the role of art in raising awareness about women's rights and the importance of an inclusive, free and democratic public sphere (see Plate 6).[29]

The first issue of *Shakmagiya*, which may be loosely translated as 'treasure chest' – it is an ornamented wooden box filled with family memorabilia that is found in many Arab homes – takes on the issue of physical, sexualized violence against women in Egypt. It was published at a time when the problem of sexual harassment was increasingly being recognized as a serious one in Egyptian media, and the magazine contains a text-only section that describes in detail the anti-harassment law recently put in force by the Egyptian authorities. Most of the content is comics, however, and they are made by women and men, including some from the *Tuk-Tuk* environment. Some of the stories are funny, such as 'The Evolution of the Egyptian Woman', in which Egyptian women have become monsters with no hair but eyes all over their skull and many arms. A depressed male teacher informs his class of deformed female students and that this evolution has occurred as a result of the constant harassment to which women are subject. First, she lost her hair so that harassers would not be attracted to her and grab her by it. Then her eyes started popping up all over her skull in order for her to spot threats in every direction early enough to escape. The final stage of the evolution was the additional arms and giant mouth, which made her capable of carrying her purse while fighting off harassers and screaming loud enough to scare them off.

Another tragicomic story tells of the woman who is beaten by her husband. She can take it no more, but to obtain a divorce she needs proof, and it is exceedingly hard to prove that she is beaten. In her desperation, she turns to two male friends and asks them to hide in the apartment to catch the husband red-handed. This doesn't get the better of the husband, who discovers the two men, grabs them by their collars and brings them outside, informing the neighbourhood that his wife has been unfaithful with no less than two men simultaneously while he was out of the house! In addition to the theme of violence and harassment the magazine contains two short fantasy stories. The first is set in a world where men have been wiped out because of a virus and only the women remain. Its message is that hatred and bigotry are found in both sexes and that the struggle for a better world is a struggle against evil persons of either sex rather than against one sex or the other. The second tells the story of a sultan who lets the sultanate's women suffer the consequences of his wazir's corruption and incompetence. In a dream he is subjected to the same unfair and cruel treatment he has reserved for the women in his realm.

Shakmagiya's second issue was very varied, and if there is a common theme to the stories it would perhaps be the importance of following one's dreams. Each of the stories is preceded by a short author's foreword, and the quote at the beginning of this chapter is from the foreword to the story 'A Critical Painting', in which a young girl recounts how she taught the rest of the family to appreciate that art is as good an occupation as any other. This second issue also includes stories told from a male perspective – such as the poor young man who inadvertently boards the women-only carriage on the metro and is verbally abused by a crowd of angry women – but the main preoccupation is with women's experiences in a male-dominated society.

The fact that there is a comic magazine devoted mostly to women's rights and women-related issues does not mean that women lead a marginalized existence in other comic outlets. *Shakmagiya*'s appearance was part of a general surge in attention to women's rights and sexualized violence in Egypt in 2011–13. The revolution made possible an unprecedented freedom of speech, and women started to speak in public about their experiences of sexual harassment and violence. After the accession to power of the Muslim Brothers in 2012 the media eagerly welcomed the gender issue as one way among many to heap blame and criticism on the Islamist government, and so there was continued attention to the issue of women's rights. There is no lack of strong female characters in Egyptian comics. As noted in chapter 2, many Egyptian comic creators have a predilection for graphic and textual hyperbole combined with caricatures of ordinary life characters, probably not unrelated to the raucous humour often seen in popular theatre productions or comedy movies. In several Egyptian comic stories men are dominated by women, but the stories are not necessarily feminist or especially preoccupied with gender issues – they just seem to take for granted that women may be strong public figures. Consider, for example, the character Rabab, in the story of the same title written by Tawfiq. In this story a pathetic male employee at a commercial film studio is bullied about by Rabab, his female boss.

Rabab is an impossibly big woman, sporting a huge, multi-layered fancy hijab, and her mouth is also oversized – everything about the way she is drawn suggests aggressive domination and self-confidence. Her employee Mr Hisham, on the other hand, is a small, thin man who is constantly harassed by all those around him.

Similarly, Anwar's story 'Umm Sudfa's House' (*Tuk-Tuk* 9) describes female steadfastness in the face of marginalization and vilification. An unsympathetic and violent business owner and landlord tries to extract the monthly rent from one of

Figure 5.2 Tawfiq, 'Rabab,' *It Really Happened* [Hadatha bi-l-fi'l], 202–3.

his tenants, an old wheelchair-bound lady whose apartment is on the first floor, isolating her from the rest of the village because she cannot descend the stairs. She has quite undeservedly been made into the bogeywoman of the neighbourhood and is feared by all the men. It is clear where the sympathy of the author lies: while the men shout abuse at both her and each other, she never utters a word, and the fact that she lives on the first floor makes for perspectives where she always looks down on men from her balcony while they always look up at her. The complete lack of any other female characters in the story contributes to the impression that the old woman is alone against a whole neighbourhood of hostile males. She wins, though: the staircase to her apartment collapses because of the lack of maintenance, leaving the landlord unable to get inside her apartment to claim his rent. He is reduced to shouting at her from the street while she stoically waters a cactus on the balcony at the end of the story.

Female experiences are important in Lebanese comics, too. The most obvious and interesting example of the strong presence of women in Lebanese comics is perhaps Lena Merhej's biography of her German mother, entitled *Murabba wa-Laban aw: Kayfa Asbahat Ummi Lubnaniyya* (jam and yoghurt, or: how my mother became Lebanese) (Figure 5.4). This story, which was serialized in *Samandal* and later published as a graphic novel, is an attempt to understand a remarkable German woman who came to Lebanon in the 1970s: what makes her 'tick' and how she has influenced her children and surroundings. Deeply personal, it is also the author's attempt to come to grips with her relationship to her mother and the experience of growing up in the midst of a civil war that lasted for 15

Figure 5.3 Anwar, 'Bayt Umm Sudfa,' *Tuk-Tuk* 9, 37.

years. The title is an allusion to her mother's German habit of combining sweet jam and sour yoghurt, which looks very strange to young Lena (the Lebanese habit being to combine yoghurt with vegetables like cucumber and *za'tar*, the famous Levantine condiment). Merhej's German mother is a character that is difficult to pin down or fit into a classification scheme of female stereotypes. Figure 5.4 shows young Lena's puzzlement at her father's phrase 'I have to remember that I didn't marry an Oriental [*sharqi*] woman' whenever her mother leaves the apartment early in the morning to go to work. It is not only the fact that her mother is German that makes her different, but also her strong personality and the curious combination of affection and sternness she displays towards her children.

Lena Merhej's mother is an enigmatic character, while the bossy film studio director in *Rabab* is an immediately recognizable Egyptian type. What the two stories and the many other tales that lie somewhere between them have in common is that they relate female experiences of the social world, a world dominated by (often violent) men – 'men with guns', as Merhej has put it.[30] These stories give voice to women.

When the comic creators are men and the genre is closer to mainstream thriller/hero stories, women are often 'mainstreamed' into the narrative. Such is the case with the two Lebanese mystery/thriller stories we looked at in chapter 3. Omar Khouri's 'Salon Tariq al-Khurafi', serialized in *Samandal* issues one to five, is a classic anti-authoritarian piece of fiction in which two young women and a man play the central roles as underground activists against a regime that forbids images. Likewise, in 'The Educator', also serialized in *Samandal*, the author relies on a girl to push the story forward. 'The Educator' exhibits influence from Alan Moore's famous graphic novel *V for Vendetta*. In the latter, which is a bleak future vision of England succumbed to fascism, a mysterious man wearing a Guy Fawkes mask teaches a young girl how to fight the system by assassinating its representatives. In 'The Educator', the roles are partly reversed: here, a male protagonist joins the battle against a *1984*-like totalitarian system, drawn into the action by a girl.

Slapstick humour and exaggerations

Having established that gender relations is a prominent issue in independent adult comics, we now move on to look at how comic artists approach it. Humour is an obvious place to start, since comics have a long tradition of playing on stereotypes, prejudice, satire and exaggeration for humorous effect. This tendency is related to cartoons and superhero comics first and foremost. In the Disney universe Uncle Scrooge with his money bin is a parody of the American tycoon stereotype, while Gladstone Gander is the dandy cousin everybody loves to hate. Scott Adams's strips on modern corporate culture in *Dilbert* are an example of how satire, stereotypes and exaggeration come together in comic strips for adults. The superhero genre is by definition exaggerating, with its tricot-wearing characters, impossible bodies and supernatural abilities. Superhero comics are a cherished object for ridicule in funny comic strips and independent comics alike. In the United States, *MAD* magazine revelled in parodies of such stories. In fact,

Figure 5.4 Lena Merhej, *Jam and Yoghurt, or: How My Mother Became a Lebanese* [Murabba wa-laban, aw: kayfa asbahat ummi lubnaniyyatan], 25.

an independent, Egyptian version of the magazine appeared in 2015, entitled, simply, *Majnun* (mad).

When it comes to gender issues, some of the funniest stories have appeared in *Tuk-Tuk* and are the creations of Makhlouf, who also works as cartoonist for the Egyptian daily *al-Misri al-Yawm*. Makhlouf has a knack for wild hyperbole, and his interest in sexuality is well above the average for Egyptian comics. His taste for the absurd, coupled with a clear concern about gender issues (he is the creator of the photographic wife-abuse story described above), has produced interesting results. Let us consider two short stories by him.

'al-Laban al-Sihri' (the magic milk, *Tuk-Tuk* 5, pp. 5–16) is one of the more surreal stories to have appeared in *Tuk-Tuk*.

For unexplained (and probably inexplicable) reasons Santa Claus has come to Cairo to deliver presents. He is not happy about it, though. There are no chimneys, the houses are too small and too close to each other and the streets are never empty of people, all of which is making his work difficult. In addition, young men in the street taunt him. Dejected, he sits down on the pavement, and then an old man approaches him to help, suggesting he relieves himself of his presents on board a bus, because there he will surely find people that really deserve a gift. Once on the bus, Santa Claus experiences the daily nightmare of so many middle- and lower-class Egyptians. The bus is very hot and full of people who are forced to squeeze together to make enough room for all the passengers. Santa Claus accidentally bumps into a lady because of the throng of people. He excuses himself, but soon starts enjoying rubbing against the woman, and from then on,

Figure 5.5   Makhlouf, 'The Magic Milk' [al-laban al-sihri], *Tuk-Tuk* 5, 8–9.

he starts hunting girls. Enter Super Makh, a ridiculous parody of Superman, with a hairstyle inspired by 1970s fashion and a floral-embroidered cape that drapes his less-than-muscular body. He hears a cry for help by a young veiled woman being chased by Santa Claus. Makh takes on Santa and saves the girl, but is beaten nearly to death by Father Christmas in the process (Santa uses Christmas candy as a weapon). 'Get me some of Umm Tartar's milk!' croaks Super Makh. The grateful girl runs off to get the milk. On the way, she must brave angry dogs and fight it out with a petty criminal. Eventually, the girl arrives at the faraway kiosk of Umm Tartar, who sells a special kind of milk with cardamom. 'For superheroes: it renews your life!' says the advertisement on the side of the little kiosk. Having drunk the milk, Super Makh returns to his old self, but he now has an admiring and very talkative girl to contend with. Super Makh is in no mood to talk or get into a relationship, but he is unable to escape. The story ends as they walk off together, she chattering happily away about how she looks forward to getting to know him better, while Super Makh sulkily tells himself that the best punishment for Santa Claus would have been to leave him with the girl.

This story is obviously connected to the serious issue of sexual harassment, which has received an increasing amount of attention in Egypt in the years leading up to and after the revolution in 2011. In particular, the key episode on the bus brings to mind the movie *Cairo 678* (2010). This movie, which won awards at the film festivals in Dubai (2010) and Montpellier (2012), depicts how three women struggle against sexual harassment in a society that tends to blame the victims. Some of the central scenes take place on bus no. 678 (hence the title of the movie). During her daily commuting to and from work on this overcrowded bus, a lower-middle-class woman repeatedly experiences men groping her – a well-known scourge of Cairo's public transport system. It is often difficult to identify the harasser for a woman since people are standing packed next to each other, and even if she does know who did it, it is hard to prove that he intended to harass her, since people inevitably bump into each other during the bus ride. Despairing of her daily humiliation and her inability to catch her tormentors red-handed, the woman starts piercing their groin with a penknife when they try to molest her. From there, the action proceeds with a lot of darkness and melodrama.

Published in 2012, Makhlouf's story might be an attempt to treat the issue of harassment in a more light-hearted way while paying homage to the movie, or conversely, to mock its melodramatic tone – or possibly both. In any case, there is no doubt where Makhlouf's sympathy lies. Santa Claus is depicted as progressively more sleazy and uncouth as Makhlouf devotes a full page to three scenes of him chasing young girls in the streets of Cairo, employing classic harassment language.

However, there is also a certain ambiguity, brought about in part by the use of panel size and frames. When Santa Claus first bumps into the woman on the bus, she does not appear to get angry; in fact, she seems to like it. At this point the frames disappear and half a page is devoted to a picture of Santa Claus and the woman rubbing against each other, without any other people around them, stars and flowers dotting the empty background. The thoughts of both are represented by symbols, perhaps to avoid direct language: the thought balloon from Santa Claus pictures a pillow as he rubs against her buttocks, while that of the woman pictures a pencil – both are unambiguous symbols for words that seem to be unspeakable even in the context of an adult comic. At the bottom-left part of this image is an inset frame picturing Santa Claus with an oily smile, saying, 'Now why do they say that there's no freedom in Egypt?' This last picture and the inset may suggest that Santa Claus's experience with the woman is just a figment of his own feverish, sexual imagination: suddenly he and the woman are alone in a separate universe, outside the frames which define the reality on the bus. It is impossible to know, of course. An alternative interpretation is that Makhlouf suggests that women are as sexually frustrated as men and might enjoy the possibilities that arise (this very idea also appears towards the end of *Cairo 678*), but that consent is a requisite for any sexually loaded behaviour, and that Egyptian men do not respect this precondition, as Santa Claus's hunt for women in the streets of Cairo shows.

An earlier story by Makhlouf, also in *Tuk-Tuk*, is no less ambiguous. In 'Shay fi sadri' (something in my chest, *Tuk-Tuk* 1, pp. 14–16) the protagonist is a cartoonist who is unable to work because his attention-demanding wife pesters him. He has finally got some time for himself and sits down at his desk, but she arrives home early with a surprise: she has had cosmetic surgery, enlarging her breasts. She insists on flirting with him, asking him to massage her breasts, but he thinks the surgery was totally unnecessary and in any case he just wants to work. When she does not get the attention she hopes for, she yells at him to make him answer. He snaps and kills her by driving his pencil into her belly. At this point he suddenly sees her enlarged breasts as if for the first time and starts massaging them, mesmerized, spittle coming out of his mouth. The twist in the story is how suddenly his attitude to her changes: as long as she lives and talks, she is just a nuisance, a talking machine (she is in fact drawn with a human body and a radio transmitter for a head in one of the panels). The protagonist takes no interest in her as a human being, and snaps when she demands his attention. As soon as she becomes only a body, however, he is consumed with lust. The consistent drawing of the woman as much bigger than the man underlines the obsession with women in male-dominated mainstream culture. A cursory look at popular music video clips from Egypt illustrates the point. A typical video features a slick young man talking dirty to a belly-dancing woman, wearing next to nothing and dancing suggestively.[31] The enormous breasts may be interpreted as the male obsession with female body parts, to the extent that men cannot concentrate on anything else when women are around them. The protagonist is literally squeezed between her breasts. A hand comes out between them as he implores her to stop: 'Baby, please, I have work to do.' The woman in this story seems to function as an allusion to the male obsession with women's bodies.

Again, as in 'al-Laban al-Sihri', another reading is possible. One may justifiably raise the question of who is being ridiculed here. The woman is not depicted in particularly flattering terms, and it is she who happily announces that she has had breast enlargement surgery, while he says that he liked the body she had. Moreover, he is trying to get some work done, while she seems to have all the time in the world for doing nothing serious. Might one not read the story as a comment on female obsession with the body and an unbearable female lightness?

One reason such ambiguities arise is that everything in Makhlouf's comic universe is ridiculous. He seems to treat any and all issues tongue-in-cheek. None of his characters are portrayed in a particularly sympathetic light, including women, whether it is the body-fixated girl who has fixed her breasts in the story 'Shay fi sadri' or the talkative hijab-wearing girl in 'al-Laban al-Sihri'. However, it is the men who receive the brunt of the ridicule. The not so heroic Super Makh in his pyjama outfit and the sweaty, dishevelled Santa Claus are both laughable characters obsessed with themselves despite their pretensions to do good for others. As for the story 'Shay fi sadri', it would be hard to sustain a misogynistic reading of it considering Makhlouf's professional activities and the environment of which he is part. Makhlouf participated in the first issue of the feminist comic magazine *Shakmagiya* with a cartoon that depicts a nervous woman walking the street wrapped in a cardboard box that has a 'fragile – handle with care' symbol on it (p. 37), a critical reference to the disrespect with which women are treated in public spaces as well as the view of women as objects. Later, he was hired to instruct up-and-coming comic artists in a workshop that resulted in the second issue of *Shakmagiya*. He has also treated the issue of domestic abuse, as mentioned above.

It is true that in both 'al-Laban al-Sihri' and 'Shay fi sadri' Makhlouf ridicules both sexes and draws on traditional gender roles: the man is the actor, the doer; the woman is the devoted lover or hanger-on. However, he breaks suddenly with this picture when the girl in 'al-Laban al-Sihri' goes to get the magic milk. She encounters a big, brutish robber, and suddenly she becomes an aggressive, self-confident fighter. While Super Makh could not handle even Santa Claus, she single-handedly fights and beats the robber. As soon as she is back with Super Makh she reverts to her old passive role. This element of the story may be read as a sarcastic comment on how traditional gender roles imprison women in a dependent position.

A final comment on Makhlouf's approach to gender roles concerns language. Both Super Makh and the girl he saves swear, using the word *aha*, which translates roughly as *fuck*, or *what the fuck*. The girl uses it to comment on Santa Claus's sexual harassment, saying, 'The guys have clearly gone crazy – fuck!' ('A7A! الرجالة اتهبلت باين'). Super Makh uses the same word, also written in Latin letters, to comment on the girl's request to touch his muscles towards the end of the story. I will have more to say about the use of profanities later, in chapter 6. Here, I will merely note that swearing is clearly unseemly behaviour for superheroes as well as their girlfriends, and it works to satirize the superhero genre as well as to ridicule the supposedly gallant character of Super Makh.

Let us turn to the Lebanese context again. The content of *Samandal* is clearly coloured by the harrowing experience of war, and most of this is not funny at all. Many stories over the 16 issues published to date (December 2016) revolve around ordinary men, women and children's experience of living in a war zone. The title of Lena Merhej's academic article 'Men with Guns', about cultural depictions of the civil war after 1991, signals the importance of the gender dimension of war. It is usually men who carry guns and fight, and the effect on ordinary social life of this kind of masculinity is destructive. Exactly this theme is pursued in two humorous stories by Wasim Mu'awwad, in which the message is brought home by the use of exaggerated symbolism and pitch-black satire. 'The Adventures of Abu Damm al-Kan'ani' (the adventures of the Bloody Canaanite) is featured in two issues of *Samandal*, no. 8, pp. 7–11, and no. 10, pp. 121–5 (in the latter his name is altered to Abu Damm the Phoenician), with a significant improvement in graphic quality from the first to the last story.

Abu Damm is a man whose arms have metamorphosed into a semi-automatic gun and a machete. This makes it exceedingly difficult for him to function as an ordinary human being, despite his best efforts. In the first story, he gets agitated when hearing that his friend the university professor is about to lose his job at the university for political reasons. His agitation makes him bang the kitchen table in anger, causing the semi-automatic gun to go off and shoot his friend in the chest.

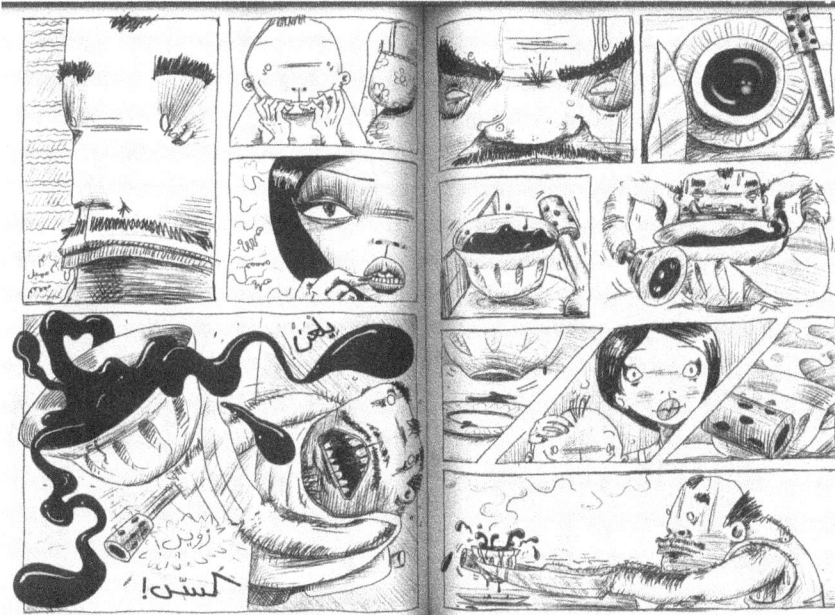

Figure 5.6 Wasim Mu'awwad, 'Abu Damm,' *Samandal* 10, 122.

As he stares at his dying friend in disbelief and dismay, his little son comes out of his room to ask what is going on. In a panic, Abu Damm yells at the son to call 999, but his agitation is such that the gun arm goes off once again and a bullet hits his son between the eyes. Shocked, Abu Damm sits down in an armchair to contemplate the bloody mess around him. His busty wife appears from nowhere to ask how the boy and the man died. Instead of replying Abu Damm requests a cup of coffee, and his wife hugs him and tells him not to worry: she will give him another son who is smarter and more beautiful. 'I love you!' she exclaims as the story ends.

The second story revolves around Abu Damm's attempt to drink a cup of delicious coffee prepared by his wife (Figure 5.6). As she and their son watch expectantly, he sniffs the coffee and licks his lips in anticipation. However, it is very difficult to raise the cup to his mouth with the machete and gun hands, and after a nerve-wracking sequence of lifting the cup to his mouth he spills the coffee just as he is about to sip it. In a rage, he screams out his curses at the 'undrinkable coffee', and once again, the gun goes off, firing bullets in the wall – and through the head of his son. He breaks down and cries in anguish – over the coffee, not his son – but his wife has a solution. She disappears into the kitchen, comes back, tells him to close his eyes, and when he opens them again, there is a plate of hummus in front of him! This he can eat using his machete arm as a spoon, and the family happiness is restored. Abu Damm embraces his wife and son (who has curiously not died, although blood is streaming out of the hole in his skull) and the story ends as the father happily exclaims, 'my beloved family!'

Abu Damm is obviously a wildly parodic figure. His nicknames, 'the Canaanite' and 'the Phoenician', suggest that he is a caricature of the militant Christian Lebanese nationalist, but the first panel of the first story depicts a cityscape dotted with minarets as well as church towers, evoking a general Lebanese milieu. Abu Damm is perhaps a generic caricature of the many Lebanese militias that ravaged the country between 1975 and 1991 and turned into bigoted political factions after the end of the civil war. Be that as it may, these two stories seem to suggest that the violent culture of the civil war years sits deep in Lebanese men, and that they continue to hurt the country even after they have laid down their weapons and engaged in normal life and politics again. Men continue to be a threat to their wives and families. As with Makhlouf's stories, the female character of Abu Damm's wife is somewhat ambiguous. Her mindless good spirits and lack of concern for her son are not particularly flattering parodies of women's reactions to the male violence that wrought havoc on Lebanon for 15 years. Alternatively, her role can be read as that of always being around to tidy up after the men have made a mess of things. The idiom of the stories is at any rate one of extreme hyperbole and blunt humour. The son, who seemingly gets killed in every episode, is reminiscent of the hapless character Kenny in the US animation series

South Park: Kenny is killed by accident in nearly every episode but always reappears in the next one.

It is perhaps time now to pause and ask why all these stories are such easy reads and how the humorous effect is achieved. The answer lies in the drawing style, I think. Most of the funny stories are drawn in the style of cartoons, short on details but rich in ideational potential. As Scott McCloud puts it: 'By de-emphasizing the *appearance* of the *physical* world in favor of the *idea* of form, the cartoon places itself in the world of *concepts*.'[32]

This is of course the time-honoured technique of the newspaper caricature, the cousin or even sister of the comic strip, and as previously noted Makhlouf – like several of the adult comic artists in Lebanon and Egypt – works as a professional cartoonist for well-known newspapers. By its simplicity and suggestiveness, the cartoon abandons any attempt at depicting concrete reality and instead focuses on ideas, letting the reader fill in both the details and the reference to reality. The pre-eminent cartoonist of gender relations in Egypt and perhaps in the entire Arab world is Du'a al-'Adl, whose cartoons for various Egyptian newspapers and magazines have won her international acclaim. Her searing graphic comments on the position of women in Arab societies often require no accompanying text nor any explanatory comment. Two good examples are found in Plate 7: the use and abuse of women for male pleasure could hardly have been better illustrated.

It is similar simple lines that Makhlouf uses to convey the idea of a ridiculous local superhero, and Wasim Mu'awwad does the same when he draws Abu Damm with a spiky moustache, hairy arms and sleeveless shirt – a well-known and instantly recognizable icon of the middle-aged Arab family man at ease in his home. This is exactly why the images are powerful – they convey an idea that is not bound to a specific time and place but by virtue of the pictorial simplicity delivers a clear message with a scope that it is left to the reader's imagination to determine.

Visual symbolism

Whether in the form of simple cartoons or elaborate drawings rich in detail, the images of comics may be strongly symbolic. Symbolism is often on display in the work of Hicham Rahma, whose story 'The Prison' I presented in chapter 4 (Figure 4.4). Rahma has also treated the question of harassment in his visually potent story 'A Terrible Disgrace' (*al-'ar bi l-zayt al-harr*), where the protagonist is a lower-class harasser named 'Ala.[33] He is depicted in an unsympathetic way, with a long, crooked nose, a big scar and a menacing grin on his face; Rahma's image of him evokes the idea of street toughs from the popular neighbourhoods of Cairo. Employing a potent metaphor, the panels show how his facial features disappear as a result of his harassment of girls in the street, and he goes to a therapist to cope with his loss of public face. In the story he attributes his loss of face to witchcraft, supposedly hiding in an object inside the girl's handbag, which she throws at him.

But of course the loss of facial features may be read as the storyteller's comment on what harassment does to the human dignity of the harasser himself, while the girl is depicted as the hero who won't stand for it. It is interesting in this regard how Rahma has drawn the curious onlookers in the second and third panels. They are featureless, passive, ghost-like beings, unable or unwilling to respond to the agitation of the offended girl. In Egyptian public debate on sexual harassment, one issue is the apathy of the public and their unwillingness to come to the rescue of girls that are being harassed. Another notable feature of Rahma's technique in this story is the relative absence of frames, the main sequencing tool in comics. As Thierry Groensteen suggests, such an absence may serve to concentrate the narrative 'only in the characters, solitary figures developed in an empty décor or one that is minimally suggested by a few elements'.[34] The story focuses not on the action but mainly on the personal development (or rather deterioration) of the protagonist, the harasser. The loss of facial features is of course a potent metaphor for a dead soul (but there is also a fine irony in the fact that he feels forced to wear a mask concealing his face because of a wrong he has committed – while many women in Egypt and elsewhere wear a mask to appear respectable (the niqab) without having done anything wrong at all). Rahma may be understood to suggest what harassment does to the human dignity of the harasser himself – one Egyptian expression to scold someone for inappropriate behaviour is 'respect yourself!'

A stylistically different but thematically similar comment on the relations between males and females is the wordless and allegorical story entitled 'Thorn' (*Shawk*) written by Rym Mokhtari (Figure 5.8).[35] The story starts with a girl who is dressed in a cactus-like bodysuit full of thorns, planted in a flower pot. She wakes up, leaves the pot and is then approached by a giant male hand that caresses her but is pricked by one of the thorns. In order not to prick the hand again the girl lets it remove her protection, the cactus suit. The giant male proceeds to pick her up, put her into his mouth and eat her alive. In contrast to Rahma's story above, here the panels are clearly marked by frames; they occur regularly three by three and the background is blank – all the attention is focused on the woman and the hand. The regularity of the panels and the straightforward progression of the story suggest a rule-based sequence of events that is reinforced by the absence of anything going on in the background that may disturb the linear narrative. The symbolism is of course obvious here: women are forced to present a hostile public face that is designed to keep male attention away, lest they get devoured by predatory men. It may also be construed as saying that for men, women are just fruit to be picked, peeled and eaten as soon as they are mature. The story is subtly humorous, but also a damning comment on male treatment of women. Having a woman come to life with her feet planted in a flower pot is a beginning that seems to be full of wry humour, suggesting as it does that women's situation is akin to that of flowers or plants, adorning the house and passively receiving whatever

Figure 5.7 A harasser loses face: Hicham Rahma, 'A Terrible Disgrace' [al-'ar bi-l-zayt al-harr], *Tuk-Tuk* 7, 49.

nourishment and care the master of the house gives them. The arrangement of panels not only indicates a slowing down towards the end, a sort of cadence, but also serves to highlight, by the increasing size of the panels in the last two strips, how male domination devours femininity (symbolized by the naked, curvaceous body of the woman), leaving only the lifeless, unfriendly shell with which women have to protect themselves from the male gaze (and hands!).[36]

Comics in Contemporary Arab Culture

Lastly, on the question of visual symbolism it is worth mentioning again the story 'The Evolution of the Egyptian Woman' (see Plate 6), created by Tawfiq and Muhammad Isma'il Amin. The four-armed, bald women with giant mouths and eyes all over their skulls are a vivid metaphor for how gender relations in the public urban space are crippling Egyptian women physically and psychologically.

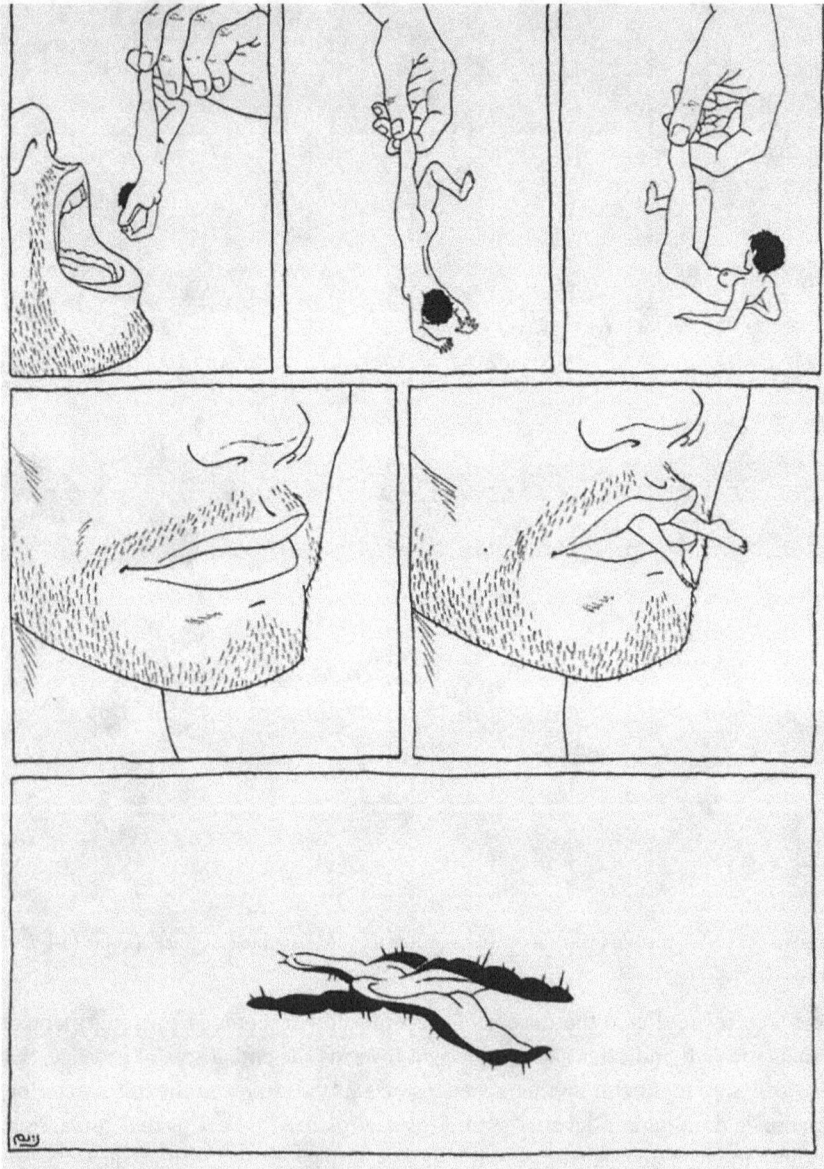

Figure 5.8 Rym, 'Thorn' [shawk], *Tuk-Tuk* 7, 37–38.

110

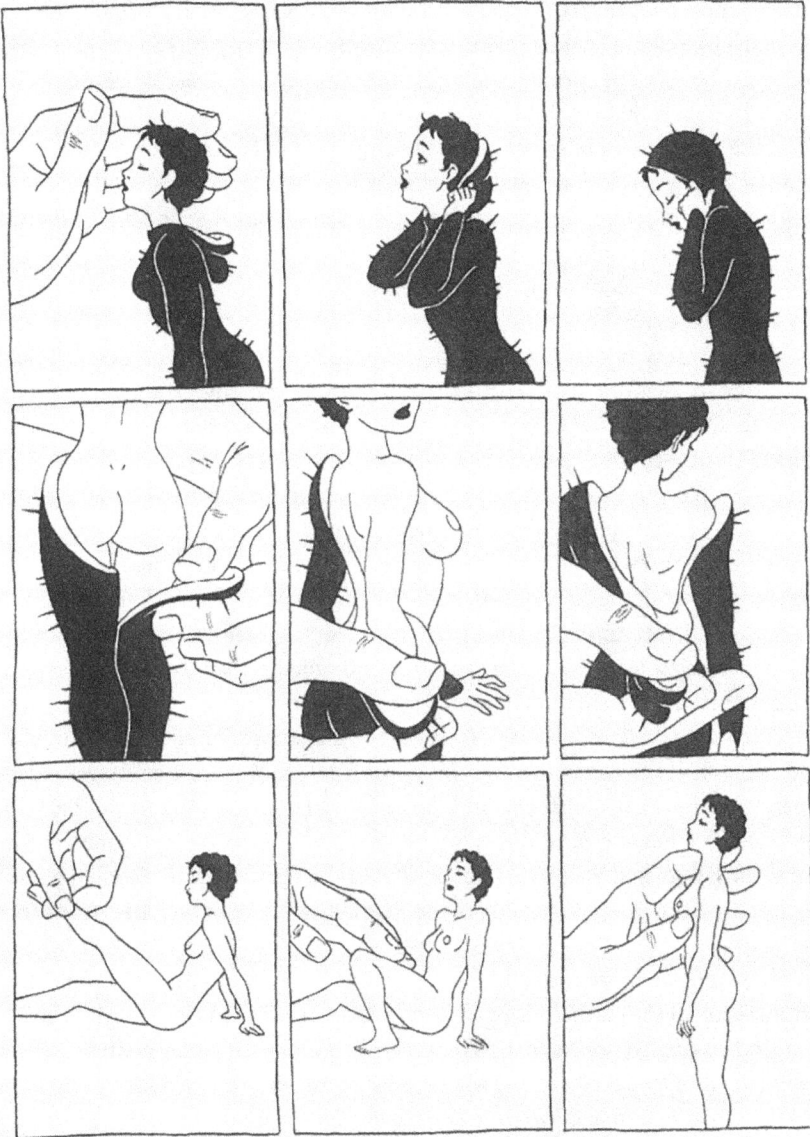

The rhetoric of the panels

Meaning in comics is created not only by images and text, but also by the arrangement of the panels. Thierry Groensteen has identified two levels of relations between images in comics. The first is the linear one, whereby a panel stands in a sequential relation to the panels preceding and succeeding it. Just as in regular text, such panels form syntagms and narrative sequences. Relations on the second level are not linear, but represent 'a more elaborated level of integration between the narrative flux [...] and the spatio-topical operation'.[37] On this second level images that are spatially distant from each other may still be closely related and contribute to the meaning and structure of the story in a non-linear way – Groensteen calls this the 'braiding effect'.

These two ways of relating images are employed to forceful rhetorical effect in some of the Egyptian and Lebanese comics that treat gender relations. We will look at three different works here: one story from *Shakmagiya* about domestic abuse, an Egyptian album of comic dialogues entitled *Ana wa-Ana* (me and myself) and a reflection from *Samandal* about women in public spaces, entitled 'Furr Furr Blues'.

I have already noted that *Shakmagiya* owes a lot to the environment around *Tuk-Tuk*, so that its style is informed by irreverent and sometimes surreal humour. However, *Shakmagiya* also brings to the fore other, less light-hearted works than those often seen in *Tuk-Tuk*. A particularly explicit example is the story 'It Is We Who Are Late' (text by al-Shayma Hamid, artwork by Muna 'Abd al-Rahman) (see Plate 8).[38] Offering snapshots of the married lives of Maryam, an upper-class housewife, and Farha, a lower-class cleaner and housemaid, it tells stories of brutal domestic violence, ending with serious injury and hospitalization for one and the death of the other's ten-year-old daughter before the two women finally decide to leave their husbands; the title of the story refers to Maryam's realization that they should have left long ago.

This story is one of several in *Shakmagiya* that are coloured rather than black and white, and the colours add to the visual rhetoric. The women's faces are red where their husbands hit them, and there is a vivid play on nuances of light and dark. Doorframes and open doors where the light pours in serve as symbolic ways out at three points in the story – and in the very last panel, the two abused women do exit through those doors, into the sunlight of a new life, free from their husbands.

However, the more systematic and striking rhetorical tool in this story is the organization of the panels. These are frameless but separated by wide white gutters in a straight-angled grid of images on each page. The wide gutter invites extensive deployment of so-called *ellipsis*, whereby the comic creator leaves it to the reader to 'fill in' her own images between the panels. This is useful in dense stories, as it saves space. Equally important, it makes it possible to suggest a disturbing level of violence without actually showing it graphically (a boy hitting his little sister to discipline her, a man abusing his wife so badly she ends up in the hospital's intensive unit). The violence occurs mostly in the gutter, as it were, and the reader can see its *results* in the panels. While the gutter allows for ellipsis, the regular grid of panels facilitates the flow and understanding of a story that jumps rather abruptly from one situation or episode to the other as it recounts the two heroines' misery. The story starts in the bedroom of Maryam and her husband the moment after he has beaten her with his trouser belt. The next sequence focuses on Farha, who works as a housemaid in the apartment block where Maryam lives. Farha comes home to find her son beaten up, and is herself battered when she asks her husband to go easier on their son. A third sequence shows Maryam and Farha talking with female friends about their problems, and the reader is then transported to a hospital in the fourth sequence, where Maryam's husband stands outside an emergency room watching her through the glass door; she has obviously been severely injured. The fifth sequence should perhaps not be regarded as a sequence at all, since it consists of only one panel: an outside view of Farha's house, where a woman or girl is screaming desperately and someone is seen running towards the house. The sixth and last sequence finally brings the two women together, Farha pushing Maryam's wheelchair out of the hospital. It turns out that while Maryam has been beaten, Farha's daughter was killed by her husband. The story ends as they walk away, heading for the house of Maryam's mother, presumably never to return to their husbands.

The organization of the panels adds its own layer of meaning to this straightforward story about domestic violence. The parallel sequences highlight that women from different social classes are subject to exactly the same kind of male violence, and this message is apparently more important than the narrative itself, since narrative flow is sacrificed in favour of presenting temporally disjointed but thematically related snapshots. The progression of the sequences furthermore seems to encourage female solidarity across class divides. Until the last sequence the two women are indirectly connected through their separate but similar experiences of male violence, but they still lead parallel lives and are not in contact with each other. In the sixth sequence they are united, one victim helping the other, together breaking free from an oppressive situation. In this way, the panels speak to each other through narrative progression, but also through parallelisms: through sequential 'syntagms' and non-temporal, thematic 'braiding', to use Groensteen's words. It is because of this visual versatility that the comic story succeeds in presenting a coherent and emotional story in a way that would have seemed disjointed if translated into moving images and would have required a lot of text if translated into verbal prose.

The second example of the rhetoric of the panels is a beautiful, meditative reflection on women and public space from Lebanon. 'Furr Furr Blues' by Mazen Kerbaj appeared in *Samandal* 12, pp. 7 – 16. Kerbaj wrote the story during a stay in Algiers, and it was inspired by this city. However, by his own account it could be a story about almost any Arab city today.[39] Starting out as a reflection on the contrasts of the cityscape at the beginning, this comic suddenly shifts gear and becomes a blues about the marginalization of women in public spaces. The comic is composed of regular, framed panels which illustrate and expand on a series of short observations made by the narrator in text boxes above the panels. It begins with panels that are empty of living beings but include the drawn letters 'f' and 'r', representing a purring sound that is heard everywhere as the light of dawn appears. The sound is revealed to come from doves, and Kerbaj proceeds to depict other birds flying silently and elegantly in the sky – even when they fly in great throngs they never collide, navigating around each other 'with the ease of the blind'. The serenity suggested by these images is further accentuated by the depiction of the sky itself, with its peaceful clouds. Then the sequence of descriptions and images turns to the contrast between the largely empty sky and the crowded streets. The images become cluttered with faces, buildings and vehicles impossibly stacked on top of each other. At first, they are dominated by men. Then, in a full-page panel, a woman is introduced as the narrator comments: 'Those with beards [i.e., religious men] – here and everywhere – spend their time claiming that they don't spend their time looking at the women who walk the streets.' From here onwards, the comic is no longer a juxtaposition of nature and city, but a comment on women in public spaces. The woman is soon squeezed out of the frames, which are filled with the eyes and mouths of men. As the sun sets, we see two women gradually losing their features and becoming empty shapes as the text reads:

> There is nothing but them [men] after sunset. How sad is the sunset which conceals the sun and the women and signals the onset of sad nights in which women [...] go and make their purring noises elsewhere.

In other words, the doves at the beginning of the story are really symbols of women. It is at the end of the story that the title becomes understandable and suitable: it really is a 'Furr Furr Blues' about the impoverishment of public spaces dominated by men, about the loss of something beautiful when women retreat to private spaces.

Kerbaj's story is powerful not only because of its melancholic personal tone, but also because of how the panels relate to each other. At first, there are regular, framed panels, six to a page, as Kerbaj moves from the sky, the domain of quiet clouds and elegant birds with their soft purring, to the city and its throngs of people, cars and pollution. In a suggestive leap, the observations of the narrator switch from a panel depicting aerial pollution to two panels which introduce men, retaining the exact same textual formula – 'a lot of pollution' is followed by 'a lot of policemen' and 'a lot of bearded men', that is, conservative religious men. The formulaic text and the juxtaposition of apparently disjointed images is a clever piece of sarcasm. Kerbaj avoids making any *explicitly* disrespectful link between urban pollution on the one hand and policemen and conservative religious men on the other, since the panels are just snapshots of different parts of the cityscape. However, it does not take much imaginative energy on the part of the reader to make the link for him/herself, given the similar formulas of the panels.

Then there is a sharp visual break, as the regular panel pattern is broken by a full-page panel introducing the main topical feature of the cityscape: a young woman depicted in the act of passing through the image. Her hair flows and there

Figure 5.9 Mazen Kerbaj, 'Furr Furr Blues,' *Samandal* 12, 9–15.

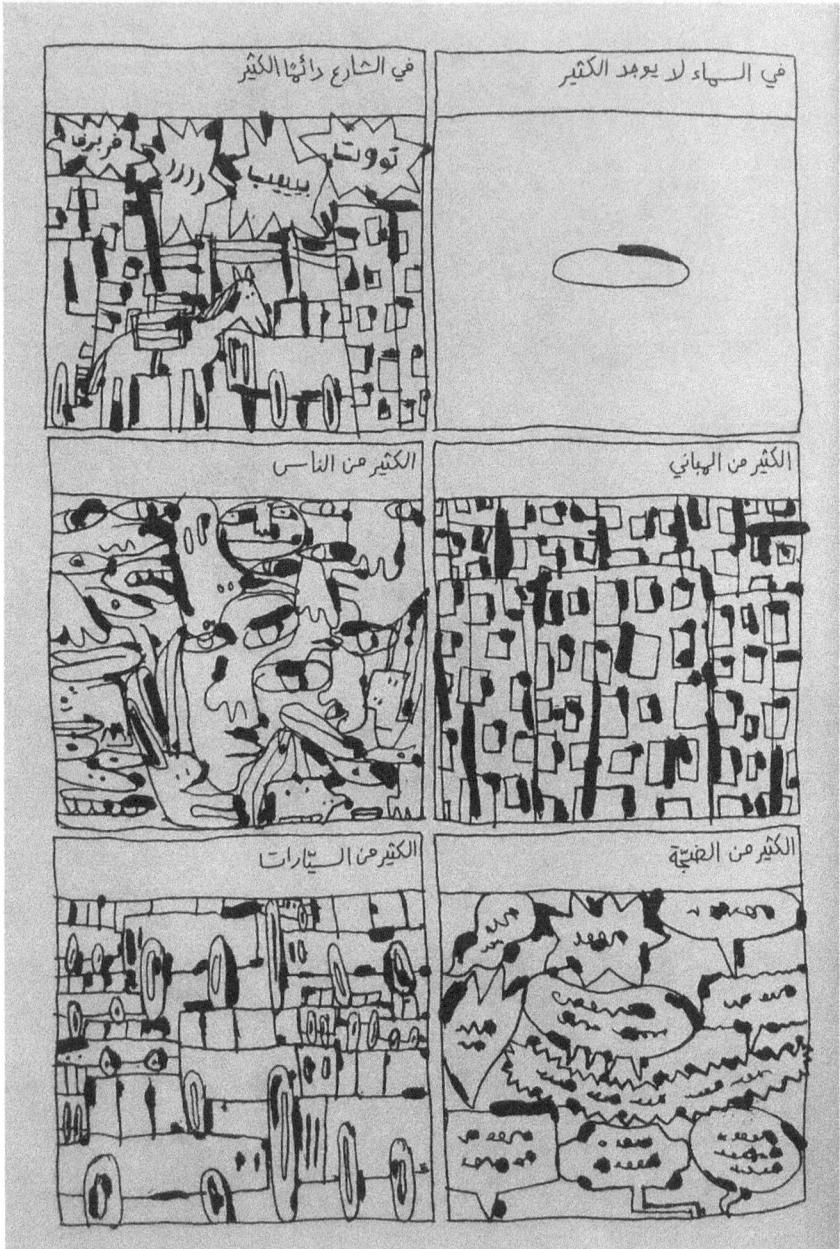

is a slight hint of a smile playing on her lips. All around her are crammed the contorted faces of men, all twisting their heads and eyes to watch her as she passes by. After this point the panels assume varying sizes before reverting back to the regular grid on the last page. The equal-sized images on that page depict women enjoying one another's company, and so the form of the panels recalls the

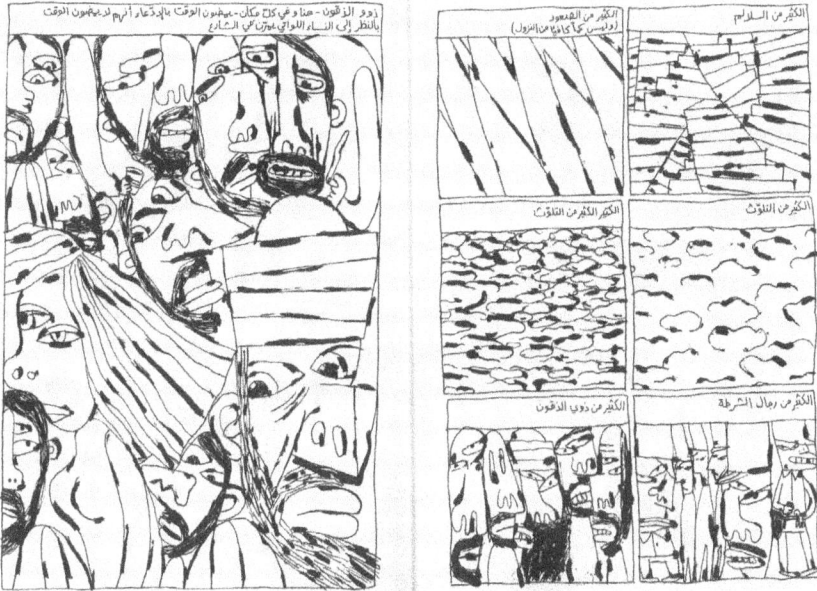

beginning of the story, which tells of the peaceful existence of doves far from the noise and bustle of the city. It is not only the title of the story that makes a connection between women and doves; so does the layout of the panels.

The combination of text and images in this comic is also eloquent. The text is sparse and appears to be little more than phrases putting into words the image of the panels, as when Kerbaj comments on his picture of policemen with the simple phrase: 'a lot of policemen'. However, while the text looks innocuous, the images convey a sense of threat and discomfort. None of the men he draws shows the slightest hint of a smile. The policemen either look mean or angry. The religious men appear as serious and disturbed at the same time, an effect Kerbaj achieves by dislocating their facial features. The impression one gets is that the street is dominated by distorted, vaguely threatening male bodies, and this impression is augmented on the following page where the contorted faces of men stare at the lone woman in the frame from every angle. On the next page, the faces of the men turn positively leering, and they start to crowd out the women in the images while the textual observations retain the same laconic tone: 'a lot of men in the street', 'a lot of men in the bars', 'a lot of men all the time and everywhere'. In the middle frame of the page, men are reduced to sets of eyes and mouths that converge on the two female heads in the picture. One of women seems to be eaten by a mouth, suggesting the erasure of women as participants in the public space. The next frame depicts the exact same female head shapes as in the previous panel, but now they are entirely white, devoid of features, mere empty shapes, an absent presence for the many male eyes in the picture. Kerbaj then turns towards nature, with

كم هو حزين هذا الغروب الذي يحجب الشمس و النساء

و يبشّر بالليالي الحزينة

which he began his story. 'How sad the sunset is, concealing the sun and the women.' And as the sun sets, the bodies and faces of two women gradually become empty white shapes: all that is left of them in the night-time public space is a memory. Towards the end, the regular six-panel page reappears to suggest affinity with the serene images at the beginning of the story. Now the images are pictures

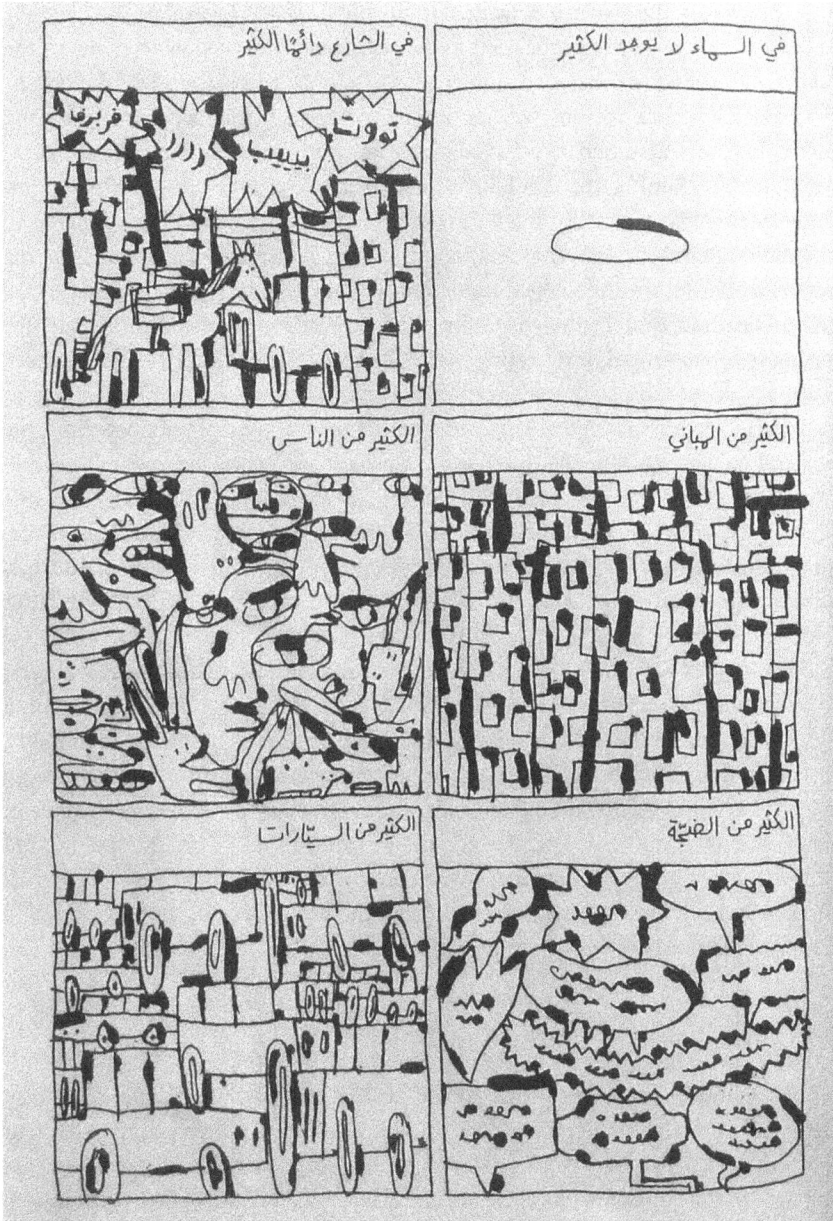

of women, and another elegant juxtaposition between words and pictures takes place. Kerbaj writes of 'beautiful' and 'ugly' women, but the two images that accompany the texts are identical, except that they are inverted versions of each other. The juxtaposition of the two opposing adjectives and two identical but inverted images suggests that for Kerbaj, appearances do not matter. He gets the blues because of the absence of women in the public space, regardless of what they look like. This point is emphasized in the subsequent images, which present the reader with veiled and unveiled women and with girls, wives, friends and mothers.

Ironically, since Kerbaj was inspired by Algiers when writing 'Furr Furr Blues', his story assumed a remarkable relevance in Beirut in late summer 2015, when the 'You Stink' campaign I mentioned in chapter 3 took off. At its high point the campaign brought as many as 30,000 people into Martyrs' Square in downtown Beirut in August, after a month of the rubbish crisis. Riot police used a variety of violent means to disperse demonstrators, from water cannons and tear gas to beatings and arrests, including keeping prisoners incommunicado for 24 hours.[40] Particularly interesting was the gender dimension of these protests; feminists and LGBT activists were a vocal part of the movement. In analyses that perfectly mirror Kerbaj's comic, the feminist activists described how the political factions and the security forces resorted to an aggressive masculinization of discourse and public space when trying to repress the protests. Masculine metaphors, such as 'iron fist', were used in the discourse of the authorities, and political leaders questioned the morality of female demonstrators, admonishing them to listen to their fathers and sectarian leaders (the latter were targeted by the protesters). Authorities and security forces also ridiculed and suppressed everything they viewed as not masculine, from homosexuality to open-minded discussion. According to the activists, their weapon in fighting against the patriarchal authorities is a discourse that insists on being feminine, a discourse that does not recognize that might is right, that openly admits to being the weaker party at the same time as it insists that this is of no consequence in deliberations about how society should be organized. They also go beyond Kerbaj's description by breaking with the strategy of withdrawal that Kerbaj mourns in his story. These activists confront the problem head-on by working to feminize public space and discourse.[41]

In favour of the sensitive man

All the examples mentioned thus far are explicit and treat the relations between men and women in antagonistic terms, the woman invariably being the victim of male violence. However, gender relations and women's emancipation are treated not only in the guise of direct criticism and clear-as-day symbolism. In conclusion, let us look at a couple of stories that focus not on repression and violence but on intimate relationships and communication between males and females. Nobody could accuse the *Tuk-Tuk* community of artists and writers of creating sensuous pieces after the fashion of Anaïs Nin, who wrote the essay I have stolen this subtitle from. However, when reading the magazine's semi-regular essay section 'al-Basla wa-l-Gazar' (green peas and carrots) penned by Andeel, one is struck by the sensitivity, openness, humour and will to self-reflection that characterizes his writing. Green peas and carrots are considered close companions in Egyptian cuisine, and 'al-Basla wa-l-Gazar' is a popular expression for male–female relations. Under this title Andeel has written a series of short texts where he tells about his early encounters with girls, from age seven until early puberty. Besides describing his relations with girls, these texts are snapshots from an Egyptian childhood and adolescence in the 1990s. Written mostly in a casual style of *fusha* with some dialect blended in, the pieces are entertaining and at times nostalgic, but their most remarkable property is the effortless blend of sarcasm and, beautiful descriptions of the innocent eroticism of children and young adolescents, free of masculine posing or chauvinism. As an example of the latter, consider Andeel's description of his first kiss at age 11:

> In short, it is a feeling from another world, a primal and abstract world, and you are baffled by your inability to control it. What was so overwhelming for me was how real it felt, and how far removed from the television images I had sketched in my imagination ... The clumsiness, the confusion, the smell of candlestick biscuits and the shy laughter – all these made the event real and full of meaning ...[42]

Such tender descriptions stand alongside funny characterizations of the newly awakened sexuality, as when he in the same piece describes his and his friends' eyes searching 'like the International Atomic Energy Agency' for the 'microscopic bulges on the girls' chests'.

It is not all harmony and fun in these pieces, however. Andeel uses 'al-Basla wa-l-Gazar' to critically review his adolescence as well as prevalent gender relations in Egypt. In a frank piece of self-criticism, he describes his first relationship with a girl, which was the result of peer pressure and vanity. Just to prove that he could do it, he got into a relationship with a girl who was generally considered to be attractive, knowing from the outset that he was not really interested in her. What followed was two weeks of tribulations as he had to explain all his jokes and sit through torturous family evenings in her home, before he came to his senses and ended the relationship. In his usual forthright tone Andeel concludes that

> I was proud to have confronted my stupidity and weakness in the face of the expectations of those around me, and because of this experience I took a second look at much of what people around me expected of me.[43]

As for Andeel's social criticism, it is inserted in an otherwise innocuous text. In the essay 'al-Banat wa-l-hurmunat' (girls and hormones) he recounts his summer flirtation with Sarah, a blue-eyed blonde who sang together with him in the choir of the Kafr al-Shaykh Centre for the Progressive (*mutatawwir*) Child (Kafr al-Shaykh, situated in the north-western part of the Nile Delta, is Andeel's hometown). Commenting on the rather pretentious name of the centre, Andeel displays the elegant, sarcastic humour which he shares with several of the Egyptian comic creators: 'For those unfamiliar with the Kafr al-Shaykh Centre for the Progressive Child, it is a centre that caters to children who are progressive.' Andeel describes the confusion and excitement of a boy who suddenly realizes that he is an object of desire. But the story is not just self-mockery. Towards the end of the humorous depictions of the two children's mutual attraction, he reflects on how Sarah made him feel good by always asking him to do things for her, to help her. As a grown man he realizes that she intuitively employed the institutionalized, skewed gender norms to make him like her.[44] And then comes the following passage:

> [T]his girl revealed to me the value of being a man. For it is only you who can stop a taxi. Only you can ask of a passer-by: 'what time is it?' Only you have the right to open the front door even if you wear nothing but your underpants [al-bita' al-tani]. And only you have to pay the cash in each and every situation that requires payment.

The last sentence serves to keep up the humorous mood of the story, and then the tale of the choir and Sarah continues. But Andeel has inserted this comment on the prerogatives of men in social life. As anyone who has been to Egypt will know, women do of course stop taxis – when they are alone. If a man and a woman are together, however, the man by default assumes the active role, and it is this difference Andeel gets at and criticizes. Underlying his comments are the implicit questions: Why would it appear unnatural if the wife hails a taxi instead of the husband? Why would it make for an awkward moment if the woman asks a passer-by what time it is, rather than her male companion? And why is it unproblematic for men to appear in little but their undergarments when some friend or acquaintance knocks on the door, while the same is unthinkable for women? He draws attention to the fact that men have a lot more social freedom than women, and by his observations he suggests that this reality is questionable. His implicit questioning of conventions that diminish the social role of women and augment that of men should be seen in connection with the whole series of texts under the 'al-Basla wa-l-Gazar' heading. The thread that runs through these texts is affection and respect for the other sex. It should also be noted here that by his last, humorous comment Andeel also suggests that the skewed gender relations in fact restrict the social freedom of men, too. The expectation that they be the ones who pay, that they are the breadwinners, can be a heavy burden to bear in contemporary Egypt. Thus, with this last comment Andeel places his little humorous essay at the intersection of some questions that haunt Egyptian social and marital life. Women are increasingly getting higher education, and they have entered the job market in rising numbers. More and more often, the woman is in fact the main breadwinner in a family. At the same time, she is supposed to take care of the household while the man is supposed to be its head, based on the traditional arrangement that *he* is the main breadwinner. And in public life, the idea that the male is the privileged actor lingers on in social norms, as Andeel suggests. The discrepancy between these expectations and the socio-economic realities of many urban Egyptians creates tensions that may in the worst case contribute to domestic violence and sexual harassment. The force of Andeel's texts, in contrast, is to argue for every individual's personal integrity and equality in social life and against norms that restrict the roles and positions women and men may acceptably occupy in social life. His texts in *Tuk-Tuk* tie in with the social commentary he regularly posts to Facebook, where he has a vast network of followers and friends. For example, on 10 May 2016 he posted a comment where he strongly condemned sexual humour at the expense of women. Such jokes might perhaps serve a taboo-breaking function in Western countries, where women at least enjoy a measure of legal protection and societal respect, he writes. But in Egypt,

> where 90 per cent of women are subjected to verbal and physical harassment in the streets, are circumcised and married off against their will, denied the same education opportunities as men, beaten by their husbands, brothers and fathers [...], frankly, I cannot at all see how jokes at the expense of a segment of society that lives under such conditions may be courageous in any way.[45]

The messages about gender relations that Andeel and his co-artists deliver in *Tuk-Tuk* are for the most part couched in more humorous terms, as we have seen in this section, but they unmistakably take the side of women (of all ages) against a system that discriminates against them and men that exploit this system.

The comic album *Ana wa-Ana* (me and myself), with texts by Michel Hanna and artwork by Rania Amin, depicts how intimate conversations between young people are affected by structural inequalities. As the title suggests it contains a number of dialogues that may be read in different ways and where the power relationship is not always clear-cut. Two of the dialogues take place between couples. In the first, an engaged couple's conversation about where to go for their honeymoon turns sour because he wants to go to Prague, while she insists on Sharm al-Shaykh – because 'that is where everybody goes'. She has no idea that Prague is a city and has not even heard of the Czech Republic, while he romanticizes about its nature, the interesting history, the people and the cultural life. The story depicts a cultural gulf between young, upper-middle-class women and men, illustrated by the physical distance between them: in the first panel, they sit at a small table, very close to each other, while in the last panel, after having engaged in a real conversation, the table has become very long, leaving them alone together, as it were, in separate lifeworlds and with little to talk about. The story nicely portrays an awkward moment of communication breakdown, but it is also

Figure 5.10 Rania Amin and Michel Hanna, *Ana wa-ana*, 53.

easily interpreted as a comment on the conformism and the expectations that especially girls are socialized into having about romanticism and the 'musts' in life.

Another story in the same album depicts a conversation between a minibus driver and his girlfriend (Figure 5.10). Before we even get to know what job the young man has, the drawings succeed in conveying a clear sense of which stratum of the population we are watching: he has a pony-tail and a casual style, wearing jeans, a T-shirt and a self-confident smile, while she is modestly dressed in a long dress and veil. The café is called The Emerald Casino. The atmosphere is somewhat evocative of the lower-middle-class environment depicted in the 1984 movie *Love Above the Pyramid Plateau,* based on the short story of the same name by Naguib Mahfouz. This story is full of warmth and sympathy for both characters, and ends in her agreeing to get engaged. However, both the dialogue and the drawings convey how skewed the power relations are. It is the man who drives the conversation forward, while his girlfriend is reduced to murmuring or answering in monosyllables. He looks directly at her and smiles winningly, while she rarely looks up and smiles modestly. Through the sophisticated interplay between text and image, the story conveys the beauty of two young persons gingerly taking their first steps towards a life together while also showing how social conventions reduce women's space for agency.

***

In this chapter and in chapters 3 and 4 I have sought to describe and analyse how comics critique patriarchal authoritarianism and prevailing gender relations in the contemporary Arab world. These two issues are by no means dominant in the new adult comics in Egypt and Lebanon, but they are a visible part of the comics landscape. They are important since they show that Arab comic creators have the will to use their art form in the service of a political mission. They do so by making use of a wide range of rhetorical tools available to comics: slapstick humour, obvious or subtle visual symbolism, and various ways of designing and relating panels so that they contribute to the message or the pace of the narrative.

Without leaving the critical impulse behind, we will move now to the constructive aspect of these comics. In the next chapter we shall investigate how they contribute to constituting the experience of youthfulness in the Arab world.

6

Youthfulness and the vernacular

In February 2016 I was in Egypt at the same time as the third EGYCon took place, on the old Greek campus of the American University in Cairo, just next to Tahrir Square. EGYCon is not only a comic convention. It is a festival devoted to anime (Japanese animation), cosplay (dressing up like superheroes), computer gaming and anime-related music (see Plate 9). It was obviously very popular among young middle-class Cairenes. For two days, the AUC's Greek campus was utterly packed with people in their late teens to early thirties, all in a festive, energetic mood. The most devoted had spent long hours designing and making their elaborate costumes, including detailed, meticulously painted cardboard replicas of futuristic weapons that have appeared in some superhero comic or movie. Walking around the grounds I encountered several American comic characters, from Superman to Rohrschach, the anti-hero of Alan Moore and Dave Gibbon's masterpiece *Watchmen*. The striking thing about EGYCon, particularly in an increasingly authoritarian Egypt in 2016, is that its whole *raison d'etre* is to encourage creativity and to have fun – innocent, raucous fun, whether it consists of dressing up like your favourite comics or animation character, singing karaoke to famous Japanese anime soundtracks (there was a big outdoor stage for this purpose) or hacking your friends to pieces in the video game *Mortal Kombat*, in front of a cheering audience. EGYCon obviously offered young people a respite from a dreary and sometimes frightening socio-political reality.

The previous two chapters have illuminated the role comics play in highlighting political and social grievances and articulating a critique of political and social realities. In this chapter, we will investigate a *constructive* aspect of comics: how they reflect and contribute to assertions of youthfulness. I argue that the independent comics are part of a wider picture where critical, youthful voices are making themselves heard through texts, art and music. Importantly, this youthfulness is often expressed in a vernacular idiom. To throw light on these points, I will broaden the empirical and analytical scope. First, we shall look at how comics construct youthfulness, and here, comics from countries other than Lebanon and Egypt are introduced. I then connect comics to the related media of independent music and to youth magazines; and lastly, I connect the assertion of youthfulness to the trend towards writing in dialect rather than in standard Arabic.

The marginalization of youth in the Arab world

Arab countries are currently seeing a so-called 'youth bulge', which means that a disproportionately high percentage of the population is young. A major survey undertaken by the Egyptian central bureau of statistics (CAPMAS) in 2009 estimated that about 62 per cent of the Egyptian population was below the age of 29.[1] Youth bulges are often called a demographic gift, since they provide a country with a large workforce and may boost the economy. However, Arab states have failed to reap the benefits of the demographic dividend represented by large cohorts of youth in recent years. Just before the revolution, unemployment among youth in Egypt (15–25 years) was 28.8 per cent, against a national average of 8 per cent. The proportion of unemployed women is significantly higher than that of men, and well-educated Egyptians suffer more from unemployment than those without higher education.[2] Lebanese youth suffer from the same kind of problems, with a youth unemployment rate of about 24 per cent, and with higher education being undervalued by employers.[3] A similar situation obtains in many other Arab countries. The result is that millions of young people with higher education are unable to find jobs and feel suspended in limbo as they grow older without being able to marry and establish themselves – a situation of 'waithood' forced upon them by the social system.[4] Continued political oppression and patriarchal structures add to the hardships of young people, as shown by Linda Herrera's interviews with young Egyptians not long before the revolution. One of her informants, a 22-year-old lower-middle-class man, stated that 'in our home the father was everything and everyone was expected to obey him'.[5] On a more systemic level, the informant deplored the clientelist system of *wasta* (access to work and social goods based on kinship and other personal connections), which is in direct opposition to citizenship rights, justice and social advancement based on merits.

Grievances like these were what moved young Egyptians to pour into the streets once a vanguard of activists started calling for mass protests in connection with Police Day on 25 January 2011. These young people had lived through all the negative social effects of Egypt's economic liberalization programme and witnessed that a small elite of businessmen and politicians monopolized the country's wealth. At the same time, they were exposed to democratic values, free speech and human rights talk as never before because of the internet. Having 'nothing to live for anymore', they were angry enough to challenge the existing order.[6]

Pervasive throughout the Arab world, *wasta* also affects Lebanese youth. In a 2016 survey, 75 per cent of Lebanese university students thought political connections were important to get a job. Twenty per cent reported having used such connections.[7] The combination of Lebanon's 'consociational democracy' and the classic Middle Eastern patron–client system makes for a thoroughly patriarchal political system. I was exposed to the informal aspect of this system while studying in Lebanon many years ago. My circle of Lebanese and non-Lebanese friends were politically outspoken, and discussions were lively. During my stay municipal elections were held in Lebanon. Asking my friends about whom they would vote for, I was flabbergasted to hear one of them, a good-humoured Druze in his late twenties, say that he did not know, because his father had not told him yet. It turned out that all the people in his extended family voted according to the instructions of the leading male member of the family. Theirs is not a unique case. In 2009, a UNDP report stated that as a result of politicization primarily within the family rather than among peers or in public discussions, as well as limited exposure to different media outlets, Lebanese youth tend to engage uncritically in politics; that is, they accept at face value what their elders tell them.[8] In sum, the social and political situation of young Egyptians and Lebanese (and their peers in other Arab countries) gives little reason for joy.

To these troubles is added the fact that they live in a region that is often associated with religious and political instability, including militant Islamism. As Bayat and Herrera put it:

> Muslim youth today are struggling to assert their youthfulness, claim rights, and make life transitions in a highly fraught post-9/11 global moment in which they are subject to media scrutiny, surveillance, a range of policy interventions to contain them, influence them, and cultivate in them a strong Islamic identity.[9]

They argue that global trends after 9/11 have construed Muslim youth as a potential factor of instability, making them into a distinct, transnational social category. I will not challenge this statement, nor their thoughtful analysis of how young Muslims deal with these pressures. However, I do want to turn the focus away from religion in this chapter. Arab youth are often overdetermined as Muslim youth, and there is a perceived need to explain what they say and do in relation to some version or other of Islam. However, as Bayat and Herrera rightly note, many of the pressures working on Arab youth are not of a religious character, and there are other ways for young Arabs to deal with the issues of identity and marginalization than through the assertion, reformulation or rejection of religion. Looking at adult comics that have appeared recently in the

Arab world, we can see one such strategy. In these works religion is largely irrelevant or relegated to the background. Instead, youthful concerns such as pop culture and fun are prominent.

Asserting youthfulness

Let us return to EGYCon for a moment. As I stood on the stairs of the old AUC library, watching the colourful, carnivalesque crowd and listening to a hopelessly out-of-tune karaoke version of a Japanese pop song, my thoughts went to Asef Bayat's wonderful article on the subversive potential of fun in the Middle East. According to Bayat fun is an affront to any exclusivist system (he singles out Islamism for in-depth treatment). Such systems tend to nurture ideals of discipline and control. For example, the Iranian Islamists propagated the Islamist 'ideal man': 'heavy, austere, warrior-like, controlled, resolute, selfless, and highly emotional – in short, an extraordinary personality who stood against the expression of lightness, carefreeness, and spontaneity, in a word, ordinariness'.[10] Let us apply these traits to contemporary Egypt. While nobody would mistake President al-Sisi for an Islamist, Bayat's description captures his public persona well. The Egyptian president, a former general, presents himself as resolute and selfless in his pursuit of the national good – a warrior in the service of the nation. He appears as an emotional, yet controlled man in his public appearances, and he governs in an exclusivist way. EGYCon is everything that al-Sisi and his regime are not. The festival inconspicuously challenges the message of austerity emanating from Egypt's authorities. Or, as Bayat concludes, 'fun disturbs exclusivist doctrinal authority because, as a source of instantaneous fulfilment, it represents a powerful rival archetype, one that stands against discipline, rigid structures, single discourse, and monopoly of truth'.[11]

EGYCon was all about innocent fun; it did not have any sharp edges. However, fun may also be naughty and explicitly subversive. Using irreverent humour and satire, comic creators in Egypt, Lebanon and elsewhere assert their independence and individuality as youths in a society dominated by values and social systems they do not approve of. A good example is provided by Muhammad Shennawy of *Tuk-Tuk*, who has a talent for satirizing social and political relations without really offending anyone.

His little story in *Tuk-Tuk* 8, entitled 'I'm Fed Up' (*zuhuqt*), expresses an effortless combination of seeming contradictions that constitutes a claim to youthfulness in a hostile environment. Shennawy's protagonist, who looks suspiciously like a caricature of himself, says that he is fed up even if he does what everybody is expected to do – and then he presents a long list where 'smoking joints on Friday night' is mentioned right after 'going to the mosque'. His outburst draws the attention of a police officer and several bystanders, none of whom sympathizes with him. Instead, the police officer heaps abuse on him and slaps

Figure 6.1 Muhammad Shennawy, 'I'm fed up', *Tuk-Tuk* 8.

him in the face. The interesting thing is that what awakens the rage of the police officer and the bystanders is not the fact that he smokes a joint now and then – illegal according to Egyptian law – but the fact that he is fed up. He is simply not allowed to vent his frustration, to say that he is tired of it all. The story is a humorous comment on the post-revolutionary situation and al-Sisi's demands

that ordinary Egyptians bear their hardships without complaining in order to make Egypt great again. Shennawy's comic also has a critical edge, as it gives voice to all the young people who feel disillusioned.

In another story that ventures deeper into the terrain of absurd humour, 'The Sponge Bob Gang' (*Tuk-Tuk* 6), Shennawy makes fun of the sexual immaturity of adolescent Egyptians and the embarrassing situations this can cause. Having rescued a kidnapped Chinese girl who does not speak Arabic, an Egyptian family of modest means employ their newly acquired machine translator to make sense of what she is trying to tell them. However, when they turn it on, it starts playing the soundtrack of what is obviously a porn movie. Flushed and stuttering, the teenage son explains that he watched a 'French movie' with his friends, and they did not know how to erase the machine's memory. The embarrassment is recognizable for everybody who has been a teenager, anywhere; there is nothing particularly Muslim or Arabic about it (see Plate 10).

Many of the stories in *Tuk-Tuk* are funny in a surreal sense and ridicule almost anything with the mocking kind of irony that is the hallmark of so many urban youth cultures. Muhammad Isma il Amin and Hicham Rahma's story about the 'third brain' is a good example ('The Third Brain', *Tuk-Tuk* 6). It is a tale of a simple farmer in an Egyptian village who compulsively watches the TV shows of the famous Islamic preacher Mustafa Mahmud, who was known for his TV shows and books on Islam and science. Influenced by Mahmud's pseudo-scientific talk-shows, the peasant is convinced that everybody has a 'third brain', a part of the brain which is normally not in use. By way of mental exercise it can be activated and thus enhance communicative and intellectual abilities. The farmer announces that he has managed to activate his third brain, and sets out to prove it for his fellow villagers by using his newfound abilities to milk a cow by telepathy. Improbably, he succeeds, but shortly after having achieved this fantastic feat he is abducted by the CIA. Eager to employ the peasant's remarkable abilities for their own purposes, they subject the poor man to all kinds of tests, only to find that there is little activity going on in his brain. Consequently, they soon dump him outside his village, where he is united with his wife (and his favourite cow). What makes this story funny is not only the wildly implausible storyline and the original artwork, but also the parody of mainstream cultural phenomena: the simplistic religio-science offered by Islamic preachers, the stereotype of the naive peasant, and the conspiratorial idea that US intelligence is 'everywhere'.

Language is also important for the sense of youthfulness one gets when reading *Tuk-Tuk*. We will look in more detail at the language of youthful cultural forms shortly, but one point is worth noting briefly here. The discourse is full of 'cool' and popular idioms, a feature that goes well with the tendency to employ dialectal Arabic rather than standard Arabic in most of the stories. A notable element in this 'cool' language is the prevalence of swearing and profanities. The favourite expression is اها (aha), which we encountered in chapter 5.

The word is written sometimes in Arabic letters, and sometimes in the Franco script, thus: 'A7A'. Its etymology is unclear, and it is not even clear what word class it belongs to. However, as one observer puts it, it is an expression of 'disdain, shock, agony, anger and a plethora of other hyperbolic emotional states'.[12] Its meaning ranges from the profane to the obscene, and it often translates approximately as 'fuck' or 'what the fuck'. The word is not new, but it rose to prominence after the 2011 uprisings. It is an indication of its popularity and implications that a Facebook

Figure 6.2 Santa Claus harasses women: Makhlouf, 'The Magic Milk,' *Tuk-Tuk* 7, 10.

group dedicated to the word was started in 2011 and currently (February 2017) has almost 700,000 likes. The page contains popular and/or political humour, and its title is 'Aha. A political, sarcastic page.'[13] In other words, this rather rude word is frequently used in sarcastic comments on the political and social state of Egypt. The way it is employed in *Tuk-Tuk* renders it an expression of youthful humour and pop culture, as in Figure 6.2, where a young woman comments on Santa Claus's harassment of women in the streets of Cairo.

The blend of youthful themes, urban coolness and surreal humour that pervades *Tuk-Tuk* inspired other Egyptian comic efforts, such as the experimental magazine *Garage*, started and edited by twins Muhammad and Haytham Raf'at. This duo is a central part of Egypt's comics scene, organizing workshops and co-organizing the yearly festival Cairocomix.[14] In the same way that Muhammad Shennawy of *Tuk-Tuk* focuses on themes associated with ordinary urban Egyptians, the Raf'at twins acknowledge the importance of the street for their art: 'We take our inspiration from the streets in Cairo [...] It's a big city and so crowded. I like watching people on the streets and in cafes and buses.'[15]

The hinterlands of the new and youthful Egyptian comics environment include the surrealistic science fiction series *Fut 'alayna bukra* (drop by us tomorrow) as well as an independent Egyptian version of *Mad* simply entitled *Majnun*, both of which have published several issues. All of these publications mix experimental impulses with a streetwise, urban humour and satire of mainstream culture. Such works are sometimes referred to as an 'Egyptian school' in comics by other Arab comic creators.

This 'school' extends beyond Egypt's borders. After the first few issues of *Tuk-Tuk* had been published, two other North African comic magazines emerged: the

Figure 6.3 Covers of *Majnun* and *Fut 'alayna bukra*.

Moroccan *Skefkef* and the Tunisian *Lab 619*. Both are self-financed, independent ventures started by collectives of graphic artists. The layout, organization and style in these two publications are similar to *Tuk-Tuk*, but they are nevertheless clearly recognizable as Moroccan and Tunisian magazines. Like their Egyptian counterparts they rely on dialectal Arabic to a large degree. But it is not only the dialect that betrays their national identities; the imagery is also infused with popular elements of Moroccan and Tunisian identity. *Skefkef* is the name of a type of stuffed pitta bread popular in Casablanca's popular quarters, and the first cover images of the magazine played on this association (see Plate 11). The very last page of each issue is entitled 'Zanqa 19/Rue 19' – juxtaposing the Arabic and the French – and it features a full-page colour image, mostly of a group of boys playing football, eating ice cream or just fooling around in a setting that evokes a popular urban neighbourhood. This feature is probably inspired by *Tuk-Tuk*'s final page feature 'Made in Egypt', also a colour page depicting some archetypical character to be found in Cairo's popular quarters. *Lab 619*'s title also refers to the magazine's national identity, as 619 is the prefix found in bar codes for all produce made in Tunisia (see Plate 12). Both magazines also emphasize the fantastic and surreal, as suggested by the artwork on the front and back covers. *Skefkef* devotes each issue to one theme which it treats with unbridled creativity, and the list of themes in its five first issues sums up its national, youthful appeal: 1) Casablanca; 2) virtual and real spaces; 3) conspiracy theories; 4) football; and 5) the 1980s.

Although playfulness and humour are the main characteristics of *Skefkef* and *Lab 619*, they do not shy away from politics, sometimes treating this issue in a more combative way than *Tuk-Tuk*, which after the 2013 military coup has had to contend with draconian and unpredictable press policies. While Tunisia has been touted as the only success story of the Arab uprisings and the Moroccan monarchy managed to steer clear of mass protests, young people are discontented and angry in both countries. The two magazines sometimes refer explicitly to this tension. In the middle of *Skefkef* 4, there is a tear-out poster of an angry, hooded demonstrator standing in front of barbed wire. The caption (which is in English) reads: 'Those who criticize our generation forget who raised it.' Similarly, the story 'It Is Not Our War' (*Lab 619*, no. 6) by 'Isam Samiri and Nuwa (artist name) uses a table football game as a metaphor for the hopeless situation of Arab citizens. Hands of monsters outside the frame (a thinly veiled reference to Arab autocrats) spin the bars. The figures pinned to the bars are the people, held in place on a board encircled by barbed wire. While they are helplessly spun around by the monsters, pawns in the hands of their masters, a chorus of voices arises from the board, reciting a poem by the famous Palestinian poet Mahmud Darwish:

> Did we not say 'no' to bribes, to corruption, to clientelism / did we not say 'revolution' in Tunisia / revolution in Egypt / revolution, revolution / until victory.

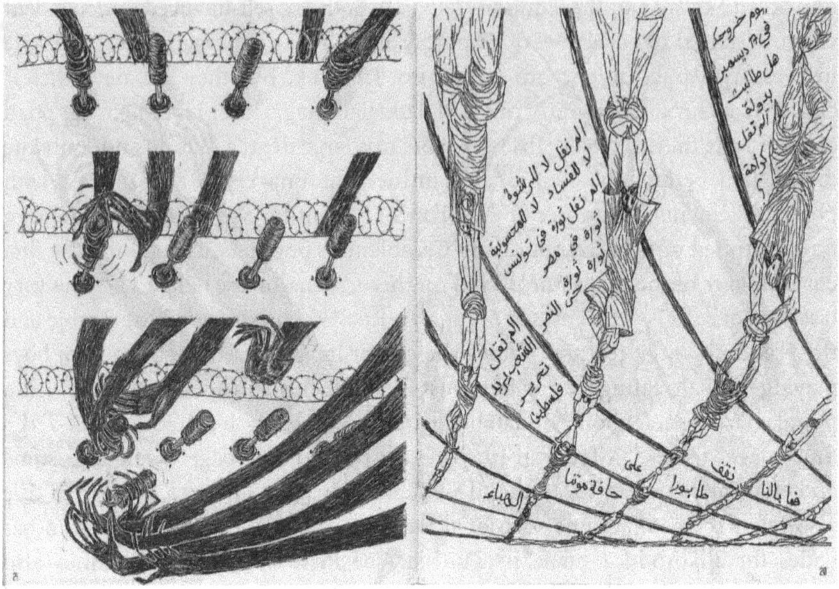

Figure 6.4 'Isam Samiri and Nuwa, 'It Is Not Our War,' *LAB619*, 6, 20-21.

Lab 619's editors always encourage their comic creators to take full advantage of the freedom of expression. 'We are very attached to the current political affairs of the country', Abir Gasmi, one of the editors, stated in an interview in 2016.[16]

Individuality and alienation

Many of these works express difficult emotions and psychological states that are often (but not exclusively) connected to the lives of young people in the Arab world. Several Arab comic artists have attested to the centrality of this issue. Hanan al-Karargi, who draws manga and Disney-inspired comics, emphasizes the importance of freeing oneself from the shackles society imposes on the individual.[17] The Jordanian comic artist The Flyin' Dutchman has stated that his narratives are 'incredibly personal, unwittingly verging on the existential'.[18] And during discussions at the 2016 Cairocomix festival, participants talked of the need to transcend issues of national identity and focus on individualism instead. Comics are a medium that seems well suited to explore profound questions about the self. Established writer-artists such as Art Spiegelman (*Maus*), Chris Ware (*Jimmy Corrigan: The Smartest Kid on Earth*) and Jason (*Hey, Wait...*) have produced haunting stories of individuals who struggle with traumas in some way or other. In contemporary Arab adult comics it is a fraught relationship between (young) protagonists and a bleak reality that is often the object of study. All the comic magazines I have mentioned in this book give room to such explorations, no matter how 'savvy' or 'cool' the image they nurture.

In Egypt one good example of such brooding pieces is the story 'Tablets of Tramadol' in *Tuk-Tuk* 7, by 'Adnan 'Umar. Tramadol is an opiate used for painkilling. In Egypt as elsewhere it is also abused to achieve a sense of wellbeing, euphoria or mellowness.

The story depicts a day in the life of a young, single Egyptian man. It starts in a metro carriage, where he has fallen asleep and is rudely awakened by an older man. The youngster is then shown at his desk at work, where he takes tramadol pills to chase away his feeling of inertia. This is followed by a livelier sequence where he meets a friend at a café and then sits down to chat and joke with a homeless beggar next to a fast food stall, before the narrative slows down again as he rides the metro home at night. In the last panel of the story he is again rudely awakened by an older man; this panel is almost identical to the one at the beginning of the story.

The story is part internal monologue, part dialogue. The shape of the frames and the rhythm they create reinforce the dreariness and apathy of the young man's life. The first page is made up of five panels that show the interior of a metro carriage from the perspective of a passenger sitting on one side of the carriage. They cover the whole width of the page. With the exception of the middle panel, they are wide and low, including only a narrow part of the field of vision. It is as if one sees the carriage and its passengers through the half-closed, sleepy eyes of a passenger. The atmosphere is oppressive. Nobody smiles, and in the middle panel, five males of all ages stare at a foreign-looking girl standing in the aisle. The layout of the page contributes to the mood of the story. The panels in the beginning of the story are wide and low. It is only when the protagonist takes the tramadol pills at work that the rhythm of the panels quickens and they vary in size and shape. This tendency peaks when he meets the old homeless beggar whom he feels at ease with. Towards the end of this encounter, when the beggar makes a joke, the frames are even broken up, and the fonts of the speech bubbles are much bigger. However, as the protagonist jumps on a metro to go home again, the frames revert back to being wide and low. The very last panel shows that the young man finds himself in a circle he cannot get out of. The same middle-aged, sweaty man who at the beginning of the story scolds him for having bad manners since he falls asleep in a public space does so again, and the panel is almost identical to the first one. But there is a suggestion of surrender: in this last panel, the lines in the background are broken, as if partly erased, and instead of reacting with a defiant scowl, the protagonist closes his eyes and hangs his head. The one thing that gives this young man respite is the painkiller tramadol. His life when not under the influence of the drug is lonely, motionless and dreary.

There are clear references to Egypt's post-revolutionary reality in this comic. At the café, where the protagonist's friend urges him to contribute to improving society instead of abusing drugs, there is an election poster showing Muhammad Mursi, the Muslim Brother who had recently been elected as president when this

Figure 6.5 'Adnan 'Umar, 'Quras Tramadol,' *Tuk-Tuk* 7, 15–22.

issue of *Tuk-Tuk* was published, and who was ousted in the July 2013 military coup. The name of the metro station has been sprayed over with graffiti, renaming the station 'The Martyrs' – a faithful depiction of the changes in downtown Cairo at the time the comic was published. The story is a piece of social realism: it depicts how life has failed to improve for young people after the heady revolutionary days.

The composition of the frames underlines this message, giving us narrow, still pictures at the beginning and end of the story.

The language is Egyptian dialect throughout. Significantly, an essential part of the text is the internal monologue, marked by grey speech balloons instead of white ones. Usually in contemporary Egyptian literature, unspoken language will be written in *fusha*. The choice of sticking to dialect throughout seems to erase the existence of a narrator, or make the protagonist and the author into one and the same person, who directs his speech directly to the reader, presuming a sense of solidarity and recognition on the part of the latter.

Let us move back to Lebanon, where youthfulness is no less central than in Egyptian comics. In *Samandal* and the Lebanese comics environment in general one often finds a palpable sense of individualism, often accompanied by a nagging feeling of unease or anxiousness. This combination is vividly on display in Barrack Rima's series of stories entitled 'A Nap Before Noon' – unsettling and even nightmarish accounts of a male protagonist's dreams (Figure 6.6). The series ran in several issues of *Samandal*. In one of the stories, the protagonist encounters an old, naked man lying in a bathtub by the road ('he looked like my mother's paternal cousin'). Later, searching for his bicycle to go home, he gets lost. Feeling the night closing in on him, he escapes the whole scene by climbing aboard a sinister-looking ship that 'was supposed to take me to my birthplace'.[19] Another and darker story is the rendition of a dream about visiting Lebanon after having spent a long time abroad. After a quarrel with his father, the protagonist goes to an isolated, decrepit cottage together with a friend. After having been attacked by a stray cat, they find a television set there, turn it on, and the protagonist sees the unhappy face of his father on the screen, being interviewed in connection with a political issue. When the father makes a reference to his personal problems, the protagonist starts crying. The atmosphere of the story is unsettling, melancholic and dark throughout, and it conveys a strong sense of not belonging, of not finding a place, of not being at ease in society.

The Lebanese scene associated with *Samandal* also offers more sardonic comments on alienation. Raphaëlle Macaron's graphic novella *Souffles courts* (short breaths) from 2015 revolves around the funeral of an old Catholic woman, gathering all her relatives in a little village in Lebanon (Figure 6.7). With humour, sarcasm and compassion Macaron depicts the dynamic in a family that is dispersed and whose members apparently have little contact with each other. The story is rich in suggestive details, but here I will emphasize the way Macaron depicts the young people, all of whom reject the company of the family and the politicized funeral ritual of the Maronite priest, seeking instead to be alone in different ways.

Figure 6.7 shows Marya, a young woman who just wants to go unnoticed because she is tired of the attempts at imposing social control on her by older members of the family. The reader shares her perspective on the left-hand page, looking into a stream of annoying faces and hearing comments she has to respond to ('When will you marry?' 'What is it you're doing for a living?'). The one person Marya seems to feel an affinity with is an outsider, the late grandmother's South Asian maid, who breaks down in tears, causing the older women of the family to complain about her 'lack of manners'. Marya seeks solace in the company of David Bowie, who implausibly appears on the scene, a total alien in this setting. His absurd appearance and the fact that he is the one who is able to console not only Marya, but also the young maid (and the dead grandmother!) underline the

كنت يا سادة
في طريق العودة في المساء
من بيروت إلى طرابلس
توقفت في مكان فيه كنيسة
ثم تابعت السير
فتبين لي أني نسيت
أغراض فعدت أبحث
عن ذلك المكان
و في الطريق مررت بالقرب
من حمام فوجدت رجلاً كبيراً في السن
كان يستلقي على أرض الحمام نائماً
وكانت المياه تجري من تحته

الرجل
يشبه
فاضل
ابن عمّ أبي
من المكسيك

Figure 6.6 Barrack Rima, 'A Nap Before Noon,' *Samandal* 8, 13.

sense of not belonging. In Macaron's narrative the extended family (and by extension the Lebanese sect, perhaps?) is a joyless site of social control where keeping up appearances is paramount, while the authenticity of lonely people's honest feelings is affirmed.

Figure 6.7   Raphaëlle Macaron, 'Souffles Courts,' (original in blue and red risograph print).

Youthfulness and the vernacular

Most of the comic works I have cited in this book, and almost all of the stories I have used as examples in this chapter and previous ones, are written wholly or mostly in dialect: Egyptian, Lebanese, Moroccan and Tunisian Arabic. This is a noteworthy fact because the default language variety when writing Arabic is *fusha*, standard Arabic. Arabic is a diglossic language, meaning it consists of two varieties that are related but structurally and functionally different. *al-Fusha* in its classical and modern forms is the standard variety, and its prestige is propped up by a language ideological edifice. It is the only codified variety and therefore also the only acknowledged written variety. The dialect, *al-'ammiyya* (approximately: common tongue), is the spoken mother tongue of all Arabs, and as usual with dialects, it varies between and within countries. We shall critically revisit the ideals and realities of diglossia in the next chapter. For the purposes of this chapter the important thing is that *fusha* has been the default variety used for writing. Especially in post-*nahda*, modern Arab culture, state-driven ideology and mass education have contributed to bolster the prestige of the high variety as the idiom for serious, consequential writing.

However, we have seen that in the Arabic adult comics, which raise a number of serious issues such as authoritarianism and gender relations, the language variety in the overwhelming majority of works is dialectal Arabic (see, for example, the text of Hicham Rahma's 'The Prison' in chapter 4, Figure 4.4).

This fact makes Arab adult comics part of a wave of cultural expressions that treat serious issues in a vernacular, casual idiom. Comics contribute to a wider vernacular trend including graffiti, cartoons, Arab indie music, youth magazines and so-called satirical literature (*adab sakhir*). These art forms cultivate a defiant sense of youthfulness and critical questioning of social and political realities. Political cartoons and graffiti are obviously connected to comics. I will not delve deeply into them here because it has already been done by others, so a few illustrations will suffice.[20] The richest current source for exploring the connection is probably Jonathan Guyer's blog *Oum Cartoon*, a reference point for anybody interested in Arabic cartoons and comics. This very blog is an illustration of the close links between comics and cartoons.[21] Guyer has made a remarkable effort to disseminate knowledge about the history and current developments of graphic art in the Arab world and their connections to politics. His blog posts and articles treat cartoons, comics and other graphic art forms in the Arab world, and many of the same names appear across genres (for references to his work, see chapter 1). Indeed, several of the comic artists we have already encountered in this book have drawn or draw cartoons and comic strips for Egyptian and Lebanese newspapers: Andeel, Makhlouf and Muhammad Anwar in Egypt, and George Khoury JAD, Mazen Kerbaj and Lena Merhej in Lebanon. As for comics and graffiti, one of the main attractions of the Cairocomix festival in 2016 was a live graffiti session, where the Moroccan street artist Normal and his Egyptian colleague 'Ammar created a piece each during a live session at the American University in Cairo's old campus (Figure 6.8). Moreover, Ganzeer, one of the main revolutionary artists in Egypt, is both a comic creator and a graffiti artist. He is a co-creator of the dark graphic novel *In the Bab al-Luq Apartment*, which won the Lebanese Mahmud

Kahil Award for best graphic novel in 2016. As a graffiti artist he made numerous pieces during the Egyptian revolutionary period, one of the most famous being the bread boy facing a military tank (Figure 6.9).

As an interesting aside, Ganzeer's piece is related to the cartoon by Shennawy depicted in chapter 4 (Figure 4.7), notwithstanding the fact that Shennawy's drawing is more light-hearted than Ganzeer's graffiti. They both juxtapose the military and the ordinary citizen, and there is no doubt about who is the more important figure. Chad Elias writes of graffiti in revolutionary Egypt that it is an activist model of consciousness-raising, adding that graffiti artists 'employ a [...] playful and self-reflexive set of semiotic strategies to engage their public', a comment that is also applicable to comics.[22]

Not only the graphic, but also the textual resources in cartoons, comics and graffiti are important elements in this playfulness, and all these art forms rely on popular wit and wordplays, expressed in dialect, for humorous effect. This was apparent in Lebanon during the 2016 'You Stink' protests. The protests were closely connected to culture and art discussions among young Lebanese, and graffiti was one of the mobilizing elements. Figure 6.10 shows a telling piece of graffiti from a wall in downtown Beirut during the protests. Two of the texts are written in Lebanese dialect, while the third can be read either in dialect or *fusha*. Two of the three also play on proverbs. The top-right text reads: 'A country in your own hand is worth ten leaders in their seats'; the top-left reads: 'To be silent

Figure 6.8 AUC graffiti workshop during CairoComix 2016, photograph by the author.

Figure 6.9 Ganzeer, tank and bread boy graffiti, central Cairo.

about injustice is to be a mute devil'; and the bottom text is simply a direct question and suggestion: 'What has your [sectarian] leader done for the country? Ask.' The blend of cheekiness and seriousness is common to comics, graffiti and political cartoons, and as they often include a textual element, it is more likely than not to be written in dialect.

Music with an attitude

In the following, I will delve more deeply into two media that are perhaps less obviously related to comics than political cartoons and graffiti but in fact are indicative of the same cultural trends among young Arabs: contemporary indie music and youth magazines.

In an article on the pop and rock music environment in Alexandria, Youssef El Chazli notes that the veritable explosion of an alternative music scene around 2010 had its roots in the cultural revival of the 2000s, with al-Sawi Culturewheel in Cairo and the Bibliotheca Alexandrina as important institutions in the birth of alternative cultural venues for young people. They catered mainly to the upper middle and upper class. While they were mostly male to begin with, women increasingly became part of the picture, especially after 2011. The alternative cultural scene was not necessarily political in and of itself, but many of the young artists were politicized quickly around the time of the revolution. The political attitudes ranged from centrist to far-left, but in cultural terms the environment was liberal.[23] This situation seems to have persisted. Many of the young artists who partake in the liberal cultural environment were politicized by the 2011 uprising, but it is important to note that just like comics, independent music, theatre and street art are not epiphenomena of the Egyptian revolution; they all appeared before that event. Populated as these art forms are by young people, they may be seen as parts of a wider social and cultural emancipatory trend that has much in common with the revolutionary ideals that went hand in hand with the political acts of mobilizing and demonstrating. The result of this convergence in

Figure 6.10 Graffiti from the 'You Stink' campaign, Beirut 2016.

the public sphere was, in the words of Egyptian author Ahdaf Soueif, 'a miraculous manifestation of the creative energy the revolution had released across the country'.[24] Soueif talks about graffiti and street art, but her comment applies equally well to music.

Music was a very important component of all the Arab uprisings. In Tunisia, the rapper El General published a music video on YouTube before Ben Ali was ousted entitled 'Rais Lebled' (president of the country). In it, El General addressed President Zine al-Abdine Ben Ali directly and criticized his rule in harsh wording. The angry rapping of El General was delivered in pure Tunisian dialect, adding to the immediacy and power of the message. It quickly went viral and functioned as efficient fuel for the revolutionary fervour. The Libyan rapper Ibn Thabit observed the events in Tunisia, and one week after Ben Ali fled he published his song 'The Question' on social media, asking if the same could happen in Libya and answering with an emphatic 'yes'.[25]

Two of the most famous indie bands with social and political messages today are Cairokee (Egypt) and Mashrou Leila (Lebanon). A particularly colourful (in the literal sense of the word) example of how comics may be wedded to other art forms to convey a critical message is found in the work of Cairokee. In 2015 the band released the music video 'Marbut bi-astik' (tied with a rubber band), in which they accuse Cairo high society of being shallow, given to hard partying and sexual harassment (Figure 6.11).[26] What was new in the Egyptian context was that the band had commissioned an illustrator to draw the narrative of the lyrics in the form of comics. The result is striking.

The artist drew the men as hyenas and the women as cat-like figures, and placed them in a fancy bar with an outdoor swimming pool. The narrator is a huge male cat, who comments that he is 'alone, as usual' and disparagingly complains that it is 'the same girls, the same stories, the only difference is the names'. Into the bar walks a girl who is 'not like the others'. She has an open face and earnest smile. The hyenas set upon her, and the giant narrator cat springs into action to protect her, hitting and killing many of the animals before he runs away with the girl. As the scene unfolds, several of the patrons tear off their faces, revealing them to be masks covering distorted bodies that are half human, half machines. Towards the end it turns out that the cat, too, is part machine, part animal, driven in the end not by valiant motives but his own lust for the girl. The comic form made it possible to augment the symbolic message of the band in the strongest terms: while the lyrics are clearly about people, the drawings depict hyenas, the lowliest of animals, as they drink, vomit and grope the bar girls.

In Lebanon as in Egypt, indie music has become very popular even as it defies social and political taboos and shuns the big media companies. The band Mashrou Leila (an overnight project), formed by American University of Beirut students in 2008, has achieved not only Arab, but international acclaim, and it is arguably even more upfront about its attitudes than Egyptian indie counterparts. The

Figure 6.11 Cairokee: 'Tied with a Rubber Band', screenshot of music video. Artwork: Ahmed Hefnawy and Muhammad Mustafa.

band's singer, Hamid Sinnu, is openly gay, and the lyrics of one of the band's most haunting songs are in a gay love poem ('Shimm al-yasmin', from the album *Mashrou Leila*, 2010). In the department of politics, the band has featured lyrics such as 'whenever you dare to ask about the worsening situation, they silence you with their slogans about all the conspiracies being woven for us'.[27] Like Cairokee, Mashrou Leila delivers its scathing criticism of political and social affairs and its cries for freedom in pure dialect. The quality of the texts belies frequent assertions in the Arab world that dialect is unsuitable for deep and complex prose. For example, the lyrics of their song '3 Minutes', from the album *Ibn al-Layl* (2015), are written in straightforward Lebanese dialect, and the direct speech expresses an eloquent message about freedom, integrity, individualism and agency:

فيي إتخبى بجلدك، فيي البس كل وجوهك. هول.
فيي إتخبى بخزانتك، فيي البس كل بدلاتك. بس قول.
فيي كونك إذا بدك، فيي غني كل كلماتك. هول.
فيي مثّل لك حياتك، لما تسمعني بمرايتك عم قول:

بس قول لي مين بدي كون علشان ارضيك
اعطيني 3 دقائق - داريني بـ 3 دقائق
بس قول لي مين بدي كون علشان ارضيك
إتركلي مهري علطاوله - شك حلمك بخلخالي

فيي أوقف إذا بدك، أو اتمدد إذا ما بدك. قول.
فيي اضحك إذا بدك، يا اما ابكي إذا انسبلك. بس قول.

ليه ليهمني اني كون بدل من اني صير؟
كل الأشياء بتعيش لتنتهي بلحن جديد.
الفرق بين الحرية والخضوع تخيير.
أنا لي اخترت. أنا لي قبلت. أنا لي قلت.
سمي الشيطان بإسمو وسمي الفنان كذاب.

149

.نصف الأشياء يلي بحسها بتجي من الخيال

،وإذا بناقد نفسي كلنا منحتوي أعداد

.أنا لي كبرت. أنا لي قبلت. أنا لي قلت

I could hide in your skin; I could wear all your faces. These (faces).
I could hide in your closet; I could wear all your suits. Just tell me to.
I could be you if you want me to; I could sing all your words. These (words).
I could act out your life, when you hear me in your mirror. And I'm saying:

Tell me who to be to please
Humour me for a three minute pop song.
Tell me who to be to please
leave the money on the nightstand; pin your fantasies to my anklet.
Standing up if you want it, or laying down if you'd prefer it. Just tell me to.
I could laugh if you want, or cry if it better suits you. Just tell me to.
Why bother being, instead of becoming?
Anyway, all things live to die as a new tune.
The difference between freedom and submission is agency.
I made the choice. I permitted it. I said it.
Call the devil by his name, and call the musician a liar.
Half the things I feel, I imagined altogether.
'If I contradict myself, we all contain multitudes.
I became larger.' I permitted it. I said it.[28]

The focus on agency, on individualism, on creativity, is the same as we have seen in the comics, and like the comics, the packaging is infused by 'coolness'. The album's cover illustration (Figure 6.16) and the song's distinct beats, synth riffs and sensual

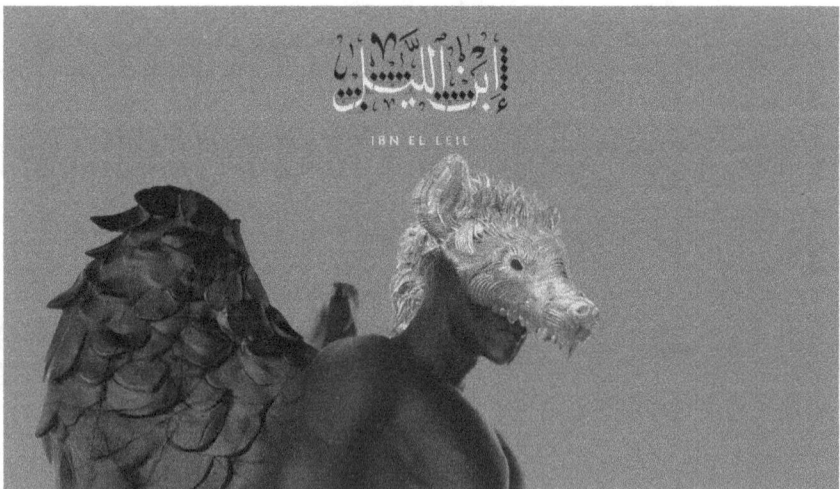

Figure 6.12   Artwork of Mashru' Layla's album *Ibn al-Layl.*

vocals all contribute to this. Like their colleagues in Cairokee, the band members of Mashrou Leila have invented a contemporary idiom saturated by rebellious youthfulness, and they use it to call for freedom, tolerance and creativity.

In Egypt, music and satire have been used by young people to 'claim their right to resist a retrograde patrimonial system that threatens every opposing voice with extinction'.[29] The same is true for Lebanese, Tunisian, Moroccan and a host of other young Arab artists today.

Youth magazines, comics and vernacular critique

In conclusion I will highlight some interesting similarities between comics and two other kinds of written publication in Egypt – youth magazines and satirical literature. I will restrict myself to the Egyptian case, noting some linguistic and stylistic similarities between *Tuk-Tuk* and two Egyptian glossy magazines for youths and young adults. The two Egyptian magazines are *Kilmitna* (our word) and *Ihna – sot gil bi-halu* (we – the voice of an entire generation). Notably, the titles of both magazines are written in Egyptian dialect.

Kilmitna and *Ihna* are magazines by youth and for youth, with the explicit purpose of nurturing a community of reader-writers.[30] *Kilmitna* is the more successful of the two. Having started in 2000, it is still published every month, and it has a relatively fixed structure. *Ihna* started in 2004 and ran until 2013, when it was discontinued, ostensibly for economic reasons. It, too, had by then acquired a recognizable design and structure. Both magazines consist of an editorial (mostly in the shape of a personal message to the readers from the editor), readers' letters, a section on social/glamour news, and then the main bulk of the magazine, which consists of personal opinion pieces, self-help articles, poems, small essays, portrait interviews, critical reportage and reviews of movies, music and books. Each issue usually runs to around 70 pages, and even considering the substantial amount of advertisements and pictures inside, they include a more than decent amount of text. Of the two, *Ihna* catered to an audience slightly older than *Kilmitna*, although there is probably some overlap: according to *Ihna*'s editor in 2012, they aimed for young adults (18–35) first and foremost, while *Kilmitna*'s editor in 2013 reckoned that the main bulk of readers were between 16 and 25 years of age.[31] Furthermore, *Ihna* was and *Kilmitna* is the Arabic-language part of two companies that also publish English-language publications (*Campus* and *Gmag* are the sister publications of *Ihna*, while *Teenstuff* is the sister publication of *Kilmitna*). The editorial staff and the content are separate for the English and the Arabic magazines. The parent companies of each magazine are both commercial actors. Although there are motives behind the magazines besides making money, they are not purely idealistic ventures.

Kilmitna and *Ihna* are both printed on glossy paper and feature interviews with celebrities, self-help pieces and entire articles devoted mostly to photographs

Figure 6.13 *Ihna* and *Kilmitna* youth magazines.

of social events. In other words, they share characteristics of 'glossy magazines' around the globe and in Egypt, where several such periodicals have come and gone over the last 20 years. However, both *Kilmitna* and *Ihna* regularly include articles about contentious social and political issues where the aim is not to entertain the reader, but make him or her reflect and engage in discussion. Some items from randomly selected front pages are telling in this regard: 'Ibrahim 'Isa: The religious discourse in Egypt is devoid of "religion"!' (*Kilmitna* March 2013); 'Harassment. . . the show goes on!' (*Kilmitna* April 2014); 'The difference between hooligans

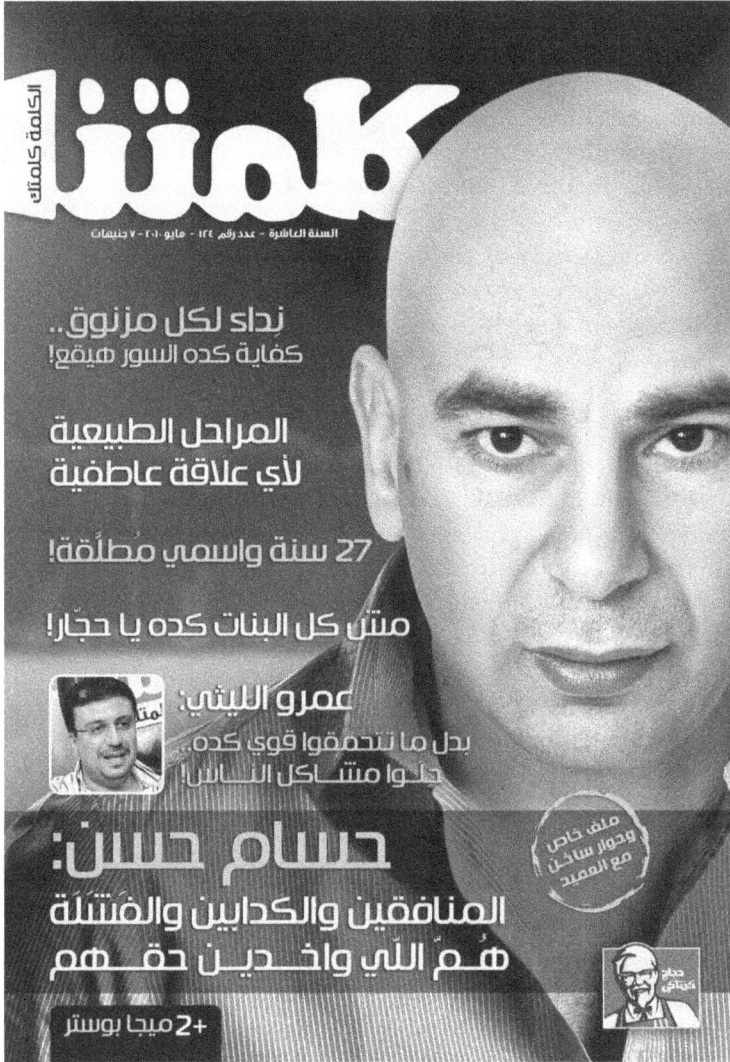

and ultras is the difference between thugs and supporters' (*Ihna* October 2012); 'Brokers of electoral IDs: the price per head varies from 50 to 200 Egyptian pounds!' (*Ihna* March 2010).

Both magazines exhibit an interesting blend of linguistic styles: predominantly *fusha* (sometimes with a word or expression in *'ammiyya* here or there); predominantly *'ammiyya* (with a few lexical or grammatical items from *fusha*); and alternation between *'ammiyya* and *fusha*. In the latter case, truly *mixed* sentences are rare. Alternation occurs on the paragraph level, or one section of an article is written in *'ammiyya* and another one in *fusha*. Occasionally a writer inserts words and expressions in English (in Latin or Arabic script).

In order to have a detailed view of the language practices in these magazines, I looked at three issues of *Ihna*, including 76 articles all in all. The linguistic distribution is as follows: 56 per cent of the articles are written in *'ammiyya*, 23 per cent in *fusha*, and 21 per cent in alternating language. As its title promises, *Ihna* is predominantly an *'ammiyya* magazine,[32] but the amount of *fusha* is far from negligible. The significant amount of texts written in *fusha* or mixed style raises the question of which variety is used for what kind of content. The table below shows the correlations between content and language code. There is not much of a clear pattern. Only two out of ten content categories are written purely in *'ammiyya*: poems and advice articles. The rest exhibit mixing to a greater or lesser degree.

Overall, *'ammiyya* is the dominant variety. In the three most frequent content categories, *'ammiyya* is clearly used much more than either of the other two. The picture when looking at *Kilmitna* is similar. Of the 30 articles in the January 2013 issue of *Kilmitna*, 15 are predominantly in *'ammiyya*, and 11 are predominantly in *fusha*, while four articles contain an even mix of codes.

The blend of codes is mirrored in the content, where there is a colourful mix of the trivial and the important, the funny and the serious, sometimes in the same article. Consider the example below, which is written entirely in *'ammiyya*. The title is 'خُدا!؟عايز ديمقراطية' (You asked for democracy? There you go!). The author of the article clearly intends to educate his readers about democracy, a serious issue if ever there was one. A central part of the article is devoted to the problem of majority rule, which he treats in a humorous manner:

يعنى تخيل أنك مسافر مع تلاتة أصحابك شرم الشيخ وقرروا إنهم ه يشغلوا طول الطريق ألبوم تامر حسنى فى العربية بدل محمد منير. عذاب، صح؟ بس ده حكم "ديكتاتورية" الأغلبية بقى

I mean, imagine that you're going to Sharm al-Shaykh with three of your friends, and they have decided to play a Tamir Husni album all the way in the car instead of Muhammad Munir. Torture, right? But there's the tyranny of the majority for you.[33]

The tone is humorous, and the author employs everyday situations and examples from pop culture to talk about a serious issue. A similar style can be found in *Kilmitna*. In the January 2013 issue there is a little reflection entitled 'Of Faults I Speak!' where the author, Muhammad Tal'at, tries to establish a basis on which to judge others as well as oneself at a time when norms and values seem to be in flux in Egypt. The background is the volatile and extremely polarized situation in the country between June 2012 and June 2013, during which the Muslim Brother Muhammad Mursi was Egypt's president until he was deposed in a military coup.

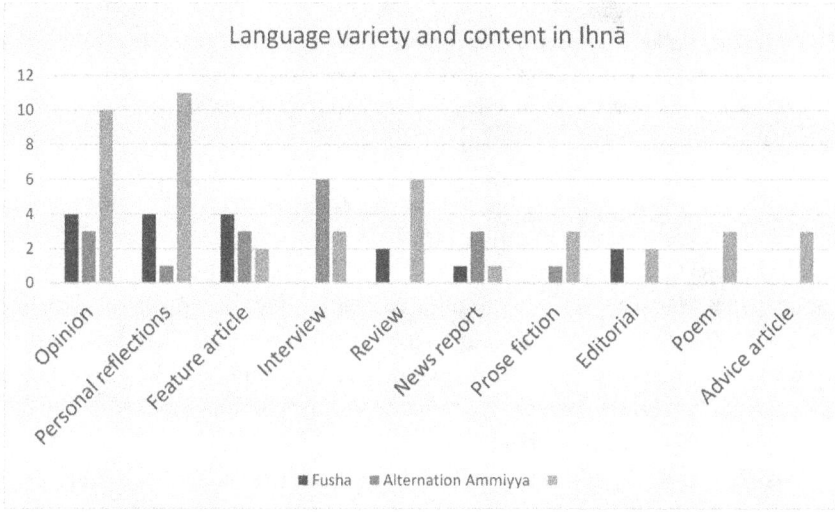

Figure 6.14   Chart: Language variety and content in *Ihna*.

قررت على الفور عمل مجلس شورى "محصن" بيني وبين أصدقائي لأسألهم أولا إيه
هو الغلط... وكانت دي ردودهم وكان ده تفسيري

> I decided right away to convene a 'fortified' advisory council among me and my friends to ask them, first, what is a fault. . . These were their answers, and this is my interpretation.

Tal'at starts this introduction to the article in *fusha*, signalled by lexis ("ala al-fawri'; 'asdiqa'i') and the use of a masdar ("amal majlis shura'), but he then turns to dialect in the adverbial part of the sentence ('ēh huwa al-ghalat'). This article also grapples with a serious issue, namely, the difficulty of disagreeing fundamentally without creating polarization and antagonism that hurt the national dialogue. As with the previous example from *Ihna*, Tal'at approaches the issue from a personal angle, sharing with the readers his discussions with his peers and his personal reflections on them. Apparently this approach lends itself to a vernacular idiom, suggesting a friendly chat with the reader about a serious issue.

Let us now compare the language/content dimension of these youth magazines with *Tuk-Tuk*. The latter exhibits a clear linguistic pattern. Purely textual pieces, such as Andeel's recurring feature "Carrots and onions" (see chapter 5) and Shennawy's presentations of popular musicians, are generally written in *fusha*, while almost all the text in the comic stories is written in *'ammiyya*. According to Shennawy, the use of either variety is not based on a programmatic approach; the instincts of the authors and the main editor determine the variety to be used, and the result shows that *'ammiyya* is generally thought to be best suited to comic narratives:

> This kind of magazine wouldn't work with *fusha*. We want a magazine that depicts reality, a magazine that is funny and at the same time critical – criticizing society. It is not logical to use *fusha* when you depict people walking the streets, or poor people. A beggar talking in *fusha*? That's absurd.[34]

By Shennawy's own account, the choice of variety is triggered by the artistic concern to depict social reality in a realistic way more than a specific social or political project. The same attitude was voiced by another prominent Egyptian comic writer, Magdi al-Shafi'i, who authored *Metro*, which also depicts life among the less privileged of urban Egyptian society (see chapter 3). al-Shafi'i stated that the problem of mainstream Egyptian comics is that they employ a language that is not truthful, for comics are a popular (*sha'bi*) art form, so one should employ the language that is used in the street.[35]

Tuk-Tuk and the two magazines I have looked at here effortlessly give room to both *fusha* and *'ammiyya*. They share the tendency to treat serious social and political issues in the vernacular idiom, which is a break with established practice. They have also challenged public morals: *Ihna* had several of its articles censored before 2011, and issues of *Tuk-Tuk* have been removed from the shelves in bookstores after complaints by customers who thought they were inappropriate.[36] In other words, there is clearly a socio-political dimension to the language/content combination in these two magazines.

What is this socio-political dimension? The vernacular style of *Ihna* and *Tuk-Tuk* reflects an urban *culture of informality*, and this is where they fit into a larger picture discernible in Cairo in the early twenty-first century. For even if the variety of publications and the number of publishing houses exploded after Egypt's 2011 revolution, the publishing industry had been revitalized well before that exhilarating moment. As I outlined in chapter 2, there was a cultural efflorescence in Egypt in the 2000s. New publishing houses such as Mirit and Dar 'Ayn appeared that brought new and unconventional authors onto the literary scene, and the established publisher Dar al-Shuruq soon followed suit. There was a new wave of so-called 'satirical literature' (*adab sakhir*) – easily digested literature in the form of essays, diaries or short stories that approaches social and sometimes political issues in a humorous way.[37] This development coincided with a new bookstore culture. Several new bookstores appeared in Egypt's urban centres Cairo and Alexandria, often sporting a café as part of the shop, many of them hosting literary and other cultural events. The new and young literature, sold in appealing café-bookstores, has an atmosphere of coolness about it, reinforced by the interior design of the stores as well as the cover designs of the books on display.

At its best the satirical literature offers riveting reads on topics that may be highly contentious. One example is *Taxi* by Khalid al-Khamisi, which consists of the author's conversations with taxi drivers during rides in Cairo in the early 2000s.[38] The conversations, reproduced in *'ammiyya*, touch on a host of aspects of Cairo (and Egyptian) life, all well known to any Cairene, conveyed with a directness and humour that make them an appealing and easy read. The same is true of *'Ayza atgawwiz* (I want to marry) by Ghada 'Abd al-'Al, and *al-Rigal min Bulaq wa-l-Nisa' min Awwal Faysal* (men are from Bulaq and women are from Faysal Street – a play on John Gray's bestseller *Men Are from Mars, Women Are from Venus*) by Ihab Mu'awwad (Figure 6.15). Similar to *Tuk-Tuk* and the youth magazines we have reviewed above, the satirical literature deals with serious issues in a humorous and straightforward way, and it is often written in a mix of *'ammiyya* and *fusha* or almost exclusively in the former variety. Much of this literature is consciously crafted for young people and seeks to connect to their lifeworld. Sometimes this includes concrete links to music, as in the case of the start-up publisher al-Riwaq. The manager, Hani 'Abdallah, explained the thinking behind the publishing house thus:

> We wanted to engage with a very important segment of society, namely the youth, the majority of the population in Egypt. To make books for young people, literary works that youth read. Satirical books, like *al-Rigal min Bulaq*, for example. Like parody. We decided to do this in a professional way that connected with youth. We made specialized music tracks to the books and posted them to Soundcloud [...] so you can feel the atmosphere of the novel.[39]

Seen as parts of this larger picture, *Ihna*, *Kilmitna* and *Tuk-Tuk* add to the phenomenon of urban informality that leads to an increasing amount of *'ammiyya* in published writing. The increase in *'ammiyya* publications is part of global sociolinguistic developments. The Egyptian case can be compared to that of late-modern European societies, where informality has become a public ideal. As Kristiansen et al. state:

> Increasing use and acceptance of features from big city vernaculars (and from capital city vernaculars in particular) may well have been a general trend of Western societies since the 1960s [...]. In the case of Denmark, attempts at explaining this trend have linked it to the development of an omnipresent media universe and this universe's remarkable turn from strict formality to ardent preoccupation with 'doing informality', a performance that draws heavily on the 'casual' image of low-status urban speech.[40]

The Cairene dialect is not necessarily 'low-status', since diglossia entails a functional divide where to some extent different scales of status apply for *fusha* and *'ammiyya*. In the hierarchy of dialects, Cairene would certainly rank high among most Egyptians. However, it does convey a 'casual image', and it does coincide with a clear turn to informality in audio-visual as well as written Egyptian media.

The same process takes place elsewhere in the Arab world. Analysing youthful, written Moroccan dialect on the internet, Dominique Caubet has coined the useful phrase 'an informal passage to literacy' about the increasing amount of writing in dialect. What she means by this phrase is that dialectal writing and reading has developed rapidly and become semi-institutionalized in the digital domain. In the beginning, dialect was used for very short pieces of text, written in Latin script because support for Arabic script was inadequate or simply for convenience when writing short SMS messages or in chat dialogues. Presently, however, Caubet sees 'a qualitative change in the texts published on the internet: writing of long elaborate prose texts in *darija*, passing from basic communication to literacy proper'.[41] People are gaining 'security, fluidity and fluency in their handling of written *darija*' through a process of unorganized but collective behaviour, repetition, and copying of the examples of others.[42]

As I have shown above, in Egypt this trend has developed beyond the largely uncontrolled sphere of the internet and into edited, published and printed writing.[43] The 'passage' that Caubet speaks of is completed, as it were, and we have actual *informal literacy*. This phenomenon is tied up with the assertion of youthfulness and a critical attitude to power and established social and political relations in Arab societies.

* * *

In this chapter I have explored the expression and meaning of youthfulness as it appears not only in comics, but also in related cultural expressions popular among youth – street art, indie music and youth magazines and satirical literature. Alongside the perennial youthful pursuit of fun, love and entertainment, all these media and art forms confront difficult social and political issues head-on, and they do so in a vernacular idiom. While the tendency to employ dialect in published writing is no doubt most widespread in Egypt, we have seen that similar trends exist elsewhere, notably in Morocco and Tunisia. Comics, independent music, and magazines are thus at the forefront of two simultaneous processes. On the one hand, they lead a trend towards informality in the public sphere, where a casual idiom and popular humour are drawn upon when addressing serious issues of great public interest, such as individual freedom, social solidarity and the political organization of society. On the other, dialect seems increasingly to be employed on both sides of the writing/speech divide in youthful culture. It is not new that song lyrics and talk-shows feature dialect. It is less common that this variety is used in writing. Adult comics and youth magazines in Egypt employ dialect, and as we have seen, the issues they grapple with are closely related to the issues taken up by immensely

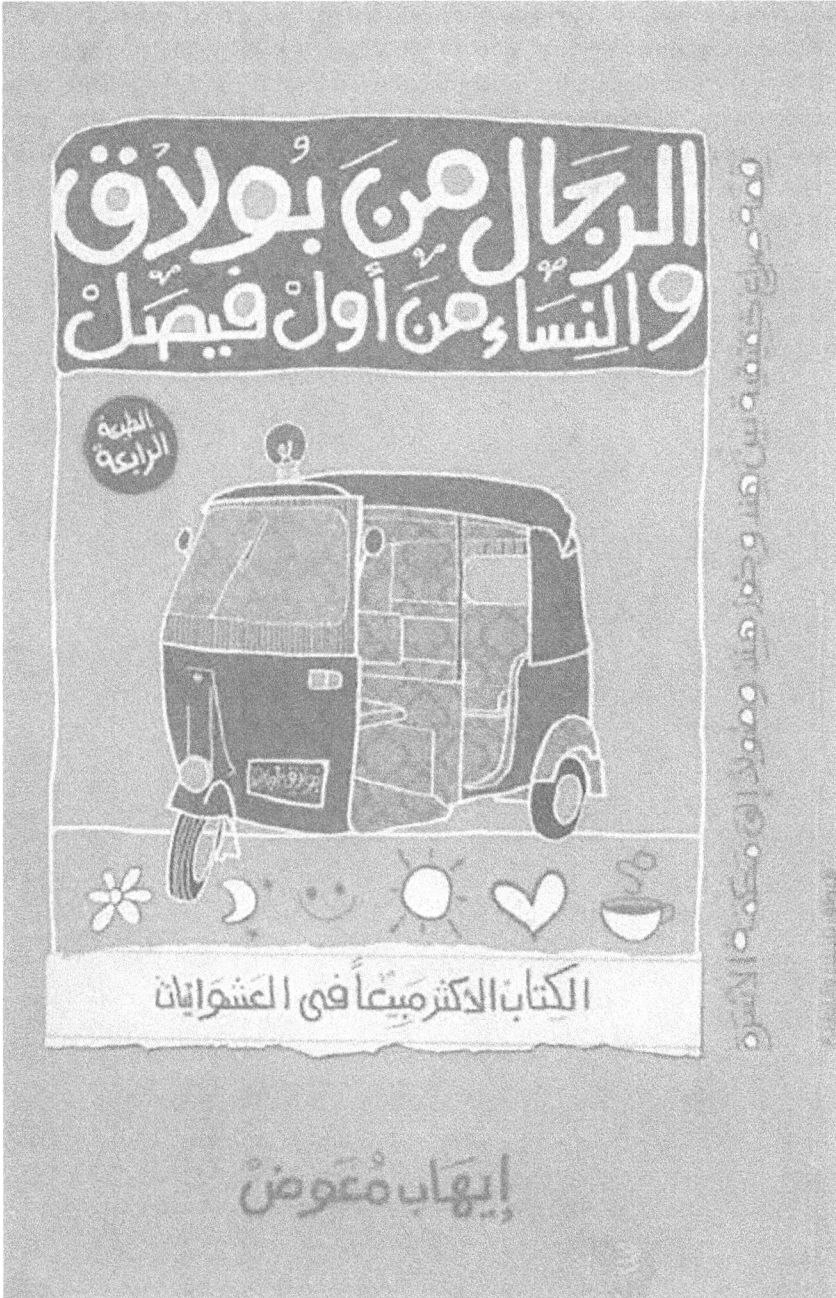

Figure 6.15 Ihab Muʿawwad, *Men Are from Bulaq and Women Are from Faysal Street*, cover page.

popular indie bands in Egypt and Lebanon today. The fact that dialect seems to be used increasingly on both sides of the writing/speech divide contributes to blurring the functional differentiation of dialect and standard Arabic that is so important to the model of diglossia. We seem to be witnessing the rapid development of informal literacy in several parts of the Arab world. In the next chapter we shall investigate the relation between this shift and the dominant language ideology in the Arab world.

7

Comics and sociolinguistics: Informal literacy, voice and language ideology

> Creative practice [...] is something that has to be situated *in the borderline zone of existing hegemonies*. It develops within hegemonies while it attempts to alter them, and so may eventually effectively alter them by shifting the borders and by creating new (contrasting) forms of consciousness; it produces 'supplements' to what is already in the archive, so to speak. The centre of this process is the individual agent, a subject often living with idiosyncratic ideas and concepts, fantasies and nightmares, who out of his/her own personal experience in society starts to feel that dominant understandings no longer work.[1]

If we regard the cultural expressions we investigated in the previous chapter – comic art, street art, song lyrics, youth magazines and satirical literature – as creative practices that take place within a restrictive social and political context, how do we account for the interplay between these creative practices and the ideological context? And how might the creative practices *affect* the existing hegemonies that Jan Blommaert talks about? We will now explore these questions from the angle of language. I focus on two questions. Towards the end of the previous chapter we established the existence of an 'informal literacy' associated with social criticism and writing in dialect. Comic art is a prominent part of this phenomenon. In the first part of the chapter I ask: what is the social and political function of the informal literacy practices we see in comics, magazines and other literature presently? The choice of *'ammiyya* for writing is not necessarily political in and of itself. However, I do think that the choice may have political implications, and I shall suggest some possible avenues for inquiry. In the second part of the chapter I turn to the language system itself, asking how informal literacy affects the issues of diglossia and language ideology.

A common claim among people who write 'ammiyya is that they do so to make it more understandable and accessible. As the former editor of the 'ammiyya-based monthly magazine *Ihna* stated: 'Everybody understands 'ammiyya, more people than understand *fusha*. Think of the popularity of Egyptian movies and songs [which are almost always in 'ammiyya].'[2] This sentiment echoes the answers in the survey on language attitudes and practices that I have referred to in previous chapters. When asked, 'do you think it is easier to understand things written in 'ammiyya?', 76 per cent of the respondents answered yes, with somewhat lower percentages (64–71 per cent) among those with higher education. From the authorial perspective, a related reason for writing in 'ammiyya or, particularly in the Lebanese context, French or English is language anxiety. Some Egyptian authors of satirical literature freely admit that they do not feel sufficiently competent to write in *fusha*.[3]

Practical considerations of linguistic competence and reader accessibility may partly explain why comic creators, authors and ordinary people may want to write texts in 'ammiyya, but they are not by themselves a satisfying explanation, for two reasons. First, there is great variation across genres and platforms. We have already seen that even within such streetwise comics as *Tuk-Tuk*, some pieces will be written in *fusha* because that variety is seen as more proper to the content and genre. As for the views of ordinary literate people, they view 'ammiyya as fitting for Facebook and SMS messages, while they tend to think that blogs, poems and newspaper columns should be written in *fusha*. If ease of understanding was the overriding concern, such variation should not have occurred across genres and platforms. Secondly, one may justifiably ask how relevant the accessibility issue is. In general, those who can read 'ammiyya can by default read *fusha*, since reading as such requires some degree of schooling, in which *fusha* is the default language introduced from the first grade. And since 'ammiyya is not a codified variety, spelling conventions and realizations of grammatical and phonological features may vary widely from author to author. For example, the particle /h/, which marks future mode in Egyptian dialect, is realized in writing as both ح and ه, and sometimes attached to the next word, sometimes not, for example حـتروح / هتروح / حـ تروح / ح تـروح (you will go). The vernacular is also more prone to include loan words from English, which make for either cumbersome spelling in Arabic or the use of Latin letters within an otherwise Arabic text. Such mixing is not necessarily good for readability and clarity. Given the high percentage of respondents who reply that written 'ammiyya is easier to understand than *fusha*, we may conclude that accessibility plays a role in people's choice of code, especially when they write personal, informal messages, but it does not provide a satisfying explanation.

In the case of comics in particular, one might turn the above argument on its head and view writing in 'ammiyya as a way of gaining distinction in the cultural field. Independent adult comics in Lebanon and Egypt straddle the boundary between what Walter Armbrust has described as 'mass culture' (TV serials, popular movies and theatre comedy) and high-brow *adab*, or serious literature.[4] The former is associated with dialect, the latter with *fusha*. In his account of the literary field in Egypt, Richard Jacquemond elaborates on this point:

> All the sections of the Egyptian intellectual elite share the same superstition regarding written material and the same over-valuation of the written word, and this elite has tended to make its specific competence – the mastery of writing – into the most important expression of the national imaginary.[5]

When Lebanese and Egyptian comic creators who are proficient *fusha* users choose to alternate between varieties, sometimes using *fusha* and sometimes *'ammiyya*, they in a sense underline comic art's in-between status as a cultural product. The restricted audience and the many sophisticated references and artwork of the comics certainly place them outside the field of mass culture, while the casual, funny and informal tone often seen in both *Tuk-Tuk* and *Samandal* separates them from traditional high-brow literature. The language choices contribute to this distinction. Writing in *'ammiyya* rather than *fusha* entails not only using a different lexicon and morphology, but also breaking grammatical and stylistic rules based on *fusha* heritage that is so dear to the literary establishment: the dual is not employed, SVO clause structure (the default in dialect and much newspaper Arabic) is routinely employed in place of the 'literary' VSO structure, and so on. I think there is much to be said for an analysis of comics in terms of Bourdieu's model of the field of cultural production.[6]

Inhabiting a third space

However, in line with the issues discussed thus far in this book, I would like to pursue the question of 'in-betweenness' not only as a position within the restricted field of cultural production, but as a position in the wider social and political context in which comics and the other vernacular print media are published.

Let us return to Jacquemond's critique of Egyptian literature for a moment. In his analysis, the elitist and culturally conservative tilt in Egyptian literature has combined with the educational system to alienate society from literary production. Schools teach Arabic based on a conservative vision of stylistics and boring, soulless textbook specimens of poetry, regarded as the highest literary form still in the educational system.

> Thus, owing to the strength of its resistance to any kind of innovation, the educational system has acted to broaden the gap between the elitist and traditionalist linguistic and literary ideology of which it is the bastion, and the real social uses made of the language and of written materials, uses that are massively out of step with this ideology. [...] By inculcating, or, rather,

by vainly attempting to inculcate, a literary ideology that has been frozen around a neoclassical norm, the Egyptian educational system has contributed to making the gap between the literary field and the social field permanent.[7]

What Jacquemond describes here is a strongly regulated writing space, in which centring institutions such as the educational system and the literary establishment have imposed a system of recognition and exclusion which effectively excludes those who do not feel at ease in a standard language idiom.[8] By contrast, the wave of digitalization since the late 1990s brought to the fore *weakly regulated writing spaces*, and comics, magazines and satirical literature reinforce such spaces and bring them into the printed, edited realm. By their dynamic switching between dialect and *fusha* (and in Lebanese comics, also French and English) and their preoccupation with the ordinary, Egyptian and Lebanese comics stand in stark contrast to the stilted, frozen idiom that Jacquemond describes in the literary field. Let us look at some examples.

Figure 7.1 Four panels from Egyptian and Lebanese comics.

day 19

after 19
days
i started
to cry

A main character in *Tuk-Tuk* who appears in most issues of the magazine is Shennawy's signature figure: a lower-middle-class, middle-aged parking lot valet with a wife and two children. This character embodies values of charity, kindness and solidarity. He and his family give refuge to a Chinese tourist who has fallen victim to trafficking, he fights and outsmarts a gang of street thugs, and he frets about the danger of his wife being subjected to sexual harassment in the street (in a feminist twist, the wife is subjected to nothing of the sort when she goes out alone to buy the groceries; instead she frightens all the men in the neighbourhood into subdued silence with the help of a broomstick and verbal abuse of any would-be harasser).

Other stories in *Tuk-Tuk* feature lonely people in the megalopolis of Cairo and alienated youngsters escaping the dreariness and hopelessness of their lives with drugs. The one I have included here is from a story by Migo which appeared in *Tuk-Tuk* 5. It is about an Alexandrian man who is about to leave middle age and enter old age and his loneliness. Since his wife passed away, he has had little social life. An old friend writes and says he will visit the city, and Migo's character eagerly goes to the train station to welcome him. The reunion is awkward, as his old friend does not recognize him and has little time to socialize. The three panels eloquently suggest the loneliness of waiting for someone who does not seem to come.

In chapter 3 I presented some prominent Lebanese war comics, including those of Mazen Kerbaj. Figure 7.1 offers another example of his work. For the duration of Israel's 2006 war on Lebanon (July–August) Mazen Kerbaj posted images and text to his blog, which became an intensely personal statement of how war affects civilians and quickly garnered much attention among Lebanese and foreigners. Although not strictly a comic, the blog is closely related to comic art and Kerbaj's work as a comic strip author. The image above is one example of the power of comic art to convey human anguish and suffering, delivered in the most unpretentious way possible: a piece of paper with a black-and-white drawing on it, scanned and uploaded to a blog server for everyone to see at no cost. Lena Merhej's comic about the same war is more traditional in form but no less powerful as a statement on how ordinary young people experienced the Israeli bombing. She describes everyday life in a city that is subjected to frequent and sudden bomb attacks in a simple, cartoonish style, which curiously serves to reduce the drama and intensify the emotional contrasts at the same time. Merhej's matter-of-fact descriptions range from the frustrations of not being able to wash her hair, via the sudden emotional changes she and her friends undergo, to her juxtaposed images of dead children in nylon bags and happy children at play.

Ihna's and *Kilmitna*'s approach to social commentary is different; after all, they are entertainment magazines filled with ads and intended to generate a profit for the publisher, and their focus is mostly on the middle and upper classes. Within these constraints they nevertheless aim to challenge both the readers and the powers that be. One issue of *Ihna* features a long interview with women who work for an Islamic TV channel and wear the niqab while on air. These women and the channel they work for were reviled and ridiculed in the mainstream Egyptian media; *Ihna* makes a point of giving them the opportunity to explain their choice without forcing them to answer provocative questions. *Ihna* has also focused on the problem of deadly family feuds in Upper Egypt, an issue that has caused suffering to thousands of Egyptians but is seldom mentioned in the Cairo-focused media. After the revolution, it opened its pages to eyewitness accounts by ordinary Cairenes who had experienced or seen torture and harassment perpetrated by the police and military. The latter was a particularly bold issue, since press freedom deteriorated sharply soon after the military took power in Egypt in the aftermath of the 2011 uprising.

In different ways, then, comics and youth magazines represent groups and concerns that are marginalized in mainstream media discourse. While the comics of *Tuk-Tuk* make visible and empathize with the millions of poor and struggling urban Egyptians, *Ihna* makes a point of focusing on groups that are anathema to many in the middle and upper classes, such as ultraconservative Islamic activists and hard-rock-loving teenagers who are (wrongly) accused of being satanic worshippers.[9] They do so in a vernacular style that represents a break with dominant written media discourse, and their stated aim for the choice of code is to depict social life truthfully and reach out to people who feel estranged from the high variety, which is nobody's mother tongue.

In line with this writing's nature of in-betweenness, the weakly regulated writing space which these publications take advantage of may also be thought of as a *third space*. Here I appropriate Homi Bhabha's notion, according to which literature may open a critical space for cultural difference, hybridity and translation instead of antagonism.[10] The notion of third space has been fruitfully drawn on in contexts comparable to the Arab one, specifically in research on written language in bilingual contexts. Bilingualism is a situation that is different from diglossia but still related to it. Crucially, it involves the existence of two language varieties and structured switches between them in speech and writing. Rakesh M. Bhatt's analysis of code-switching between Hindi and English in India suggests that switching reflects social struggles, and writers'/speakers' switches between the two codes express their position in relation to these struggles.[11] Bhatt draws on Homi Bhabha to argue that when prominent English-language newspapers in India employ Hindi words and phrases, they create a discursive space that is shared symbolically by those who imagine themselves in-between: neither traditional nor necessarily modern.[12] This third space offers them 'the possibility of a new representation, of meaning-making, and of agency'.[13]

Similarly, it has been observed that Bruneian bilingual youth use different languages in unregulated and regulated settings.[14] The Arabic-based *Jawi* script is associated with Islamic settings and formal affairs in Brunei. Youth from affluent English-language homes conform to the standard use of *Jawi* in regulated settings, such as in school and formal letters. However, when communicating with friends on digital media such as mobile phone applications, they employ code-switching between English and Malay, but always written in Roman script. Mukul Saxena's findings show how youth negotiate identities with their language and script choices. Importantly, she notes that this code-switching

> had not been learned in the regulated, institutional spaces of their lives but had been learned within their peer group and through participation in social networking sites and in computer-mediated communication. What we see in their digital literary practices is an illustration of the ways in which the global seeps into the local[.][15]

Both Bhatt and Saxena draw attention to the informal, unofficial nature of this code-switching, and its association with youthful culture and values. In other words, they describe the same kind of informal literacy practices we have identified in the Arabic context. Bhatt's evocation of Bhabha's third space hints at an interesting socio-political dimension to the Egyptian informal written language. Bhatt's remark about the element of social struggle in code-switching is relevant to the Egyptian context in particular. A persistent feature of Egyptian elite discourse before and after the 2011 revolution has been its xenophobic attitude. This attitude, prevalent under Mubarak to shore up his legitimacy, has been supported by the ruling military elite and the Islamists after February 2011. In this discourse, activists and demonstrators critical of the powers that be (before June 2013 the Islamists; after the 2013 coup the military leadership) are described as people who have dubious connections to 'foreign' elements and agendas harmful to the Egyptian national interest. In this climate, the choice to publish critical articles and stories in a mix of 'ammiyya and *fusha* is interesting. Many of the writers belong to a stratum of society that is multilingual, and where especially English is widespread both in speech and writing. There are and have been English-language publications that resemble *Ihna* in many respects, such as *Campus* and *Cairo Times* magazines. By opting to write in Arabic script and for a large part in the Cairene urban vernacular, *Ihna*'s contributors at once reach out to an audience that is wider than the cosmopolitan Anglophile crowd and simultaneously place themselves within the Egyptian Arab identity sphere. In this way, their choice of code helps them navigate a complex cultural and social landscape and signals that they are in-between: they do not subscribe to high-blown nationalist rhetoric, but nor do they wish to place themselves outside the national community, and this is signalled by their writing in their native language instead of a foreign one.

It is here that the cultural in-betweenness of Arab comics and other informal literacy practices expands to become also a social and political in-betweenness, a mediator between high and low culture, between the well-known and the foreign. The intention to translate between cultures and to open a critical dialogue by using difference creatively is a hallmark of adult comics and youth magazines. *Tuk-Tuk*'s main editor Muhammad Shennawy freely acknowledges his debt to French fanzines and other contemporary European graphic art in creating stories about contemporary Egyptian society. And the mix of *fusha* and 'ammiyya in the magazine's presentations of famous Arab and international musicians serves to translate and encourage contact: he translates the lyrics of songs in other Arab dialects and European languages into Egyptian dialect, while the presentation of the musician is written in *fusha*. *Samandal* incorporates the desire to traverse cultures in its very subtitle: *Picture Stories from Here and There*. It is also cosmopolitan in its outlook, featuring stories in English and French as well as Arabic and opening its pages to comic creators from all over the world (several contributions have been made by French and American artists). As for *Ihna* and *Kilmitna*, their play on combinations of genres, content and code is evidence of a refusal to let the content or the issue at hand determine the tone and the style of writing. By treating serious issues like democratization and conservative religion in a playful and informal language, the writers encourage hybridity and translation between high and low, conservative and liberal cultures and idioms.

Charles Hirschkind has noted a related development in the Egyptian blogosphere, where religious differences are overcome and a critical ideology developed through a common, unifying language marked by code-switching between *fusha* and *'ammiyya*. In the blogosphere, he notes, there is 'recognition of the necessity of creating a language of political agency capable of encompassing the heterogeneity of commitments – religious and otherwise – that characterize Egyptian society'.[16] As I have tried to show in this section, it seems probable that written *'ammiyya* has the potential to be used in a boundary-breaking and critical sense, and that the comic artists and young aspiring journalists have seized this opportunity.

Voice

Most importantly, however, and related to the carving out of a third space, is the way in which the use of dialect and an informal idiom gives *voice* to young Arabs outside the media and literary establishment. Dell Hymes developed this concept in terms of a vision consisting of two parts:

> One is a kind of negative freedom, freedom from denial of opportunity due to something linguistic, whether in speaking or reading or writing. One is a kind of positive freedom, freedom for satisfaction in the use of language, for language to be a source of imaginative life and satisfying form. In my own mind I would unite the two kinds of freedom in the notion of *voice*.[17]

Let us for a moment go back to the views of some of the Egyptian and Lebanese comic creators on language and language choice. Magdi al-Shafi'i, who wrote *Metro* and was also the editor of the human-rights-focused comic magazine *Dushma*, realized that the formal Arabic he had used when writing comics for children was not 'truthful', and so he started inserting more Egyptian dialect into his work. Talking about the changes that have taken place in Egyptian writing during the last couple of decades, he glowed with enthusiasm:

> The real linguistic empowerment took place at the hands of the Egyptian bloggers. These are the prophets of the new age in Egypt. Seriously. They have changed the language. Before them, the written language was a hypocritical Arabic language that did not communicate with simple people; it was not truthful, not real. The bloggers started using Egyptian terms [...] There was a tremendous development [in prose writing] as a result of this. Wa'il 'Abbas is a good example. And 'Ala ['Abd al-Fattah] and Ahmad Gharbiyya are real connoisseurs of comics [...] These people made a new linguistic awakening [*ba'th*]. Ahmad Sarraf al-'Asab, Ahmad al-'Ayidi, 'Umar Tahir, Bilal Fadl – they have no inhibitions. *They represent a linguistic liberation in mixing the Arabic [i.e. fusha] and the Egyptian.*[18]

It is worth noting here that among the writers al-Shafi'i mentions, the last two are well-known – in the case of Bilal Fadl celebrated – satirical writers (see chapter 6). al-Shafi'i clearly feels that the trend towards writing in dialect and alternating between it and *fusha* liberates and empowers him, makes him able to communicate in an idiom that feels authentic and truthful – in other words, he talks about linguistic freedom, in Hymes's terms. The same feeling was expressed by George Khoury JAD, the Lebanese comics pioneer, who switched from French (his language of education) to Lebanese Arabic because he felt it expressed his identity better.[19] And Shennawy of *Tuk-Tuk* prioritizes atmosphere and authenticity over the standard language ideology when he writes his humorous comics about ordinary Egyptians.

The point here is not that writing in *'ammiyya per se* gives voice to these comic creators; sometimes they choose to write in *fusha* because they deem it more appropriate. At other times, especially in *Samandal* but also in Moroccan comics, French or English may be employed. The point is rather that the comics medium allows people who master two or several varieties the freedom to choose among them at will, using language as 'a source of imaginative life and satisfying form'.

By allowing and even encouraging young people to write in a non-standard idiom in which they feel at ease, comics, street art, youth magazines and colloquial literature enable young people to make themselves heard, or rather *read*, despite not employing the institutionally sanctioned resource for making meaning: the modern standard Arabic variety. The institutionalized diglossic ideology imposes a standard – *al-fusha* – which is not the natural idiom for any speaker of Arabic (that is, nobody learns it as his/her mother tongue). According to this norm, writing, particularly published writing, is supposed to be composed in *fusha*. Hapless Arab writers and would-be writers have experienced the power of this norm over the centuries, as their grammatical errors and alleged stylistic weaknesses made them objects of ridicule and scorn. As Jan Blommaert notes, '[i]nstitutions have the tendency to "freeze" the conditions for voice: unless you speak or write *in this particular* way, you will not be heard or read'.[20] However, today there seems to be growing acceptance of non-standard writing in a number of media. Young people experience the negative freedom that Hymes talks about – they are not denied the opportunity to express themselves in writing 'due to something linguistic'. And the comic creators and other writers we have been studying in this book also increasingly feel free to gain pleasure from writing, exactly by being able to write in *fusha*, *'ammiyya*, French or English, and mix those languages as they see fit.

But the concept of voice also has an important socio-political dimension. In the contemporary Arab world, young people feel that they are marginalized and disenfranchised. Their concerns go largely unheeded and there are few public arenas for them to express their opinions and participate in forming society. The Egyptian uprising, initiated by youths, was partly about such grievances, as was Lebanon's 'You Stink' protest. There is a linguistic dimension to this marginalization connected to the concept of voice. *Fusha* is the code of high culture, of officialdom and weighty words. It is a code that does not sit well with the casual, informal idiom in popular culture which is embraced by young people. This is where the significance of *Kilmitna* and *Ihna*'s linguistic *laissez-faire* policy comes into view. These magazines are made by young people for young people. Karim al-Dugwi, the editor of *Ihna*, explained that the reason his magazine employed dialect was to make it more accessible to people who were not used to reading much. When I interviewed *Kilmitna*'s director Marwa 'Awad in 2014 she told me that the main idea driving *Kilmitna* is that young people get a chance to express what is inside them, and that they write themselves, not that somebody writes about them. The magazine is a place where they can learn and experiment with new skills, so they get a chance to practise before they begin their career.[21]

Ihna and *Kilmitna* explicitly encourage readers to write articles. They are built on the idea of a community of reader-writers, and many of the articles are contributed by non-staff, freelance journalists or quite simply amateur writers who wish to publish their writing. Both magazines explicitly encourage their readers to submit articles, poems, essays or the like, putting the threshold quite low for accepted contributions, judging from some of the articles that have appeared in certain issues. The community aspect of the magazines is alluded to in their very names: *We – The Voice of an Entire Generation* and *Our Word*. There is an implication of community and solidarity between young people in these two magazines that is not found to the same extent in other magazines that are more purely for entertainment and profit. At times it is quite explicit. Thus Manal al-Mahdi, the owner of the publishing company that publishes *Kilmitna*, ended her regular column in issue 1/2013 with the words:

> January 2013 is the 13th anniversary of *Kilmitna* [...] 13 years in which we have been a pulpit for youth, to spread positivity, and we will continue – God willing – with youth and for youth, so that they can express themselves and realize their dreams and aspirations. Congratulations to each creative and influential *kalamawi* in Egypt.

These two magazines offer youth a place where they can write and read about the things that are on their minds – in an idiom in which they feel at home. Some choose a simple form of *fusha*, others *'ammiyya*. The point is that the magazines accommodate a youthful discourse and that they are flexible about the choice of code, prioritizing the effort to get young people to write over linguistic orthodoxy. And they serve as vehicles for unabashed social and political criticism.

An issue of *Ihna* shortly before it closed down in 2012 illustrates this point well. It shows that the young editors felt they had a political mission to spread young people's version of Egypt's post-revolutionary reality. The January 2012 issue was devoted to eyewitness accounts of the Egyptian military's abuse of power after Mubarak stepped down on 8 February 2011. The editor Karim al-Degwi, who normally wrote in *'ammiyya*, composed the whole leader article in *fusha*, perhaps because he felt the issue to be so grave; the accounts inside the issue were written in both varieties according to the choice of the individual authors. Here is Degwi's opening salvo:

هذا العدد يختلف عن غيره كثيراً، فقد انتهى زمن السكوت! هذا العدد هو توثيق لما يقرب من عام من حكم المجلس العسكري للبلاد، عام من الوعود والبيانات، عام من الأحداث، عام من الجرائم التى لم يعاقب مرتكبوها، عام من الشهداء مل أهلهم طلب القصاص!

[…]

قد تختلف معنا، وقد نتفق سويا، لكن فى النهاية نحملك أمانة، أن تعطى هذا العدد بعد قراءته لشخص لا يملك حسابا على فيس بوك وتويتر، شخص لا يشاهد أون تى فى ول الجزيرة … شخص لم تصله الحقيقة بعد […]

This issue differs a lot from others, for the era of silence has come to an end! This issue documents nearly one year of the rule of the Military Council [i.e. the Supreme Council of the Armed Forces] over the country – a year of promises and declarations, of events, of crimes whose perpetrators have not been punished; a year of martyrs whose families have tired of demanding retribution!

[…]

You may disagree with us, or we may agree, but in either case we entrust you with a task: that after reading this issue you give it to a person who does not have a Facebook or Twitter account, someone who does not watch ON TV [an independent TV channel at the time] or al-Jazira… A person whom the truth has not yet reached […].

The importance of gaining a voice could hardly have been illustrated better. The era of silence has ended; young people now stand up and fearlessly raise their voice in the face of power. Since the military coup in 2013 the atmosphere has changed, obviously, and fear has taken the place of heady enthusiasm among many young people. But we will do well to remember that many Egyptians still engage in criticism of the powers that be and their ideology, and at huge personal risk. Several of these activists were and are closely associated with the Egyptian comics scene, for example Muzn Hasan, the director of Naẓra, the feminist NGO that produced *Shakmagiya* (see chapter 5). She had her assets frozen in January 2017 and faces an uncertain future. Andeel, who is one of the extremely few artists to have drawn caricatures of President al-Sisi, used to be on the creative team of Basim Yusuf's immensely popular talk-show *al-Barnamig*, which was taken off air in 2014 (Yusuf now resides in the United States with his family, deeming it unsafe to stay in Egypt).

Diglossia and written Arabic

Let us now turn to the second concern of this chapter. The informal literacy practices that Arab comics champion have implications for the Arabic language system and its attendant language ideology. To understand why, we first need to look a bit closer at the concept of diglossia. The most widely cited definition is the classic formulation by Charles Ferguson in 1959:

> DIGLOSSIA is a relatively stable language situation in which, in addition to the primary dialects of the language (which may include a standard or regional standards), there is a very divergent, highly codified (often grammatically more complex) superposed variety, the vehicle of a large and respected body of written literature, either of an earlier period or in another speech community, which is learned largely by formal education and is used for most written and formal spoken purposes but is not used by any sector of the community for ordinary conversation.[22]

Ferguson himself drew extensively on Arabic to illustrate this model. *Fusha* diverges from *'ammiyya* in terms of syntax, morphology and lexicon, but the two are clearly related varieties and not separate languages. The former is indeed the vehicle of a large and respected body of literature and not least the sacred language of the Qur'an. It is nobody's mother tongue, but learnt at school, and is used for most written and many formal spoken purposes. The various Arabic dialects are people's actual mother tongues, but they have not been codified. Throughout Islamic history, cultural and religious elites have tended to regard them as inferior to *fusha*, or even as distortions of a supposed pure Arabic – despite the fact that people, including the elites, often wrote in a style that mixed elements from *fusha* and *'ammiyya*.

The functional divide was never as clear-cut as the ideal model makes it out to be. Ferguson himself noted the existence of 'unstable intermediate forms of the language' in his original article, and very soon it became obvious that the divide between *fusha* and *'ammiyya* is full of grey areas. Starting with Badawi's classic study of the levels of spoken Arabic,[23] this research has, *inter alia*, treated questions of how to even define *fusha*,[24] attempts at identifying distinct spoken varieties on the *fusha – 'ammiyya* continuum,[25] and critical applications and reviews of the notion of diglossia in relation to Arabic.[26] In spoken Arabic, so-called 'mixed styles' – styles with only partially structured switching between *fusha* and *'ammiyya* – are a common occurrence in semi-formal and formal situations, and such styles are recognized as a distinct variety of speech by language users.[27] The fact that speakers tend to mix and switch codes is of course connected to the fluidity of many social situations: how many participants there are, what their social positions are relative to the speaker's, which particular topic is being discussed, whether or not the tone is serious or jocular, and so on. Attempts at finding clear patterns usually end in only partial success at best. One author has described mixed styles as being 'somewhere between order and chaos'.[28]

Notice that I have mentioned only speakers and spoken language so far. This is because, while some of the contributions include reflections on written Arabic, the focus in Arabic sociolinguistics has been on the spoken language. Needless to say, the two modes are very different, and in this book, we deal with written language. If mixed and intermediate forms are inherently part of the language system in the spoken mode, what is the accepted view of the written forms of the language?

Originally, diglossia was in fact conceived of in terms of a dichotomy between written and spoken language instead of Ferguson's H(igh) and L(ow) divide. The first scholar to use the term in a systematic way, William Marçais, defined diglossia in the following way:

> La langue arabe se présente à nous sous deux aspects sensiblement différents; 1° une langue littéraire dite arabe écrit (c'est le terme que nous adopterons) [...], qui seule a été partout et toujours écrite dans le passé [...]); 2° des idiomes parlés [...] dont aucun n'a jamais été écrit [...]).[29]

As for Ferguson, while he did not give pride of place to the spoken/written distinction, he certainly did not neglect it, commenting in retrospect that 'there was one superposed variety to be used for written purposes and for many formal spoken purposes, but not spoken by anyone as the ordinary medium of conversation'.[30] In light of our focus on comics, it is an interesting fact that Ferguson developed the idea of diglossia from looking at 'popular political magazines', where he noticed that the texts were in the H variety, while the captions accompanying the political cartoons were in the L variety across languages and cultures.[31]

Later contributions have highlighted the importance of writing to diglossia. The perhaps most forceful statement is found in Florian Coulmas's recent book on writing and society.[32] Coulmas argues that '[i]n the final analysis, *diglossia is an outgrowth of the introduction of writing into human communication*. It is not a necessary consequence of writing and literacy, but a factual one'.[33] His point of departure is the concepts of *abstand* and *ausbau* languages.[34] An *ausbau* language has been shaped or reshaped from a natural, spoken (*abstand*) language to become a standardized tool of literary expression. Afrikaans, split from Dutch in this way, is one example, Arabic another. Coulmas argues that when *ausbau* languages coexist with a pre-existent vernacular variety and there is a clear division of functional domains, we have diglossia.

Language ideology and the illusion of zero-sum games

Inherent to Coulmas's dynamic model is the possibility that the language situation may change as the result of new language practices. This is a crucial point, because the informal literacy furthered by comics, magazines and the like in the Arab world contributed to such change by making dialect a more acceptable variety in written communication. And importantly, this development is highly contentious.

At this point we leave the descriptive approach to diglossia and move into the terrain of language ideology.

Diglossia has always been tied up with power and ideology; grammar and norms of correctness served as tools of power in medieval Arab societies.[35] However, for our purposes we need not go back longer than the late nineteenth century, when Arab nationalism was expressed in the cultural renaissance (*nahda*) movement. Arab nationalism was invested in a common Arabic tongue, and so it tended to reinforce the perceived supremacy of *fusha* over Arab dialects. Pan-Arab ideologues defined belonging to the Arab nation in linguistic terms, and this is a potent symbolic tool, since, allowing for stylistic and rhetorical variation, *fusha* has been the code for written language and formal speech for centuries and functions as a unifying factor across the Arab world. The dual framework of Islam and nationalism has served to reinforce the symbolic importance of *fusha*, and it is a truism that Arabs today regard it as the 'real' Arabic language, while the various Arabic vernaculars are seen as distortions of the ideal. Thus, the entry on language attitudes in the standard reference work *Encyclopedia of Arabic Language and Linguistics* states that 'the language itself [i.e. *fusha*] has become linked to Islam in ways that many believers, especially Arab believers, experience as essentialist'.[36] As for the link with Arab nationalism, Yasir Suleiman writes that '[f]ormulations of Arab nationalism [...] are invariably built around the potential and capacity of Arabic in its standard form to act as the linchpin of the identity of all those who share it as their common language'.[37] The prestige of *fusha* is supported by the state and religious as well as cultural authorities. Accordingly, and despite radical reform suggestions by some Arab nationalist thinkers, a conservative attitude to Arabic has prevailed into the present.

John Eisele has offered the most succinct description of this conservative view of the language. Eisele identifies a linguistic 'dominant regime of authority' in the Arab world. This regime accompanies education policy and language policy in Arab countries and is characterized by four central themes: unity, purity, continuity and competition.[38] According to the regime, Arabic (meaning *fusha*) unites all Arabs and should therefore be a single language for a single culture; it is in competition with foreign cultures and languages and needs to be protected from contamination by them and also by Arabic dialects, which represent corruptions of the norm; and for unity and purity to be achieved, it is necessary to preserve the classical linguistic system. Taken together, the emphasis on *fusha*'s association with Islam and Arabism and the dominant regime of authority, we have a fully-fledged *language ideology*, in the sense of a set of 'cultural conceptions of the nature, form, and purpose of language, and of communicative behavior as an enactment of a collective order'.[39] According to this ideology, only *fusha* and not the vernacular should be used for writing, and there is a strong preoccupation with norms of correctness, leading sometimes to widespread linguistic insecurity.[40] Contemporary high culture is associated with modernist nationalism, and the cultural high–low divide correlates with the *fusha* – *ʿammiyya* divide.[41] Furthermore, *fusha* is the official language of the state and almost all written news media: it is the variety of seriousness and officialdom.

In line with this view of language, contemporary Arab elites do not only believe that the domain of print media is overwhelmingly mediated by *fusha*, they also believe that this is how it *should* be. The few attempts at language reform that have involved meddling with the writing system have failed, often facing harsh criticism. Writing in *ʿammiyya* is 'resisted because it breaks with what is in effect a "cultural taboo" whose ideological validity is sanctioned by tradition and historical practice'.[42] The tradition and historical practice in question here are of course associated with religious ideology (*fusha* as the sacred language of the Qur'an) and Arab nationalism.

Thus, not only conservative religious authorities, but everyone with pan-Arab sentiments has a vested interest in upholding the ideal of *fusha* as the *real* Arabic language, and certainly the only acceptable written form. The literary establishment is a central pillar in the ideological edifice. The modernism of many Arab authors contrasts with the conservative linguistic attitudes that suffuse the literary field:

> [T]he ancient idea of adab includes conformity to linguistic norms, such as those governing purity and correctness, as well as aesthetic ones [...]. The idea of adab's necessarily conforming to certain linguistic norms was at the center of the nahda's project to revive the Arabic language, and it continues to be important today when one of the tasks of literary criticism is to ensure that works conform to linguistic standards.[43]

In the wider intellectual environment, the self-professed 'Islamic leftist' Hasan Hanafi illustrates well the concern of many Arab intellectuals. He laments Arabs' current tendency to communicate in foreign languages and *ʿammiyya*, and he blames cultural alienation. For Hanafi, the linguistic fragmentation he purports to see has two causes. First, the global, neoliberal practices connected to the contemporary modernizing efforts of Arab states. Secondly, Salafism, which is a widespread reaction to this neoliberal ideology, expresses itself in an idiom that is backward-looking and strongly connected to a reactionary *fusha* ideology. Both trends alienate the great mass of Arabs, Hanafi claims. Rejecting both these idioms, ordinary people resort to *ʿammiyya* so that it spreads throughout society.[44] The result is that modern *fusha*, the vehicle of Arab identity, corrodes:

> *ʿammiyya* as a vehicle of communication eats its way into the centre in Egypt. This is so not only in public life, but also in the scientific sphere, in teaching at the universities, in the media [for example in] the public and private satellite channels. For some time now there have even been calls to write in *ʿammiyya*, and for a dialect literature [...] And when [people]

talk in *fusha* it will be full of errors, even when the speaker in question is the minister of culture [...][45]

A similarly purist view also informs reformist endeavours, as can be seen from the Arab Human Development Reports. The 2003 Report calls for reform through linguistic research and the making of new dictionaries 'incorporating words common to both colloquial and classical Arabic', besides 'the gradual simplification and rationalization of grammar leading to a median language [*lugha wusta* in the Arabic version] that neither lapses into the colloquial nor replicates the rigid old structures that are difficult to use'.[46] On the next page, however, the Arabic language (to be understood here as *fusha*) is described as the main pillar of Arab solidarity, national unification and Arab cultural unity. 'Further still, Arabic is the bulwark against fragmentation emanating from "Information Age Orientalists" who defend the multiplicity of Arabic dialects.'[47] This is the basis on which the 'Arabic in danger' rhetoric and the genre of language policing (*qul wa-la taqul*) build. The internet is full of activists that have taken it upon themselves to correct the *fusha* errors of others, and during the past 40 years, more than 20 books on the topic of language mistakes have been published in the Arab world.[48] It is a regular occurrence in the public sphere that one religious, political or intellectual figure or other raises his voice (it is mostly men) to warn against the imminent collapse of the Arabic language, that is, *fusha*.

Opposed to the purists are the radical reformers. For example, Hisham Sharabi identifies a neo-patriarchal 'discourse' that is both a language system and systematized ways of speaking and writing. In his scheme, the religious tradition, the Arab renaissance, or *nahda*, and the classical language itself are to blame in equal measure for the Arab world's failure to embrace modern rationality. The religious tradition of learning never taught people to *read* the Qur'an, merely to recite or chant it, and thus the potential for critical interpretation has been severely circumscribed, leading to the culture of monologue that reinforces authority and hierarchy. At the same time, the classical language – *fusha* – somehow structures thought in a decisive way, and thus enjoys agency on its own:

> This is not only because of the essentially ideological character of this language with its rigid religious and patriarchal framework, but also because of its inherent tendency to 'think itself,' that is to say, to impose its own patterns and structures on all linguistic production.[49]

According to Sharabi, this reality has had momentous consequences in religious and secular discourse alike. The influential religious specialists perpetuate a discourse aimed at imposing submission to (religious) authority by restricting the mode of discourse to the traditional categories of commentary, exegesis and recitation. These modes impose meaning instead of communicating or clarifying, according to Sharabi. On the other hand, the reformist secularists of the Arab awakening (*nahda*) were, by dint of their incomplete liberation from the classical language and its discourse, unable to mould a new, rational way of thinking. Instead of replacing classical language and thought structures with modern, critical thinking and a similarly modern and critical style of writing, they merely refurbished and modernized them. The incomplete liberation from traditional modes of thought and expression is apparent in the modern form of *fusha*, which Sharabi terms 'newspaper Arabic'. For Sharabi, this is a simplified form of classical Arabic that is 'neither fully traditional nor really modern'.[50] As a result of this double (religious and secular) failure to develop a critical, rational attitude, the Arab awakening never got past the fetish for European modernism to a properly critical interrogation of the Arab past that could have paved the way for an authentic Arab modernization.

The evidence suggests that Sharabi is too schematic and determinist when he draws a line of causation from a linguistic division to a social rift. The reality is more complex. First, the idiom of *fusha* is not necessarily tied to neo-patriarchal discourse, as Sharabi implies. During the 1990s in Egypt, the most eloquent critique of the elitist and patriarchal Islamic discourse was written in flawless *fusha* by a professor of Arabic at Cairo University, Nasr Hamid Abu Zayd. In several books, notably *The Concept of the Text* and *Critique of Religious Discourse*, he advocated a historical-critical reading of the Islamic scriptures and a farewell to the elitism of Islamic scholarship's stark division of Muslims into *khassa* (elite) and *'amma* (the masses) – and he did so in a clear and eloquent style of *fusha*. More recently, in the period before the 2011 Egyptian revolution, the novelist 'Ala' al-Aswani wrote a long series of op-eds in the independent Egyptian daily *al-Misri al-Yawm* severely criticizing the regime, ending each piece with the sentence 'al-dimuqratiyya hiya al-hall' (democracy is the solution), a progressive spin on the Muslim Brothers' famous slogan 'al-islam huwa al-hall' (Islam is the solution), thereby carving out a position that was both anti-patriarchal and secular. Secondly, dialect is by no means the medium of the downtrodden and marginalized only. The poet Ahmad Fu'ad Nigm and the singer Shaykh Imam were stars among the intellectual elite of the 1970s, Imam providing the music to Nigm's powerful poetry, which definitely leaned towards the leftist end of the political spectrum. As the other side of this coin, one could mention the fact that dialect ideology has been part of fascistoid, separatist projects, as in the case of Lebanese Sa'id 'Aql, who ran publications in the Lebanese vernacular.[51]

What the purists and radical critics such as Sharabi have in common is the tendency to see the *fusha – 'ammiyya* pair in terms of a zero-sum game: if one of the varieties prospers the other must necessarily wither, and either option comes with profound socio-political consequences. On this view, the writing practices in comics, youth magazines and satirical literature seem to be part of the radical language ideological agenda. But are comic writers and young magazine journalists really language ideological iconoclasts? Let us look at language history as well as the views and practices of young writers to illuminate this question.

A brief look at the history of written Arabic suggests that variation in writing is nothing new, and that both the purists and the radical reformers are in fact blind to some historical and contemporary linguistic realities in the Arab world. I will cite two prominent trends here. First, there is the centuries-old tradition of what Jérôme Lentin has called *Middle Arabic*. In Lentin's definition,

> Middle Arabic encompasses all the attested written layers of the language which can be defined as entirely belonging neither to Classical Arabic nor to colloquial Arabic, and as an intermediate, multiform variety, product of the interference of the two polar varieties on the continuum they bound, a variety that, for this very reason, has its own distinctive characteristics.[52]

Middle Arabic (MA) thus exhibits forms that are both colloquial and standard, and in addition to these, a third type that is neither, for example the negator 'lam' to negate nouns (rather than verbs) and the construction لما أن to express the word 'when' instead of simply لما. From being a widely used variety throughout the centuries, MA largely disappeared with the advent of the Arab renaissance, the *nahda*, for unknown reasons.

Lentin describes MA as a mixed language.[53] Writers who knew how to write sophisticated *fusha* used it, as well as writers who were probably not comfortable with writing *fusha*, even though they had a level of active competence in it. In any case, it was not a substandard variety for the semiliterate. However, its *audience* may well have been semiliterates and illiterates, because MA served as a 'cultural mediator' between literate and illiterate culture.[54] *A Thousand and One Nights* was written in MA, as were a lot of popular poetry and travel diaries, and Lentin speculates that there might have been 'some kind of "parallel (cultural) market" for *some* writings in MA, more or less restricted to the middle classes'.[55] We do not know why people chose to write in this variety, since we have only the texts themselves as evidence. Lentin proposes as possible explanations ease of reading, and (for the learned texts) that writers sometimes wished to avoid hyperclassical language. There were also some literary rebels who abandoned *fusha* to write in MA, probably because they wanted to flout the conventions. The existence of MA has important implications for the concept of diglossia. Ferguson maintained, also in later contributions, that there were only two poles in diglossia, H and L. However, as Lentin argues, MA fills a space between these two poles. By dint of being a standardized and distinct variety, it constitutes a *third pole*.[56] It does so in its capacity as a *written* variety that served as a mediator between high literary and colloquial culture.

MA and colloquial writing are two different varieties. Written colloquial is also widely found, in proverbs, songs, riddles, folk tales, and so on. In this form, it has been called 'artistic colloquial Arabic'.[57] It is close to ordinary spoken language, but may be a bit more refined than it, and it may be difficult to understand since it often draws on centuries of colloquial linguistic history. As Doss and Davies show in a recent historical anthology of Egyptian texts written in dialect, it has existed for centuries,[58] and it is also documented that writing in Egyptian dialect was crucial for the emergence and form of Egyptian nationalism in the early twentieth century.[59]

Similar to Lentin, who has found his material in Levantine sources, Nelly Hanna has documented that the emergence of an affluent Egyptian middle class in the sixteenth to the eighteenth centuries brought with it a new kind of book, different from the elitist and mostly religious works that had monopolized the scene before that. In the new type of book, the oral tradition was put into writing (the funny *Juha* stories, for example), the life of the ordinary man and woman was described, and there was more attention to local culture, not least the activities and position of women. The development is noticeable from the middle of the seventeenth century. Together with this topical development there was also a change of language towards the oral idiom and style:

> The extensive use of a vernacular language close to the spoken word became prevalent in written texts at the beginning of the seventeenth century. As a result, the written word became more accessible, more inclusive, potentially even more marketable, as the language used was modified and made simpler.[60]

There are also dictionaries of dialectal Arabic from the same period, suggesting that the dialect led a vibrant life in the written domain. Nelly Hanna notes that one probable reason for this literature's popularity was that people could understand and identify with it, since it expressed local, as opposed to a universal Ottoman or Islamic, culture.[61] Later, dialectal cultural production served as a vehicle not only for identification with local culture, but for nationalist sentiments. In turn-of-the-century Egypt, where illiteracy was massive, nationalist, satirical writings in dialect were transmitted orally in cafés and other public gatherings, thereby contributing to the growth of a popular nationalism in the country. At the height of this vernacular nationalist period between 1890 and 1909, up to 24 per cent of Egypt's periodicals were in dialect.[62] This high number of dialectal periodicals 'indicated not only the amount of disaffection caused by the tremendous changes taking place in Egyptian society but also the need for a more popular and accessible forum to express these frustrations and perhaps harness it politically'.[63]

It was probably not until late in the Arab *nahda* that non-standard varieties of written Arabic became thoroughly marginalized and deplored. From this point in time, the function of diglossia as *ideology* is especially clear.[64] It seems to have gained a solid hold in Arab culture sometime between the beginning of the twentieth century and World War II, a period characterized by resistance to colonialism and the struggle for independence in the Arab world. In *fusha*, the

Arab intellectual elite had a language that was closely associated with Islam, the majority religion in the Arab world, and it was shared among all Arabs, with only minor differences from country to country. Not least, there was a vast heritage of literary and scientific work written in *fusha* from the late seventh century onwards. All this made *fusha* an ideal vehicle for Arab nationalism, the engine for the various independence movements in the Arab world in the twentieth century, and consequently it was also invested symbolically in the new states that emerged during the middle of that century and that as a rule turned more and more authoritarian before long. The dual framework of Islam and nationalism has served to reinforce the symbolic importance of *fusha*, and the end result is the conservative 'dominant regime of authority' described above.

However, as we have just seen, this view does not accurately reflect the actual language history. Then what about the views and practices of young writers – do they come across as radical language iconoclasts? The comics and other vernacular literature introduced in the previous chapter indicate a renewed trend towards a resurgence of written *'ammiyya* in the public sphere, quite possibly of unprecedented magnitude. *'ammiyya* is being used freely in Egypt in advertisements, popular magazines, short stories, novels and poetry.[65] A similar development can be observed in Tunisia[66] and Morocco,[67] respectively. In Egypt this development is reflected in the publishing industry, which was revitalized well before the 2011 uprising. Noting the increased usage of *'ammiyya* in written genres in Egypt, Gabriel Rosenbaum suggests that *'ammiyya* 'has become a second written Arabic language [...], in addition to *fusha*'.[68] A similar situation obtains in Morocco, where writing in *darija* (the Moroccan Arabic vernacular) 'runs the gamut of genres, themes, and styles of writing'.[69] The trend towards writing in dialect is particularly evident in the new, electronic and social media: young people freely use mixed language in SMS messages and in internet chat forums.[70] On Facebook *'ammiyya* is largely the order of the day, also for Arabs other than Egyptians. Digital media has played a key role in increasing writing in Arabic dialects. After an intermediary stage of writing Arabic with Latin letters, so-called Latinized Arabic,[71] support for Arabic script on computers and mobile phones is now so good that Arabic is written in Arabic script. *'ammiyya* is the most frequently used variety not only on Facebook and in instant messaging, but also in 'slower' and more in-depth digital media like blogs.[72]

Popular language attitudes and practices point in the same direction. As part of a recent research project I led an investigation into how urban, literate Egyptians and Moroccans relate to writing in dialect. We conducted two major surveys among literate people in Cairo and Rabat, comprising about 2,900 individuals. We were surprised at how little resistance there was to the idea of written dialect as an acceptable variety, and how many people reported using dialect in their own writing. Figures 7.2 and 7.3 show some salient results from the surveys.

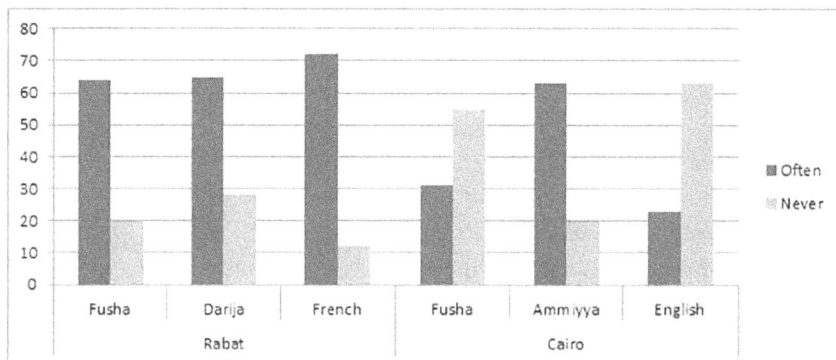

Figure 7.2 Chart: Frequency of writing in dialect in Morocco and Egypt (often=weekly or daily).[73]

There are considerable differences between the Cairo and Rabat samples, illustrating my comment towards the end of chapter 6 that Egypt has come further on the path of informal literacy than Morocco. In addition, the language ideological debate in Morocco has been at times acrimonious, and the situation is more complex than in Egypt, since Amazigh is an official language variety and the country has an important French colonial heritage. All this has led to more polarization in the public on linguistic issues. Nevertheless, also in Morocco the percentage of people who write in dialect and think that it is a variety that is suitable for writing is relatively high, considering the strong standard language ideology in the Arab world.

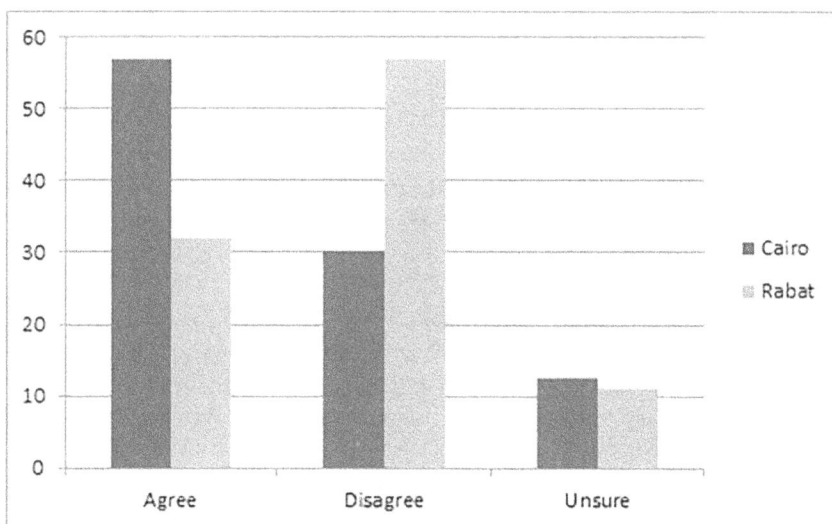

Figure 7.3 Chart: Percentage that agree that dialect has a place as a written language.[74]

The survey of historical and contemporary writing practices and attitudes above suggests that when comic creators, young journalists and authors write extensively in dialect, they are not language ideological iconoclasts – on the contrary, they contribute to a widespread trend in the Arab world today. In fact, I would say that they are at the forefront of this trend towards writing in dialect, because *they normalize a development where 'ammiyya is routinely and as a matter of course employed in published writing.*

Unlike the situation in Egypt in the late 1800s, the reason for writing in dialect today is not to reach out to illiterates, since both the writers and readers of the publications we have been discussing are literate. The question remains: if the informal literacy practices we have identified in comics are at the forefront of a widespread trend, what are the implications for diglossia as a system and for language ideology in the Arab world? Are the purists right to worry about linguistic fragmentation and the slow demise of *fusha*? This question has to do with the attitudes and intentions of those who write in dialect as well as the objective, observable trends in writing. We will examine both. Let us first look at the explicit attitudes of comic creators, writers and journalists.

There is a conscious drive among many writers to use *'ammiyya*, and their motives are sometimes ideological. In the case of the Egyptian environment surrounding *Tuk-Tuk* and Cairocomix, the very project is critical and challenges the elite culture of public writing and reading. As Magdi al-Shafi'i states, his aim is to be a popular (*sha'bi*) artist: 'I want to reach out to ordinary people.'[75] In his view, using *fusha* when depicting the lives of ordinary Egyptians would not be truthful.

Other comic creators tend to take a pragmatic approach to the issue of *'ammiyya/fusha*. As we saw in the previous chapter, Muhammad Shennawy of *Tuk-Tuk* felt there would be a dissonance between images from the Egyptian street and dialogues in *fusha*, and so opted mostly for *'ammiyya*. At the same time, *fusha* was important to him for other purposes: 'If you want to explain something I think it is better to do that in *fusha*. That kind of speech and its terms are more serious and accurate.'[76] Lena Merhej, one of the founders of *Samandal*, usually writes dialect in dialogues and *fusha* in the narrative parts. She cited politeness and ease of communication as reasons for her writing strategy. She does not particularly enjoy reading long stretches of text in dialect herself:

> OK, I read one or two sentences [in dialect]. But if someone sends me a whole text I wouldn't read it. I would say, you know, it's not very polite to do this [...] The problem is that the words [in dialect] are written differently by different people, which leads to confusion. If there is a rule, then fine. Often with the same person we develop the same spelling.... Now I have some correspondence with Egyptians, and I often think 'do they understand my *'ammiyya*?' – but I do it. For one sentence, it's fine .... I think that *fusha* has to be respected. It's the one language that unifies us all. It's the one that makes me able to communicate with many, many people.[77]

Comics and sociolinguistics

Among comic creators the motivations for writing dialect vary, but none of them harbour a dislike for *fusha* or display any wish to alter the writing system. The same may be said for writers of satirical literature. In her survey of such literature in Egypt, Eva Marie Håland shows that the authors are often highly conscious of their language, inserting meta-linguistic comments in the preface or within chapters of their books. One such comment, by one of the advocates of *'ammiyya* within satirical literature, is worth quoting in full. He gives the following reasons for writing in dialect:

> Firstly, I am more than fond of Egyptian *'ammiyya* because it is my mother language/tongue (لُغَتي الأُم) (not my dialect, no, my language, I really do consider it that), and secondly for its amazing richness, and thirdly, my emotional connection and complete control (تحَكُّمي الكامل) of it. And maybe more important than all of that: because I feel that it is mine... and after all of that as well, because I feel it is more related than fusha, to this era of Egyptian writing and the type of writing (النوع من الكتابة) that I write, and to those who read me. And I want to be close to those who read me and listen to me, I want to reach them ... (عايز أوْصَلُه).[78]

While this author states his preference for dialect in more absolute terms than the comic creators I have interviewed, there is no aversion to *fusha* or desire to diminish its prestige in his words. His preference for dialect is stated not in negative but in positive terms, as having to do with identity and voice.

What about the youth magazines? The writing practices in *Ihna* and *Kilmitna* betray a desire to present *'ammiyya* as an inherent part of the written Arabic language system, apparent in the fact that they mix the varieties within the same article and that the script used for *'ammiyya* is not distinguished from that of *fusha*, or it is distinguished only to a small degree. In *Ihna* the dialectal b-prefix in the present tense is written detached from the rest of the verb, to show that it is not part of *fusha* morphology. In *Kilmitna* there are no such markers. The reluctance to set *'ammiyya* apart in terms of script may be compared to the case of written Creole in the UK. Few who write it use the writing system invented by academics. They prefer to use the English alphabet in order not to make Creole seem separate and alien.[79]

In the eyes of the self-appointed guardians of *fusha*, these two youth magazines go against all the elements of the dominant regime of authority, making written Arabic 'impure' and less unified. However, it does not appear that the mixing found in *Ihna* and *Kilmitna* is motivated by any iconoclastic impulse, or a wish to heighten the prestige of *'ammiyya* at the cost of *fusha*. When I asked Marwa 'Awad, the director of *Kilmitna*, when she would use each variety, she answered:

> *Fusha* for literary things, *'ammiyya* perhaps for sarcastic things, or some specific experience described in an article. But *'ammiyya* also has its

standards. There is street 'ammiyya, things you can hear in the popular markets [...] Yes, there is a kind of language that is not suitable for a magazine. There are phrases we won't use at all. There is taste also in 'ammiyya, it's not a free-for-all. There are limits. Of course the best option for me is... I like the simple fusha (al-fusha al-sahla). It's not all 'ammiyya.[80]

'Awad did not seem entirely comfortable with the fact that a lot of the texts in Kilmitna are written in dialect, and attempted to play down the use of this variety to some degree. She also connected the recent wave of Egyptian literature partly written in dialect to a general linguistic deterioration (tadahwur). The same kind of attitude is often on display among comic creators and authors: a stated preference for fusha if the issue at hand is considered to be 'serious' – and this preference is quite often acted on in practice, too.

There is clearly a reverence for fusha at play here, and again, similar attitudes are widespread among the literate population in Cairo and Rabat. In the above-mentioned survey among literate Cairenes, 73 per cent thought that fusha was important or very important on the personal level, while 93 per cent thought it was important for Egypt as a country. The corresponding figures for 'ammiyya were 91 per cent and 96 per cent, respectively.[81] Considering that 'ammiyya is, after all, the mother tongue of all Egyptians, the sense of personal and national pride in fusha is high. The reverence for fusha that is at the base of Eisele's dominant regime of authority is still widespread, including among people who write a lot in 'ammiyya.

Informal literacy and the ideology of diglossia

We can conclude that neither comic creators, other authors nor ordinary literate people intend to diminish the standing of fusha to the benefit of 'ammiyya. At the same time, it is an undisputable fact that there is currently a lot of published and private writing in dialect in the Arab world. How does it impinge on the language system? It is a seductive idea that we might be seeing the evolution of a new, written variety – a kind of revival of Lentin's third pole, Middle Arabic. That would have important implications for the language system. However, the texts we have been looking at in this and previous chapters give little support for such a notion. They are characterized instead by rather clear-cut alternations between relatively long sections of either variety, and for the most part it is a straightforward task to determine which parts of a text are in fusha and which ones are in 'ammiyya.

Rather than identifying new varieties, I think the key to understanding current writing trends lies in the dual emergence of new domains for written Arabic and informal literacy practices. We do not have language ideological iconoclasm or erosion of the standing of fusha. What we do have, though, is sociolinguistic change that gives more room for dialect as a written variety. This happens because there are more media, and crucially, more private or semi-private media, in which writing is the normal mode of communication, and there are more literate, young Arabs who populate these media. I am thinking here of e-mailing, Facebook, Twitter, blogs and mobile text messaging. It is alongside this development that dialectal writing has risen to such prominence also in certain printed media like the ones we are concerned with in this book. What these digital and print media have in common is that they are all vehicles for domains of informality. What seems to have happened is that new forms of writing have appeared where 'ammiyya is accepted, but for the established forms of writing the hold of *fusha* has not lessened. There is simply more writing going on, and substantial parts of it take place in dialect. But this does not mean that *fusha* suffers. There is still a functional differentiation. When students write e-mails to their professors they are likely to express themselves in *fusha*; when they write to each other they prefer 'ammiyya.[82] By the same token comics, magazine articles and satirical literature are often written in dialect since by their very nature, these media are given to an informal idiom. However, for serious writing and high-brow articles *fusha* is mostly preferred.

Arabic is not a unique case. Similar characteristics have been found in Czech literature.[83] Colloquial Czech and literary Czech are the L and H variety in a setup that until recently conformed pretty well to Ferguson's restricted definition of diglossia. However, new domains were introduced after the fall of Communism: advertising, digital communication and public political debates. And '[i]n the new domains, typically, distinctions were blurred between formality and informality, and between spoken and written'.[84] This was connected to the global turn towards more informality in the public sphere and the introduction of intimate discourse in the mass media. In Czech literary fiction there is a move from the L variety being used in dialogue to being used also in narrative to a greater or lesser degree. The L variety is also widely used in written interviews. This situation is strikingly similar to developments in the Arab world. Colloquial in literary dialogues has long been accepted, especially in Egypt, while its use in narrative parts is still rare – the satirical literature is breaking new ground in this respect. And we have seen that in the youth magazines *Kilmitna* and *Ihna* interview transcripts are invariably written in dialect.

Given the historical heritage of writing in different varieties and the current surge of dialectal writing, neither Arab language purists nor radical reformers are particularly good guides to understanding the language situation in the Arab world. Both groups seem to be engaged in quixotic tilting at linguistic windmills: the Arabic language in its standard and dialectal varieties is alive and well, as it has always been, and nobody is out to promote one variety at the cost of the other. What has happened is simply that in the late-modern, digitalized public sphere, there are more domains available for written communication, and this opportunity has been seized upon eagerly, mainly by young people who feel at home with informal literacy practices that resemble spoken language to some degree.

While nobody is out to attack *fusha*, the new informal literacy does have a bearing on the very concept of diglossia. As one observer recently stated with reference to the Maghreb countries:

> The fact that diglossic code-switching happens in oral and written forms and in formal and informal contexts indicates that the separation of domains, which has often been claimed as the central feature of diglossia, is not as categorical as had been thought.[85]

As I have referred to above, mixed styles, grey areas and extensive code-switching are commonplace in spoken Arabic, but in written language they are not. We have seen that writing is crucial to the notion of diglossia, and that the high/low divide is associated, sometimes perhaps even equated, with the distinction between written and spoken language. How do the informal literacy practices impinge on the concept of diglossia?

I think the answer lies in redefining our approach to the question, treating diglossia as an ideological construct rather than an analytic concept. The informal literacy practices spearheaded by comics, magazines and satirical literature along with social media do not threaten the existence or wellbeing of *fusha*. Instead, they challenge the standard language ideology that has been propagated by Arab state elites since the *nahda* in the early twentieth century, a language ideology which extols *fusha* and regards it as intrinsically more valuable than dialect. This is the discursive hegemony that Jan Blommaert refers to in the quote that introduced this chapter. I follow Kristen Brustad here, who has recently redefined diglossia as ideology. Brustad notes that when Ferguson described how native speakers conceived of the H/L divide, he employed terms that pointed to ideology rather than objective linguistic facts:

> In using words like 'feeling,' 'belief,' and 'regarded as,' Ferguson himself indicates what we now call language ideology (a term that did not exist during his career). It is not that h is superior to l or more real or beautiful, but that the speakers of this culture feel and believe that it is – even those for whom h is not part of their daily lives. In other words, it is a shared belief among all members of this culture. This is the core of the definition of language ideology.
>
> Moreover, it is likely that the ideology of diglossia itself has helped engender a sociolinguistic process of erasure that renders mixed or ʿammiyya texts invisible. In other words, the ideology of diglossia leads us to expect written texts in fusha, and to see them as normative; the texts that do not fit the model are brushed off, or, in the naḥda and 20th century, physically erased, either through the 'correction' process or exclusion from publishing.[86]

She notes that today, the process of erasure is much less effective since there are so many new and uncensored arenas in which people write – in other words, the informal domains we have just discussed. Brustad's redefinition of diglossia as ideology has obvious parallels to Eisele's 'dominant regime of authority', which emphasizes unity, purity, continuity and competition. Both may be seen as expressions of *a standard language ideology*, a term Brustad explicitly invokes. The idea of standard language ideology was originally conceived of in the British context by James Milroy and Lesley Milroy:

> The standard ideology is promoted through public channels: in the past, standardisation has first affected the writing system, and literacy has subsequently become the main influence in promoting the consciousness of the standard ideology. The norms of written and formal English have then been codified in dictionaries, grammars and handbooks of usage and inculcated by prescription through the educational system. Standardisation through prescription has clearly been the most successful in the written channel: in the daily conversation of ordinary speakers, however, it has been less effective. Indeed, the norms of the colloquial, as against formal, English have not been codified to any extent. [...] [T]here is a general belief that there is only one form of correct, i.e. legitimate, English, and a feeling that colloquial and non-standard forms are perverse and deliberate deviations from what is approved by 'law'; i.e. they are 'illegitimate'.[87]

Arab language guardians, with their complaint tradition and their linguistic policing, certainly fit the picture of a standard language ideology at work against the background of a much more messy and vibrant reality. However, the reconceptualization of diglossia as ideology also highlights a weakness in several scholarly accounts. There is a difference between a systemic and a dynamic or 'processual' analysis, and the views of diglossia among both scholars and Arab intellectuals may have focused too much on the systemic end of the analytical spectrum. Diglossia is often regarded as a relatively stable situation. One central account argues that the protection of L as the native language in a diglossic system makes for stability, since the H variety is restricted to certain functions and will not marginalize the colloquial. *If* stability is upset, one would expect either that there is a shift from H to L in formal domains of interaction, or that a new L standard emerges at the expense of the H variety.[88] Such systemic approaches implicitly accept the purist view of the Arab language guardians (without the normative component, of course), and are ill suited to take account of the variation, mixing and volatility that have probably been part of spoken *and* written Arabic for centuries.

What is needed when trying to make sense of the changes in written Arabic is more of the dynamic analytical spirit that has made headway in studies of *spoken* Arabic. The substantial number of studies that have identified intermediate varieties and constant code-switching between them shows that diglossia is far from being a black-and-white picture. Commenting on the mixed forms of spoken discourse witnessed in several Arab countries today, Mejdell argues for a more flexible view of language varieties: 'The interplay between the [H and L] varieties and "the intermediate forms of the language" [Ferguson's term] should become part of the definition of diglossia itself.'[89] Building on an analysis of spoken Arabic, Boussofara-Omar actually argues for a 'reconceptualization' of diglossia that is focused not on notions of clash or intrusion but on the 'complex patterns and configurations of use that arise out of their [H and L's] coexistence'.[90]

Exactly coexistence and a symbiotic relationship between *fusha* and *'ammiyya* are the outcomes of the attitudes and practices among the mostly young writers of informal Arabic. The new adult comics represent a way of relating to language whereby young Arabs have discarded the zero-sum logic and instead use diglossia as a resource for being authentic. In this scheme, there is no one, fixed value attached to the use of any variety, whether in sociolinguistic or political terms. While the Arab state has invested considerable energy in language policies, organic language practices keep defying the dominant standard ideology.

Again, the parallel to Czech may be instructive. Karen Gammelgaard argues that Czech is moving away from a diglossic situation, or has moved away from it, towards a situation with graded registers and mixed language across and within domains.[91] Her mention of 'registers' is interesting, since it brings to mind Michael Halliday's functional approach to language analysis. His definition of 'register' is useful to interpret the meaning of everyday writing as well as published writing in *'ammiyya*:

> Register refers to the fact that the language we speak or write varies according to the type of situation. [...] The main question is 'which kinds of situational factor determine which kinds of selection in the linguistic system['].[92]

For Halliday, the register is an intermediate level between language system and individual instances of text. It thus provides us with a less ideologized and/or compartmentalizing notion than diglossia to approach variation in written Arabic. Such a framework takes the linguistic practices of young literate Arabs down from the level of ideological considerations to the everyday semiotic settings of which they are part – daily scribblings of personal household notes, postings on Facebook, text messages to friends and colleagues, or published texts that are meant to convey a sense of everyday, streetwise life. Seen from this perspective, the frequent usage of *'ammiyya* in these channels is the main constituent of a register that signals that the interaction is meant to be informal and personal. This register also allows for jocular colloquialisms to a much greater degree than pure *fusha* does.

This reorientation in analysing the use of dialect in written Arabic opens our eyes to interesting possibilities for evolution in the language system in the longer run. For if written *'ammiyya* at some point is considered one register among several in a system of which *fusha* is also a part, then both varieties are parts of one whole, rather than being separate (as implied by the notion of diglossia and by many Arabs' refusal to view *'ammiyya* as a language variety on a par with *fusha*). And if *'ammiyya* is now starting to become established as a *written* register, the whole edifice, central to diglossia, of a strict separation between *'ammiyya* and *fusha* (already weak in spoken discourse, but traditionally more solid in written discourse) crumbles. This contributes to the volatility that Badawi, Carter and Gully describe in their grammar of modern written Arabic.[93] It is not inconceivable that this volatility may eventually give way to a more flexible writing system where *'ammiyya* is officially recognized as a legitimate variant.

8

Conclusion: Ideology, resistance and voice

Arabic comics for adults are a remarkable phenomenon. Having been virtually non-existent before 2007, in just five years they developed into a veritable movement that now brings together artists from all over the Arab world. They share their work by extensive use of social media and whenever they meet during big and small comics events in Egypt, Lebanon, France, Algeria and elsewhere. It is a truly pan-Arab and cosmopolitan environment. It is also a small community of producers and consumers, however, and while independent comics have a dedicated audience of avid readers, their impact in Arab society is probably minuscule; most people have not even heard of them. Why then spend a whole book writing about them?

In the preceding chapters, I hope to have shown that there are two main reasons why we should pay attention to Arab adult comics. First, they have intrinsic value as cultural products. My aim in including a substantial number of illustrations in this book has partly been to show that a new and sophisticated form of art has emerged in the Arab world. Comics straddle the divide between high and low culture, between entertainment media – evident in many Egyptian comics – and something that is closer to curated graphic art, represented by contributions to *Samandal* magazine over the years. The independent comics I have analysed in this book are a colourful and often thought-provoking form of art. In a region where future prospects are for the most part bleak, comics offer a gateway into Arab culture that is a lively alternative to academic and media focus on issues such as civil wars, jihadism, IS and dysfunctional states. And while their combination of text and images makes for easy reads, they are often no less profound than traditional, serious literature – and equally, if not more immersive. In short, independent adult comics in the Arab world are a medium that deserves more attention among Arabs and observers of the Arab world alike because of their inherent qualities.

Conclusion

However, my main concern in this book has been with the second reason for studying comics, which is that they are a little-known but exciting expression of a larger cultural and social trend. This trend is about critique, vernacular culture and voice in the Arab world today. I have argued that the adult comics that appeared from 2007 onwards voice a criticism of and an alternative to authoritarianism and patriarchy. These are features of many Arab countries that undergird unequal and oppressive social systems – strategies for keeping certain people powerful and others powerless. In the new adult comics, these social structures and ways of thinking are often recognized for what they are and do, and with this recognition comes criticism and resistance.

In the preceding pages I have described and analysed how adult comics criticize and resist the oppressive and violent political system and its marginalization of women and youth. As argued in chapter 4, overtly political comics were part and parcel of the revolutionary atmosphere during the Arab Spring, but they have a history that is much longer than that and that has been expressed by Lebanese as well as Egyptian comic creators in explicit and implicit ways. However, it is obvious that 2010–11 was a watershed for Arab comics. The uprisings in several countries coincided with the coming of age of many comic artists who had ambitions to do more than create children's comics or political cartoons in newspapers, and this coincidence laid the ground for the rapid growth of independent adult comics across the Arab world. Egyptian and Lebanese comic creators have vividly described the stifling political atmosphere in their countries, the feeling of living in a prison, or in a highly controlled, closed-circuit system where the authorities always manipulate the public in ways reminiscent of George Orwell's *1984*. However, I have also sought to show that the depressing reality of political oppression is often addressed with a liberating sense of humour and satire. These are the moments when James C. Scott's 'hidden transcripts' – the criticism, contempt and irreverence towards the powerful that ordinary people privately share – become public by way of ambiguity and thinly veiled references, whether it is a Lebanese patriarch with weapons instead of normal arms (Figure 5.7) or it is a Cairene valet finding a parking spot for an army tank (Figure 4.8).

In chapter 5 I explored how comics deal with the oppression of women and the question of gender relations in general. Here, too, humour is an important rhetorical tool. But in this chapter I dedicated more space to trying to describe how visual symbolism and the system of panels – semiotic and structural tools at the disposal of comic artists – play a role in adding meaning to the stories concerning gender issues. It is when exploring the remarkable versatility of comics as a meaning-making device that one really understands why they are a medium and art form that is inherently interesting, and also how sophisticated Arab comic creators are.

I then shifted the analytical focus and moved on to the question of youthfulness and its subversive potential in an authoritarian, patriarchal system.

Here, I concentrated less on the criticism, or the deconstructive aspects of comics, and more on how they contribute to creating a space that is an alternative to the patriarchal system: a space for autonomy, individuality and vernacular culture more in tune with young people's experiences and idiom than more formal kinds of cultural production. When looked at in this way, it becomes clear that the new adult comics are part of a wave of youthful cultural production: street art, music, glossy magazines, satirical literature and comics. They are obviously different in many respects, but the people who inhabit this cultural space share an impulse to challenge taboos and speak their minds. They also share a common idiom, which I identified as informal literacy. This is the tendency to write naturally and unapologetically in the Arabic dialects, using socially agreed-upon conventions for spelling, and creating often long, elaborate prose texts in this variety. The informal literacy is visible in new digital media and in media that allow for a jocular or casual style, such as comics and magazines.

This insight served as a bridge to an exploration of how comics and the cultural wave they are part of connect to a set of sociolinguistic questions in the Arab world. First, I argued that the discursive space opened up by the informal literacy and the media associated with it is a hybrid, 'third' space that embraces impurities and variation rather than abhorring them. Moreover, and most importantly, the increasing acceptability of writing in dialect contributed to giving young people in the Arab world *voice* – freedom to express themselves and to be heard on their own terms. In a social and political reality that is shaped by patriarchal, authoritarian forces, this ability to acquire voice is important to young Arabs, as they struggle to survive and navigate a social and political system that puts up hindrances at every turn. A precondition for changing reality is the opportunity to speak about it, and comics are one of the channels for doing so in today's Arab world.

I then tried to assess what the increasing amount of dialect writing does to the notion of diglossia. When we realize that dialectal writing seems to always have been around, we open the analytic path of treating diglossia as a contingent and never clear-cut reality that owes its existence to a strong standard ideology. According to this ideology Arabic (meaning *fusha*) is inherently superior and must not be contaminated by other languages or the Arabic dialects, which are regarded as inferior to it. Such a view implies a zero-sum game between the Arabic standard and the dialects, and to the extent that the dialect is written this constitutes an invasion of the territory supposedly held by the Arabic standard. I argued that the language ideology implicit in comics and other dialectal media rejects the notion of a zero-sum game. For these writers diglossia is a resource rather than a problem, and they freely write in dialect without having the slightest intention of devaluing *fusha*. Surveys done in Cairo and Rabat suggest that this open, *laissez-faire* linguistic attitude is widespread in two of the most populous Arab countries, and we may be witnessing a slow change in progress in the entire Arabic language system.

Conclusion

I hope I have succeeded in showing that Arab adult comics are good windows through which to understand current political, social and linguistic developments in the Arab world. However, there is also another sense in which comics are important for anyone who tries to understand the contemporary Arab world: they defy the dominant narrative of a struggle between actors that are all repressive in one way or the other, whether it is al-Sisi's regime, militant Islamists or powerful Lebanese elites vying for power over the state apparatus. Comics tell funny, beautiful and sometimes powerful stories about ordinary people and their lifeworld, desires and ambitions, and so offer us a picture of the Arab world that is more nuanced than the usual stories of war and violent conflict suggest.

The history of independent adult comics in the Arab world is short, and their future is naturally uncertain. Underground, independent comics in the United States and Great Britain led precarious lives and disappeared after a relatively short while, and they faced far fewer obstacles than Arabic comics do. Still, new initiatives keep showing up, and a certain degree of institutionalization has been achieved with the annual Mahmud Kahil Awards at the American University of Beirut and the Cairocomix festival in Cairo. One hopes that the trend will continue and that the phenomenon of adult comics keeps growing in the Arab world. In any case, it is a cultural expression that deserves to be better known among Arabs as well as non-Arabs who are interested in graphic art and the social and political affairs of the Arab world. The Arab comic creators have already made stories that can serve as artistic and political inspiration for those who come after them and as useful documents for observers of Arab society and politics. Hopefully, I have managed to document their efforts well enough to inspire further research into the topic.

Notes

1 Introduction

1. Joe Sacco, *Footnotes in Gaza: A Graphic Novel* (New York: Metropolitan Books, 2010); Joe Sacco, *Palestine*, 1st edition (Seattle, WA: Fantagraphics, 2001); Marjane Satrapi, *Persepolis: The Story of a Childhood*, 1st edition (New York: Pantheon, 2004); Guy Delisle, *Jerusalem: Chronicles from the Holy City*, trans. Helge Dascher (Montreal, QC: Drawn and Quarterly, 2012); Riad Sattouf, *The Arab of the Future: A Childhood in the Middle East, 1978–1984: A Graphic Memoir* (New York: Metropolitan Books, 2015).
2. Jean-Pierre Filiu and David B., *Best of Enemies: A History of US and Middle East Relations, Part One: 1783–1953* (London: Harry N. Abrams, 2012).
3. The Moroccan magazine *Skefkef* is inspired by *Tuk-Tuk* and produced by a Casablanca collective. In Tunisia, *Lab 619* is a similar kind of comic magazine. The acclaimed comic artist The Flyin' Dutchman hails from Jordan, and there is also an alternative comics environment in war-ravaged Iraq.
4. Ariel Dorfman and Armand Mattelart, *How to Read Donald Duck: Imperialist Ideology in the Disney Comic* (New York: International General, 1984); Adam Riches, Tim Parker and Robert Frankland, *When the Comics Went to War: Comic Book War Heroes* (Edinburgh: Mainstream, 2009); Binita Mehta and Pia Mukherji (eds), *Postcolonial Comics: Texts, Events, Identities* (New York: Routledge, 2015).
5. Allen Douglas and Fedwa Malti-Douglas, *Arab Comic Strips: Politics of an Emerging Mass Culture* (Bloomington: Indiana University Press, 1994).
6. Thierry Groensteen, *The System of Comics* (Jackson: University Press of Mississippi, 2007); Scott McCloud, *Understanding Comics: The Invisible Art*, reprint (New York: William Morrow Paperbacks, 1994); Charles Hatfield, *Alternative Comics: An Emerging Literature* (Jackson: University Press of Mississippi, 2005).
7. The blog is found at http://oumcartoon.tumblr.com/.
8. See, for example, Jonathan Guyer, 'On the Arab Page', *Le Monde Diplomatique*, 1 January 2017, http://mondediplo.com/2017/01/15cartoons; Jonathan Guyer, 'Arabs of the Future: Beirut in the Present Tense', *Institute of Current World Affairs* (blog), 2015, http://www.icwa.org/arabs-of-the-future-beirut-in-the-present-tense/; Jonathan Guyer, 'Understanding Arab Comics', *Los Angeles Review of Books*, 9 July 2016, https://lareviewofbooks.org/article/understanding-arab-comics/; Jonathan Guyer, 'The Case of the Arabic Noirs', *Paris Review Daily* (blog), 20 August 2014, http://www.theparis review.org/blog/2014/08/20/the-case-of-the-arabic-noirs/.
9. Rikke Platz Cortsen, Erin La Cour and Anne Magnussen, *Comics and Power: Representing and Questioning Culture, Subjects and Communities* (Newcastle upon Tyne: Cambridge Scholars Publishing, 2015); Matthew P. McAllister, Edward H. Sewell and Ian Gordon, 'Introducing Comics and Ideology', in *Comics & Ideology*

(New York: Peter Lang, 2006), 1–15; Randy Duncan and Matthew J. Smith, *The Power of Comics: History, Form and Culture* (New York and London: Continuum, 2009), 246–69; Martin Barker, *Comics: Ideology, Power, and the Critics* (Manchester University Press, 1989).

10. Duncan and Smith, *The Power of Comics*, 246–55; Riches, Parker and Frankland, *When the Comics Went to War*.
11. For a full discussion, see Douglas and Malti-Douglas, *Arab Comic Strips*, 27–45.
12. The blog *Oum Cartoon* by Jonathan Guyer provides the thematically and geographically most comprehensive guide to Arab comics that I know of. See http://oumcartoon.tumblr.com/.
13. Clifford Geertz, *The Interpretation of Cultures: Selected Essays* (New York: Basic Books, 1973), 221.
14. There is a large literature that explains the emergence and persistence of Arab authoritarianism, also after the Arab Spring. For some of the more recent contributions, see Eva Bellin, 'The Robustness of Authoritarianism in the Middle East: Exceptionalism in Comparative Perspective', *Comparative Politics* 36, no. 2 (2004): 139–57, https://doi.org/10.2307/4150140; Eva Bellin, 'Reconsidering the Robustness of Authoritarianism in the Middle East: Lessons from the Arab Spring', *Comparative Politics* 44, no. 2 (2012): 127–49, https://doi.org/10.5129/001041512798838021; Jason Brownlee, '... And yet They Persist: Explaining Survival and Transition in Neopatrimonial Regimes', *Studies in Comparative International Development* 37, no. 3 (2002): 35–63, https://doi.org/10.1007/BF02686230; Rex Brynen et al., *Beyond the Arab Spring: Authoritarianism & Democratization in the Arab World* (Boulder; London: Lynne Rienner Publishers, 2012); Raymond Hinnebusch, 'Authoritarian Persistence, Democratization Theory and the Middle East: An Overview and Critique', *Democratization* 13, no. 3 (2006): 373–95, https://doi.org/10.1080/13510340600579243.
15. Hisham Sharabi, *Neopatriarchy: A Theory of Distorted Change in Arab Society* (New York: Oxford University Press, 1988), 47.
16. Alan Richards and John Waterbury, *A Political Economy of the Middle East* (Boulder, CO: Westview Press, 1996), 345.
17. Ibid., 41.
18. Just for the record, it should be noted that this fetishization of females is by no means exclusive to the Arab (or Muslim) world. Women continue to be exploited as symbols of cultural values in Europe and the United States; see Lila Abu-Lughod, 'Do Muslim Women Really Need Saving? Anthropological Reflections on Cultural Relativism and Its Others', *American Anthropologist* 104, no. 3 (2002): 783–90, https://doi.org/10.1525/aa.2002.104.3.783.
19. Shereen Abouelnaga, 'Reconstructing Gender in Post-Revolution Egypt', in *Rethinking Gender in Revolutions and Resistance: Lessons from the Arab World*, ed. Maha El Said, Lena Meari and Nicola Pratt (London: Zed Books, 2015), 40.
20. Amnesty International, *'Circles of Hell': Domestic, Public and State Violence Against Women in Egypt* (London: Amnesty International, 2015), http://www.amnestyusa.org/sites/default/files/mde_120042015.pdf.
21. Asef Bayat, 'Islamism and the Politics of Fun', *Public Culture* 19, no. 3 (2007): 433–59; Asef Bayat, *Life as Politics: How Ordinary People Change the Middle East* (Stanford, CA: Stanford University Press, 2010), 115–37.
22. United Nations Development Programme, *Arab Human Development Report 2016: Youth and the Prospects for Human Development in a Changing Reality* (New York: UNDP, Regional Bureau for Arab States, 2016), 41.

23. On this trend, see the contributions in Jacob Høigilt and Gunvor Mejdell (eds), *The Politics of Written Language in the Arab World: Writing Change* (Leiden; Boston: Brill, 2017).

24. Kathryn A. Woolard and Bambi B. Schieffelin, 'Language Ideology', *Annual Review of Anthropology* 23 (1994): 55–82.

25. Jan Blommaert, *Discourse: A Critical Introduction* (New York: Cambridge University Press, 2005), 3.

26. See, for instance, José Antonio Flores Farfán and Anna Holzscheiter, 'The Power of Discourse and the Discourse of Power', in *The SAGE Handbook of Sociolinguistics*, ed. Ruth Wodak, Barbara Johnstone and Paul E. Kerswill (London: Sage Publications Ltd, 2010).

27. Paul Ricoeur, *From Text to Action: Essays in Hermeneutics, II*, trans. Kathleen Blamey and John B. Thompson (London and New York: Continuum, 2008).

28. Quentin Skinner, *Visions of Politics: Regarding Method, Volume 1* (Cambridge, UK: Cambridge University Press, 2002), 101–2; Alan McKee, *Textual Analysis* (London: SAGE Publications Ltd, 2003), 63–6.

29. McCloud, *Understanding Comics*, 30.

30. Ibid., 118–37.

31. Hatfield, *Alternative Comics*, 36.

32. Ibid.

33. Guyer, 'Understanding Arab Comics'.

2   Mapping the scene

1. Paul Gravett, *Comics Art* (London: Tate Publishing, 2013), 73.

2. Walid Tahir, cited in Jonathan Guyer, 'Yes and No!', *Oum Cartoon* أم كرتون, 14 January 2014, http://oumcartoon.tumblr.com/post/73306371896/yes-and-no-as-egyptians-head-to-the-polls-today.

3. A thorough analysis of *al-Tanabila* is found in Allen Douglas and Fedwa Malti-Douglas, *Arab Comic Strips: Politics of an Emerging Mass Culture* (Bloomington: Indiana University Press, 1994), chapter 5.

4. Douglas and Malti-Douglas, *Arab Comic Strips*, 62.

5. Shennawy and Makhlouf, 'حجازي أبو التنابلة المجتهد', *Tuk-Tuk* no. 1 (2011): 9–11.

6. I would like to thank Eva Marie Håland for getting hold of a copy of the magazine. They are difficult to come by, and I have not been able to find references to the magazine in the literature.

7. Menna Taher, 'New Wave of Comic Books Flourishes in Egypt', *Ahram Online*, 24 October 2011, http://english.ahram.org.eg/NewsContent/5/25/25015/Arts–Culture/Visual-Art/New-wave-of-comic-books-flourishes-in-Egypt.aspx.

8. Makhlouf, 'عن البكباشي ناصر.. توثيق تاريخي في قصة مصورة', *al-Fann al-Tasi'* 5 (2012): 5. This quote and all other quotes attributed to Arabic texts are my own translations.

9. George Khoury (JAD), 'La Bande Dessinée D'expression Arabe de 1950 À Nos Jours', *Takam Titou*, 2011, http://takamtikou.bnf.fr/dossiers/dossier-2011-la-bande-dessinee/la-bande-dessinee-d-expression-arabe-de-1950-a-nos-jours.

10. Massimo Di Ricco, 'Drawing for a New Public: Middle Eastern 9th Art and the Emergence of a Transnational Graphic Movement', in *Postcolonial Comics: Texts, Events, Identities*, ed. Binita Mehta and Pia Mukherji (New York: Routledge, 2015), 187–204.

11. There is a significant amount of multilingualism apparent in this movement, but I focus on works written in Arabic, since one main aim of this book is to explore the relationship between dialect and standard language in written Arabic.

12. Charles Hatfield, *Alternative Comics: An Emerging Literature* (Jackson: University Press of Mississippi, 2005).

13. Pierre Bourdieu, *The Field of Cultural Production* (New York: Columbia University Press, 1993), 54 and passim.

14. Tamir ʿAbd al-Hamid, 'الكومكس.. تحليق إبداعي.. على ارتفاع منخفض', *Ibda*ʿ magazine, nos. 36– 7 (2015), 147.

15. Islah Bakhat, 'Arab Comic Strips Experience Their Own Spring', *SWI Swissinfo.ch*, 2013, http://www.swissinfo.ch/eng/culture/picture-power_arab-comic-strips-experience-their-own-spring/35337848.

16. http://www.comicsgate.net/home/.

17. The website is located at http://kotobna.net/Home/Index.

18. This funding enabled the team behind the magazine to publish new issues on a regular basis, and it also made possible the creation of a short magazine devoted to comics and graphic design, *al-Fann al-tasi*ʿ (the ninth art), produced by the team behind *Tuk-Tuk*.

19. Interview with Muhammad Shennawy Cairo, 10 December 2012. This quote and all other quotes from interviews conducted by me are my own translations.

20. Sally al-Haqq and Mustafa Shawqi, *Comics in Arabic: The Egyptian Scene (in Arabic)* (Cairo: Association for the Freedom of Thought and Expression, 2016), 12, http://afteegypt.org/freedom_creativity/2016/02/02/11609-afteegypt.html.

21. Rowan El Shimi, 'Women Artists Do Well as CairoComix Launches', *Mada Masr*, 1 October 2015, http://www.madamasr.com/sections/culture/woman-artists-do-well-cairocomix-launches.

22. Richard Jacquemond and David Tresilian, *Conscience of the Nation: Writers, State, and Society in Modern Egypt* (Cairo, Egypt; New York, NY: American University in Cairo Press, 2008).

23. Ibid., 42.

24. Bakhat, 'Arab Comic Strips Experience Their Own Spring'.

25. Interview with Lena Merhej, Beirut, 15 November 2015.

26. His latest work, *Solar Grid*, is a science fiction graphic novel published on the Kickstarter platform. See http://thesolargrid.net/.

27. Zeina Abirached, *A Game for Swallows: To Die, to Leave, to Return*, Single Titles edition (New York: Graphic Universe, 2012).

28. Interview with Majdī al-Shafiʿī, 11 December 2012.

29. Interview with the Hanan al-Kararji, Cairo, 7 February 2016.

30. Roger Sabin, *Adult Comics* (London: Routledge, 2013), 36–52.

31. Mark James Estren, *A History of Underground Comics* (Berkeley, CA: Ronin Publishing, 1993), 17.

32. Hatfield, Alternative Comics, 12.

33. Santiago García, *On the Graphic Novel*, trans. Bruce Campbell (Jackson: University Press of Mississippi, 2015), 126.

34. Tewodros Aragie Kebede, Kristian Takvam Kindt and Jacob Høigilt, *Language Change in Egypt: Social and Cultural Indicators* (Oslo: Fafo, 2013), 51.

35. Soraya Morayef, 'Arab Comic Artists Discuss Adversity and Censorship', *Middle East Eye*, 19 August 2015, http://www.middleeasteye.net/fr/node/45520.

36. Interview with Shennawy, Cairo, 12 December 2012.

37. Walter Armbrust, *Mass Culture and Modernism in Egypt* (Cambridge: Cambridge University Press, 1996), 212–18.

38. Jacquemond and Tresilian, *Conscience of the Nation*.
39. Sune Haugbølle, 'The Leftist, the Liberal, and the Space in Between', *Arab Studies Journal* 24, no. 1 (2016): 170–93.
40. It is symptomatic of the situation for the press in Egypt today that *Mada Masr* exists only online.
41. This award-winning documentary was directed by Sara Taksler. See http://ticklinggiants.com for details.
42. Adel Iskandar, 'Big Words on Art: The School Playground and the Cloud of Bollocks', part 3, *Status Hour*, 22 December 2014, http://www.statushour.com/andeel.html.

3 Resistance against authoritarianism and war: Adult comics before 2011

1. President Mubarak in a televised speech to the nation on 8 February 2011, three days before he was forced to resign.
2. Raymond Hinnebusch, 'Authoritarian Persistence, Democratization Theory and the Middle East: An Overview and Critique', *Democratization* 13, no. 3 (2006): 373–95, https://doi.org/10.1080/13510340600579243; Daniel Brumberg, 'The Trap of Liberalized Autocracy', *Journal of Democracy* 13, no. 4 (2002): 56–68, https://doi.org/10.1353/jod.2002.0064; see also Steven Heydemann, 'Upgrading Authoritarianism in the Arab World', Brookings Institution, Analysis Paper no. 13, October 2007.
3. Hinnebusch, 'Authoritarian Persistence', 386.
4. Eberhard Kienle, *A Grand Delusion: Democracy and Economic Reform in Egypt* (London; New York: I.B.Tauris, 2001), 144–60.
5. Ibid., 23.
6. Jack Shenker, *The Egyptians: A Radical History of Egypt's Unfinished Revolution* (New York; London: The New Press, 2017), 73–4. Shenker provides several striking observations about the extreme inequality in Egypt in the 2000s.
7. Hisham Sharabi, *Neopatriarchy: A Theory of Distorted Change in Arab Society* (New York: Oxford University Press, 1988), 40–49.
8. Ibid., 47.
9. Salwa Ismail, *Rethinking Islamist Politics: Culture, the State and Islamism* (London: Tauris, 2003), 63; see also Samia Mehrez, *Egypt's Culture Wars: Politics and Practice*, Routledge Advances in Middle East and Islamic Studies, 13 (London; New York: Routledge, 2008). It should be noted that the Coptic Church's official stance is also deeply conservative and supportive of al-Sisi's regime.
10. Mehrez, *Egypt's Culture Wars*; Kienle, *A Grand Delusion*, 164–7.
11. John Chalcraft, *Popular Politics in the Making of the Modern Middle East* (Cambridge, UK: Cambridge University Press, 2016), 507.
12. Salwa Ismail, *Political Life in Cairo's New Quarters: Encountering the Everyday State* (Minneapolis: University of Minnesota Press, 2006).
13. Gravett, *Comics Art*, 73.
14. Interview with Magdi el-Shafee, Cairo, 11 December 2012.
15. Theodor Hanf, Coexistence in Wartime Lebanon: Decline of a State and Rise of a Nation (London: I.B.Tauris, 1993), 73, 87.
16. Joseph Maila and Fida Nasrallah, *The Document of National Understanding: A Commentary* (Oxford: Centre for Lebanese Studies, 1992), 62–72.
17. Hassan Krayem, 'The Lebanese Civil War and the Taif Agreement', in *Conflict Resolution in the Arab World: Selected Essays*, ed. Paul Salem (American

University of Beirut, 1997), 411–36, http://ddc.aub.edu.lb/projects/pspa/conflict-resolution.html.

18. Farid El-Khazen, *Lebanon's First Postwar Parliamentary Election, 1992: An Imposed Choice.* (Oxford: Centre for Lebanese Studies, 1998), 69–73.

19. Sharabi, *Neopatriarchy*, 35.

20. Ziad Abu-Rish, 'Garbage Politics', *Jadaliyya.com*, 2016, http://www.jadaliyya.com/pages/index/24713/garbage-politics.

21. *Lebanon National Human Development Report: Toward a Citizen's State* (UNDP, 2009), 165, http://www.lb.undp.org/content/lebanon/en/home/library/democratic_governance/the-national-human-development-report-2008-2009–toward-a-citize0.html.

22. Bassel Salloukh et al., *The Politics of Sectarianism in Postwar Lebanon* (London: Pluto Press, 2015), 7.

23. Lena Irmgard Merhej, 'Men with Guns', in *Postcolonial Comics: Texts, Events, Identities*, ed. Binita Mehta and Pia Mukherji, Kindle edition (New York; Oxford: Routledge, 2015), sec. 5003.

24. 'The People VS Samandal Comics', *Indiegogo*, 2015, https://www.indiegogo.com/projects/1512356.

25. Lena Merhej, 'Wasfat Lubnaniyya li l-Intiqam', *Samandal* no. 7 (2009): 79–87.

26. Valfret, 'Ecce Homo', *Samandal* no. 7 (2009): 258–66.

27. Elias Mhanna, 'The Fate of a Joke in Lebanon', *The New Yorker*, 26 September 2015, http://www.newyorker.com/news/news-desk/the-fate-of-a-joke-in-lebanon.

28. E-mail interview with Fouad Mezher, 1 December 2016 (on file with author).

29. Qifa Nabki, 'An Interview with Omar Khouri', *Qifa Nabki*, 6 November 2014, https://qifanabki.com/2014/11/06/an-interview-with-omar-khouri/.

4 Comics in revolutionary and post-revolutionary Egypt

1. 'Sisi: Don't Listen to Anyone but Me', *Mada Masr*, 24 February 2016, http://www.madamasr.com/news/sisi-dont-listen-anyone-me.

2. The recording is available on YouTube: https://www.youtube.com/watch?time_continue=5073&v=iiht9hEkiAE (accessed 30 June 2016).

3. David D. Kirkpatrick, 'Egypt's New Strongman, Sisi Knows Best', *The New York Times*, 24 May 2014, http://www.nytimes.com/2014/05/25/world/middleeast/egypts-new-autocrat-sisi-knows-best.html.

4. 'Permission to Speak, Sir', *The Economist*, 23 April 2016, 29.

5. Samiha Shafy, '"Horribly Humiliating": Egyptian Woman Tells of "Virginity Tests"', *Spiegel Online*, 10 June 2011, International sec., http://www.spiegel.de/international/world/horribly-humiliating-egyptian-woman-tells-of-virginity-tests-a-767365.html.

6. Jonathan Guyer, 'Inside the Strange Saga of a Cairo Novelist Imprisoned for Obscenity', *Rolling Stone*, 24 February 2017, http://www.rollingstone.com/culture/features/cairo-novelist-imprisoned-for-obscenity-in-egypt-tells-story-w468084.

7. 'Government Shuts Down 3rd Library Owned by Rights Activist Gamal Eid', *Mada Masr*, 20 December 2016, https://www.madamasr.com/en/2016/12/20/news/u/government-shuts-down-3rd-library-owned-by-rights-activist-gamal-eid/.

8. David D. Kirkpatrick, 'Human Rights Groups in Egypt Brace for Crackdown Under New Law', *The New York Times*, 26 December 2014, http://www.nytimes.com/2014/

12/27/world/middleeast/human-rights-groups-in-egypt-brace-for-crackdown-under-new-law.html.

9. See the Egypt monitor of the International Center for Not-for-Profit Law: http://www.icnl.org/research/monitor/egypt.html (accessed 17 October 2017).

10. 'Timeline of Egypt's Escalating Campaign Against Civil Society | Project on Middle East Democracy (POMED)', http://pomed.org/blog-post/egypts-escalating-campaign-against-the-ngo-community/?utm_source=Project%20on%20Middle%20East%20Democracy%20-%20All%20Contacts&utm_campaign = 6ea204fec0-Egypt_Coup_Resources&utm_medium = email&utm_term=0_75a06056d7-6ea204fec0-215935721 (accessed 3 July 2016).

11. 'Background on Case No. 173 – The "Foreign Funding Case"', *Egyptian Initiative for Personal Rights*, 2016, http://eipr.org/en/pressrelease/2016/03/21/2569.

12. Sally al-Haqq and Mustafa Shawqi, *Comics in Arabic: The Egyptian Scene (in Arabic)* (Cairo: Association for the Freedom of Thought and Expression, 2016), 25, http://afteegypt.org/freedom_creativity/2016/02/02/11609-afteegypt.html.

13. Joe Sacco, *Palestine*, 1st edition (Seattle, WA: Fantagraphics, 2001); Joe Sacco and Christopher Hitchens, *Safe Area Gorazde: The War in Eastern Bosnia 1992–1995* (Seattle, WA: Fantagraphics, 2002); Guy Delisle, *Jerusalem: Chronicles from the Holy City*, trans. Helge Dascher (Montreal, QC: Drawn and Quarterly, 2012).

14. Paul Gravett, *Comics Art* (London: Tate Publishing, 2013), 54–63.

15. *Tuk-Tuk* no. 1 (2011): 12.

16. Makhlouf, 'al-Sanafir ḍa'irun', *Tuk-Tuk* no. 3 (2011): 16–21.

17. Tristan Berteloot, 'Academic: Are the Smurfs Crypto-Fascists?', *Time*, 8 June 2011, http://content.time.com/time/world/article/0,8599,2076353,00.html.

18. Abdallah, 'Sharīt/Strip', *Tuk-Tuk* no. 4 (2011): 26–7.

19. Scott McCloud, *Understanding Comics: The Invisible Art*, reprint (New York: William Morrow Paperbacks, 1994), 41.

20. This is a famous proverb used when a person gets into a lot of trouble by engaging in something that seemed innocent and unproblematic at the outset. Its origin is worth citing, since it is a good example of popular wit. A man opened a *hammam* and put up a sign saying that entrance was free of charge. When the clients had undressed and entered the bath, he took away their clothes. When they were finished bathing and wanted to leave, he refused to hand them back their clothes unless they paid him a sum that was equal to the common price for using a *hammam*. Enraged, the customers referred to the sign he had put up outside, to which the man shrugged and said: 'Entering the *hammam* is not the same as leaving it.'

21. Featured in *Tuk-Tuk* no. 5 (2012).

22. Michael Collins Dunn, 'MEI Editor's Blog: Why Is a Taboo Word Taboo? The Curious Case of أح (a7a)', 2014, http://mideasti.blogspot.com/2014/01/why-is-taboo-word-taboo-curious-case-of.html.

23. Interview with the author, Cairo, 8 February 2016.

24. Interview with the author, Cairo, 11 December 2012.

25. *Tuk-Tuk* no. 8 (2012): 2.

26. James C. Scott, *Domination and the Arts of Resistance: Hidden Transcripts* (New Haven: Yale University Press, 1992).

27. Samer S. Shehata, 'The Politics of Laughter: Nasser, Sadat, and Mubarek in Egyptian Political Jokes,' *Folklore*, vol. 103, no. 1 (1992), 82.

28. Lisa Wedeen, *Ambiguities of Domination: Politics, Rhetoric, and Symbols in Contemporary Syria* (Chicago: University of Chicago Press, 1999).

5 Gender relations

1. From the introduction to Muhammad's story 'A Critical Painting' in *Shakmagiya* online, 2016. The online magazine is found at http://kotobna.net.
2. Amnesty International, *'Circles of Hell': Domestic, Public and State Violence Against Women in Egypt* (London: Amnesty International, 2015), 12, http://www.amnestyusa.org/sites/default/files/mde_120042015.pdf.
3. Ibid., 25. These figures are high, but it should be made clear that Egypt is not an exception when it comes to violence against women. Norway, the author's home country, is commonly considered to be among the world's most advanced countries as far as women's rights are concerned, and has a well-developed legal framework to deal with domestic violence. Nonetheless, in a 2005 nationwide survey 14.4 per cent of the surveyed women reported having been the victim of 'less serious' domestic violence, while 8.2 per cent had experienced serious violence (kicking, strangulation, etc.). See the Norwegian Women's Shelter website: http://www.krisesenter.com/tall-og-fakta/nasjonal-statistikk.
4. Amnesty International, *'Circles of Hell'*, 45–7.
5. Sylvia Walby, *Theorizing Patriarchy* (Oxford, UK; Cambridge, MA: Wiley-Blackwell, 1990), 135.
6. Ahdaf Soueif, 'Image of Unknown Woman Beaten by Egypt's Military Echoes Around World', *The Guardian*, 18 December 2011, Comment is Free edition, http://www.theguardian.com/commentisfree/2011/dec/18/egypt-military-beating-female-protester-tahrir-square.
7. *Egypt: Keeping Women Out. Sexual Violence Against Women in the Public Sphere* (Cairo: FIDH, Nazra for Feminist Studies, New Women Foundation, Uprising of Women in the Arab World, 2014), https://www.fidh.org/IMG/pdf/egypt_women_final_english.pdf.
8. Deniz Kandiyoti, 'Bargaining with Patriarchy', *Gender & Society* 2, no. 3 (1988): 283, doi:10.1177/089124388002003004.
9. Salwa Ismail, 'Confronting the Other: Identity, Culture, Politics, and Conservative Islamism in Egypt', *International Journal of Middle East Studies* 30, no. 2 (1998): 199–225, doi:10.1017/S0020743800065879.
10. Farha Ghannam, *Live and Die Like a Man: Gender Dynamics in Urban Egypt* (Stanford, CA: Stanford University Press, 2013), 118.
11. 'Al-Sisi Takes on "Sexual Terrorism" and Orders the Minister of Interior to Confront the Phenomenon of Harassment', *Al-Hayat*, 11 June 2014, http://www.alhayat.com/Articles/2892577/السيسي-يتحدى-الإرهاب-الجنسي-ويأمر-وزير-الداخلية-بمواجهة-ظاهرة-التحرش; Amnesty International, *'Circles of Hell'*.
12. Paul Amar, 'Turning the Gendered Politics of the Security State Inside Out?', *International Feminist Journal of Politics* 13, no. 3 (2011): 299–328.
13. Hisham Sharabi, *Neopatriarchy: A Theory of Distorted Change in Arab Society* (New York: Oxford University Press, 1988), 65.
14. John Thompson, Ideology and Modern Culture: Critical Social Theory in the Era of Mass Communication, 1st edition (Stanford, CA: Stanford University Press, 1991), 60.
15. 'متابعات', "محيط | والي: المرأة المصرية الولد وعمود الخيمة لحماية المجتمع', *Moheet*, 2 June 2016, http://www.moheet.com/2016/06/02/2433673/والي-المرأة-المصرية-الولد-وعمود-الخي.html.
16. Salwa Ismail, *Rethinking Islamist Politics: Culture, the State and Islamism* (London: Tauris, 2003), 28.
17. Shereen El Feki, *Sex and the Citadel: Intimate Life in a Changing Arab World* (London: Vintage, 2014), 84.

18. *Lebanon National Human Development Report: Toward a Citizen's State* (UNDP, 2009), 72, http://www.lb.undp.org/content/lebanon/en/home/library/democratic_governance/the-national-human-development-report-2008-2009 – toward-a-citize0. html.
19. Lamia Rustum Shehadeh, 'Coverture in Lebanon', *Feminist Review* 76, no. 1 (2004): 85, doi:10.1057/palgrave.fr.9400133.
20. Jinan Usta, JoAnn M. Farver and Christine Sylva Hamieh, 'Effects of Socialization on Gender Discrimination and Violence Against Women in Lebanon', *Violence Against Women*, vol. 22, no. 4 (2016), 426.
21. Nadine Moawad, 'The Bigger Struggle for Women in Municipalities', *Sawt Al Niswa | صوت النسوة* 16 May 2016, http://www.sawtalniswa.org/article/557.
22. Roger Sabin, *Adult Comics* (London: Routledge, 2013), 224–32.
23. Shereen Abouelnaga, 'Reconstructing Gender in Post-Revolution Egypt', in *Rethinking Gender in Revolutions and Resistance: Lessons from the Arab World*, ed. Maha El Said, Lena Meari and Nicola Pratt (London: Zed Books, 2015), 35–59.
24. Hala G. Sami, 'A Strategic Use of Culture: Egyptian Women's Subversion and Resignification of Gender Norms', in *Rethinking Gender in Revolutions and Resistance*, ed. Maha El Said, Lena Meari and Nicola Pratt, 86–109.
25. Gravett made these comments in a lecture during the festival at which the author was present.
26. Skype interview with Naif al-Muttawa, 2 April 2013.
27. Sabin, *Adult Comics*, 224. For some examples of male chauvinistic underground comics, see Patrick Rosenkranz, *Rebel Visions: The Underground Comix Revolution, 1963–1975* (Seattle, WA: Fantagraphics Books, 2002), 171–85.
28. The protagonist is a curly-haired woman (*limma* means 'curl'). As far as I can understand, the title here is a double entendre. 'Limma' written with a *damma* (*lumma*) means 'calamity', so the title may be read as either 'Miss Curly' or 'Miss Trouble'.
29. See the 'Who we are' section at its website, http://www.nazra.org/نحن-من (accessed 12 May 2016).
30. Lena Irmgard Merhej, 'Men with Guns', in *Postcolonial Comics: Texts, Events, Identities*, ed. Binita Mehta and Pia Mukherji, Kindle edition (New York; Oxford: Routledge, 2015).
31. The specific reference here is to the music video 'I Will Pet You', by *sha'bi* singer Sa'id Hamid; see https://www.youtube.com/watch?v=GFINjMA4BFk.
32. Scott McCloud, *Understanding Comics: The Invisible Art*, reprint (New York: William Morrow Paperbacks, 1994), 41.
33. 'Al-'ar bi l-zayt al-ḥarr', *Tuk-Tuk* no. 7 (2012): 48–58.
34. Thierry Groensteen, *The System of Comics* (Jackson: University Press of Mississippi, 2007), 44.
35. 'Shawk', *Tuk-Tuk* no. 7 (2012): 35–8.
36. For an analysis of how panels contribute to the form and meaning of comics, see Groensteen, *The System of Comics*, 39–57.
37. Ibid., 22.
38. Muna 'Abd al-Rahman and al-Shayma Hamid, 'إحنا اللي اتأخرنا!', *Shakmagiya*, 2014.
39. Personal communication with the author, Cairo, 1 October 2016.
40. Ziad Abu-Rish, 'Garbage Politics', *Jadaliyya.com*, 2016, http://www.jadaliyya.com/pages/index/24713/garbage-politics; Josie Ensor, 'Thousands of Lebanese Mass in "You Stink" Rally', *The Telegraph*, 29 August 2015, World sec., http://www.telegraph.co.uk/news/worldnews/middleeast/lebanon/11833292/Thousands-of-Lebanese-mass-in-You-Stink-rally.html.

41. The Asfari Institute, *Gender Dimensions of the Protests*, Protest Series, https://soundcloud.com/the-asfari-institute/police-brutality-panelwav (accessed 18 August 2016).

42. 'Ahl al-Qimma' (those at the summit), *Tuk-Tuk* no. 5 (2012): 40–2.

43. 'The Evils of Men', *Tuk-Tuk* no. 8: 26–7.

44. Andeel and Hicham Rahma, 'Girls and Hormones', *Tuk-Tuk* no. 3 (2011): 40–2.

45. Andeel, 10 May 2016, Facebook. Available at https://www.facebook.com/Andeel?fref=ts.

6 Youthfulness and the vernacular

1. R. Roushdy et al., *Survey of Young People in Egypt: Final Report* (Cairo: Population Council, 2010), 2, http://www.popline.org/node/217332.

2. Jad Chaaban, *Job Creation in the Arab Economies: Navigating Through Difficult Waters*, Arab Human Development Report Research Paper Series (United Nations Development Programme Regional Bureau for Arab States, 2010), 20–1, http://www.arab-hdr.org/publications/other/ahdrps/paper03-en.pdf; Roushdy et al., *Survey of Young People in Egypt*, 97.

3. Mary Kawar and Zafiris Tzannatos, *Youth Employment in Lebanon: Skilled and Jobless* (Beirut: The Lebanese Center for Policy Studies, 2013), 20–1, http://www.lcps-lebanon.org/publications/1368538726-youth_enemployment.pdf. In this study, 'youth' means 20–29-year-olds.

4. Diane Singerman, 'The Economic Imperatives of Marriage: Emerging Practices and Identities Among Youth in the Middle East' (Wolfensohn Center for Development and Dubai School of Government, 2007), http://www.shababinclusion.org/content/document/detail/559/; for a good summary of the situation in the Arab world at large, see Jean-Pierre Filiu, *The Arab Revolution: Ten Lessons from the Democratic Uprising*, 1st edition (Oxford; New York: Oxford University Press, 2011), 32–3.

5. Linda Herrera, 'Young Egyptians' Quest for Jobs and Justice', in *Being Young and Muslim: New Cultural Politics in the Global South and North*, ed. Asef Bayat and Linda Herrera (New York: Oxford University Press, 2010), 132.

6. Selim H. Shahine, 'Youth and the Revolution in Egypt', *Anthropology Today* 27, no. 2 (2011): 1–3, doi:10.1111/j.1467-8322.2011.00792.x.

7. 'Lebanese Cronyism: Hire Power', *The Economist*, 23 July 2016.

8. *Lebanon National Human Development Report: Toward a Citizen's State* (UNDP, 2009), 31, http://www.lb.undp.org/content/lebanon/en/home/library/democratic_governance/the-national-human-development-report-2008-2009–toward-a-citize0.html.

9. Linda Herrera and Asef Bayat, *Being Young and Muslim: New Cultural Politics in the Global South and North* (New York: Oxford University Press, 2010), 10.

10. A. Bayat, 'Islamism and the Politics of Fun', *Public Culture* 19, no. 3 (2007): 438.

11. Ibid., 457.

12. Michael Collins Dunn, 'MEI Editor's Blog: Why Is a Taboo Word Taboo? The Curious Case of أها (a7a)', 2014, http://mideasti.blogspot.com/2014/01/why-is-taboo-word-taboo-curious-case-of.html.

13. The Facebook page is at https://www.facebook.com/A7a.Kbira/ (accessed 13 February 2017).

14. M. Lynx Qualey, 'Another Pop-Literary Comics Magazine Launches in Egypt: "Garage"', *Arabic Literature (in English)*, http://arablit.org/2015/08/31/garage/ (accessed 7 September 2015).

15. Katie de Klee, 'Egyptian Twins Bring Comic Love to Cairo', *Design Indaba*, 30 April 2015, http://www.designindaba.com/articles/point-view/egyptian-twins-bring-comic-love-cairo.
16. Emmanuel Haddad, 'Ebullition', *Le Courrier*, 1 April 2016, http://www.lecourrier.ch/137895/ebullition.
17. Sally al-Haqq and Mustafa Shawqi, *Comics in Arabic: The Egyptian Scene (in Arabic)* (Cairo: Association for the Freedom of Thought and Expression, 2016), 25, http://afteegypt.org/freedom_creativity/2016/02/02/11609-afteegypt.html.
18. Jonathan Guyer, 'Arabs of the Future: Beirut in the Present Tense', *Institute of Current World Affairs* (blog), 2015, http://www.icwa.org/arabs-of-the-future-beirut-in-the-present-tense/.
19. Barrack Rima, 'قيلولة قبل ضهر', *Samandal* no. 8 (2010): 11–21.
20. A notable book on the street art of the Egyptian uprising is Don STONE Karl and Basma Hamdy, *Walls of Freedom: Street Art of the Egyptian Revolution* (Malta: From Here to Fame, 2014).
21. The blog is found at http://oumcartoon.tumblr.com.
22. Karl and Hamdy, *Walls of Freedom*, 89.
23. Youssef El Chazli, 'Alexandrins en fusion: Itinéraires de musiciens égyptiens, des milieux alternatifs à la révolution', in *Jeunesses arabes*, ed. Laurent Bonnefoy and Myriam Catusse (Paris: La Découverte, 2013), 363–4.
24. Ahdaf Soueif, 'Foreword', in *Walls of Freedom: Street Art of the Egyptian Revolution*, ed. Don STONE Karl and Basma Hamdy (Malta: From Here to Fame, 2014), 5.
25. Opendemocracy's interview with Ibn Thabit, London, 17 March 2012: https://www.youtube.com/watch?v=KOkExdgjqQg&index=2&list=PLF70A-m8_LNc_IaaqRxxdyj9QwgOTtamp.
26. The music video may be found on the band's official YouTube page, https://www.youtube.com/user/Cairokee (accessed 5 October 2016).
27. 'Li-l-waṭan' (for the homeland), featured on the album *Raʼʼasuk* (they made you dance), 2013.
28. Lyrics and translation taken from the website musixmatch.com, https://www.musixmatch.com/lyrics/3/2-ليلى-مشروع-minutes/translation/english. Translated by Hamid Shavarean.
29. Albrecht Hofheinz, '#Sisi_vs_Youth: Who Has a Voice in Egypt?', *Journal of Arabic and Islamic Studies* 16 (2016): 327.
30. For the purposes of this analysis, I rely on six randomly chosen issues of *Ihna* (ranging from March 2010 to November 2012) and ten issues of *Kilmitna* (ranging from October 2012 to May 2014).
31. Interviews with Karīm al-Dawjī (editor of *Ihna*) and Marwa ʿAwad (director of *Kilmitna*), Cairo, 10 April 2011 and 24 June 2014, respectively.
32. *Iḥna* is the ʿammiyya variant for the first-person plural pronoun. The *fusha* equivalent is *naḥnu*.
33. Joseph Nasr, 'You Asked for Democracy? There You Go!', *Ihna* 11 (2011): 39.
34. Interview with Muhammad Shennawy, Cairo, 10 December 2012.
35. Interview with Magdī al-Shafiʿī, Cairo, 11 December 2012.
36. Interview with Karim al-Degwi, editor-in-chief of *Ihna*, Cairo, 10 April 2011, and Muhammad Shennawy, 10 December 2012, respectively.
37. Eva Marie Håland, 'Adab Sakhir (Satirical Literature) and the Use of Egyptian Vernacular', in *The Politics of Written Language in the Arab World*, ed. Jacob Høigilt and Gunvor Mejdell (Leiden: Brill, 2017), 142–65.

38. The first edition was published in 2006. By 2009, it had reached its 14th edition, a remarkable feat in a market characterized by very low sales figures.
39. Interview with Hani 'Abdallah, Cairo 25 June 2014.
40. Tore Kristiansen, Peter Garrett and Nikolas Coupland, 'Introducing Subjectivities in Language Variation and Change', *Acta Linguistica Hafniensia* 37, no. 1 (2005): 14, doi:10.1080/03740463.2005.10416081.
41. Dominique Caubet, 'Morocco: An Informal Passage to Literacy in Darija (Moroccan Arabic)', in *The Politics of Written Language in the Arab World*, ed. Jacob Høigilt and Gunvor Mejdell (Leiden: Brill, 2017), 122.
42. Ibid., 137.
43. Published dialectal work seems to be gaining acceptance also in Morocco. See Alexander Elinson, 'Darija and Changing Writing Practices in Morocco', *International Journal of Middle East Studies* 45, no. 4 (2013): 715–30.

7 Comics and sociolinguistics: Informal literacy, voice and language ideology

1. Jan Blommaert, *Discourse: A Critical Introduction* (New York: Cambridge University Press, 2005), 106.
2. Interview with Karim al-Degwi, Cairo, 10 April 2011.
3. Eva Marie Håland, 'Adab Sakhir (Satirical Literature) and the Use of Egyptian Vernacular', in *The Politics of Written Language in the Arab World*, ed. Jacob Høigilt and Gunvor Mejdell (Leiden: Brill, 2017), 156–7.
4. Walter Armbrust, *Mass Culture and Modernism in Egypt* (Cambridge: Cambridge University Press, 1996).
5. Richard Jacquemond and David Tresilian, *Conscience of the Nation: Writers, State, and Society in Modern Egypt* (Cairo, Egypt; New York, NY: American University in Cairo Press, 2008), 42.
6. Pierre Bourdieu, *The Field of Cultural Production* (New York: Columbia University Press, 1993).
7. Jacquemond and Tresilian, *Conscience of the Nation*, 51.
8. Theresa M. Lillis, *The Sociolinguistics of Writing* (Edinburgh: Edinburgh University Press, 2013), 136–9; Blommaert, *Discourse*, 73–5.
9. For the latter controversy, see Mark LeVine, *Heavy Metal Islam: Rock, Resistance, and the Struggle for the Soul of Islam* (New York: Three Rivers Press, 2008), 62–8.
10. Homi K. Bhabha, *The Location of Culture* (Oxford; New York: Routledge, 2004), 28–57.
11. Rakesh M. Bhatt, 'In Other Words: Language Mixing, Identity Representations, and Third Space', *Journal of Sociolinguistics* 12, no. 2 (2008): 177–200, doi:10.1111/j.1467-9841.2008.00363.x.
12. Bhabha, The Location of Culture.
13. Bhatt, 'In Other Words', 182.
14. Mukul Saxena, 'Reified Languages and Scripts Versus Real Literacy Values and Practices: Insights from Research with Young Bilinguals in an Islamic State', *Compare: A Journal of Comparative and International Education* 41, no. 2 (2011): 277–92, doi:10.1080/03057925.2011.547290.
15. Ibid., 290.
16. Charles Hirschkind, 'New Media and Political Dissent in Egypt', *Revista de Dialectologia Y Tradiciones Populares* 65, no. 1 (2010): 144.

17. Dell Hymes, Ethnography, Linguistics, Narrative Inequality: Toward an Under-standing of Voice (Exeter: Taylor & Francis, 2003), 64.
18. Interview with the author, Cairo, 11 December 2012 (my italics).
19. Personal communication with the author, Beirut, 16 November 2016.
20. Jan Blommaert, 'Bernstein and Poetics Revisited: Voice, Globalization and Education', Discourse & Society 19, no. 4 (2008): 428.
21. Interview with Marwa 'Awad, Cairo, 24 June 2014.
22. Charles A. Ferguson, 'Diglossia', Word 15, no. 2 (1959): 336.
23. As-Said Muhámmad Badawi, Mustawayat al-arabiyya al-muasira fi Misr (Cairo: Dar al-maarif, 1973).
24. Dilworth B. Parkinson, 'Searching for Modern Fusha: Real-Life Formal Arabic', Al-'Arabiyya 24 (1991): 31–64; Dilworth B. Parkinson, 'Knowing Standard Arabic: Testing Egyptians' MSA Abilities', in Current Issues in Linguistic Theory, ed. Mushira Eid and Clive Holes (Amsterdam: John Benjamins Publishing Company, 1993), https://benjamins.com/#catalog/books/cilt.101.05par/details.
25. Enam Al-Wer, 'Arabic Between Reality and Ideology', International Journal of Applied Linguistics 7, no. 2 (1997): 251–65, doi:10.1111/j.1473-4192.1997.tb00117.x; Gunvor Mejdell, Mixed Styles in Spoken Arabic in Egypt: Somewhere Between Order and Chaos (Leiden: Brill, 2006).
26. E.g. Keith Walters, 'Fergie's Prescience: The Changing Nature of Diglossia in Tunisia', International Journal of the Sociology of Language 2003, no. 163 (2003): 77–109, doi:10.1515/ijsl.2003.048; Naima Boussofara-Omar, 'Diglossia', in Encyclopedia of Arabic Language and Linguistics, ed. Kees Versteegh (Leiden: Brill, 2006); Gunvor Mejdell, 'Diglossia, Code Switching, Style Variation, and Congruence', Al-'Arabiyya nos. 44–5 (2012): 29–39; Lotfi Sayahi, Diglossia and Language Contact: Language Variation and Change in North Africa, 1st edition (New York: Cambridge University Press, 2014); Kristen Brustad, 'Diglossia as Ideology', in The Politics of Written Language in the Arab World, ed. Jacob Høigilt and Gunvor Mejdell (Leiden: Brill, 2017), 41–67.
27. Mejdell, Mixed Styles in Spoken Arabic in Egypt, 398 and passim.
28. Mejdell, Mixed Styles in Spoken Arabic in Egypt.
29. William Marçais, 'La langue arabe', in Articles et conférences (Alger: Adrien-Maisonneuve, 1961), 83–110, cited in Catherine Taine-Cheikh, 'Arabe(s) et Berbère En Mauritanie : Bilinguisme, Diglossie et Mixité Lingistique', in High vs. Low and Mixed Varieties: Status, Norms and Functions Across Time and Languages, ed. Lutz Edzard and Gunvor Mejdell (Wiesbaden: Otto Harrassowitz, 2012), 88–109.
30. Charles A. Ferguson, 'Diglossia Revisited', Southwest Journal of Linguistics 10, no. 1 (1991): 52.
31. Ibid., 54.
32. Florian Coulmas, Writing and Society: An Introduction (New York: Cambridge University Press, 2013).
33. Ibid., 57, my emphasis.
34. Heinz Kloss, '"Abstand Languages" and "Ausbau Languages"', Anthropological Linguistics 9, no. 7 (1967): 29–41.
35. Michael G. Carter, 'Language Control as People Control in Medieval Islam: The Aims of the Grammarians in the Cultural Context', Al-Abhath 31 (1983): 65–84; Kristen Brustad, 'The Story of Al-'Arabiyya, or: How the Abbasids Got a Standard Language Ideology' (Leuven: Tenth Conference of the School of Abbasid Studies, 2010), http://www.abbasidstudies.org/?page_id=341; Brustad, 'Diglossia as Ideology', 41–67.

36. Keith Walters, 'Language Attitudes', in *Encyclopedia of Arabic Language and Linguistics*, ed. Kees Versteegh (Leiden: Brill, 2007), 654.

37. Yasir Suleiman, The Arabic Language and National Identity: A Study in Ideology (Edinburgh University Press, 2003), 224.

38. John Eisele, 'Myth, Values, and Practice in the Representation of Arabic', *International Journal of the Sociology of Language* 2003, no. 163 (2003): 43–59, doi:10.1515/ijsl.2003.045.

39. Susan Gal and Kathryn Ann Woolard, *Languages and Publics: The Making of Authority* (Manchester: St. Jerome Publishing, 2001), 1.

40. Dilworth B. Parkinson, 'Verbal Features in Oral Fusha Performances in Cairo', *International Journal of the Sociology of Language* 2003, no. 163 (2003): 27–41, doi:10.1515/ijsl.2003.044; Parkinson, 'Knowing Standard Arabic', 47.

41. Armbrust, *Mass Culture and Modernism in Egypt*, 54.

42. Yasir Suleiman, *A War of Words: Language and Conflict in the Middle East* (Cambridge: Cambridge University Press, 2004), 72.

43. Jacquemond and Tresilian, *Conscience of the Nation*, 9–10.

44. Hasan Hanafi, 'Identity and Alienation in the Arab Consciousness', in *Language and Identity in the Arab World: Historical, Cultural and Political Problematics* (Beirut: Arab Center for Research and Policy Studies, 2013), 199.

45. Ibid., 196.

46. UNDP, *Arab Human Development Report 2003: Building a Knowledge Society*, Arab Human Development Report (Amman: UNDP, 2003), 125, http://www.arab-hdr.org/publications/other/ahdr/ahdr2003e.pdf.

47. Ibid., 126.

48. Brustad, 'Diglossia as Ideology', 50.

49. Hisham Sharabi, *Neopatriarchy: A Theory of Distorted Change in Arab Society* (New York: Oxford University Press, 1988), 86.

50. Ibid., 98.

51. Arkadiusz Płonka, 'Le Nationalisme Linguistique Au Liban Autour de Saʿīd ʿAql et L'idée de Langue Libanaise Dans La revue "Lebnaan" en Nouvel Alphabet', *Arabica* 53, no. 4 (2006): 423–71.

52. Jérôme Lentin, 'Middle Arabic', in *Encyclopedia of Arabic Language and Linguistics*, ed. Kees Versteegh (Leiden: Brill, 2008), 216.

53. Jérôme Lentin, 'Reflections on Middle Arabic', in *High vs. Low and Mixed Varieties: Status, Norms and Functions Across Time and Languages*, ed. Lutz Edzard and Gunvor Mejdell (Wiesbaden: Otto Harrassowitz, 2012), 39–40.

54. Lentin, 'Middle Arabic', 219.

55. Lentin, 'Reflections on Middle Arabic', 45.

56. Ibid., 49.

57. Heikki Palva, *Artistic Colloquial Arabic: Traditional Narratives and Poems from Al-Balqa' (Jordan)*, vol. 69, Studia Orientalia (Helsinki: Federation of Finnish Learned Societies/Bookstore Tiedekirja, 1992).

58. Madiha Doss and Humphrey Davies, العامية المصرية المكتوبة (*Written Egyptian Dialect*) (Cairo: The General Egyptian Book Organization, 2013).

59. Ziad Fahmy, Ordinary Egyptians: Creating the Modern Nation Through Popular Culture (Palo Alto: Stanford University Press, 2011).

60. Nelly Hanna, In Praise of Books: A Cultural History of Cairo's Middle Class, Sixteenth to the Eighteenth Century (Syracuse, NY: Syracuse University Press, 2003), 128.

61. Ibid.

62. Fahmy, Ordinary Egyptians, 74.

63. Ibid., 75.
64. Brustad, 'Diglossia as Ideology'.
65. Madiha Doss, 'Cultural Dynamics and Linguistic Practice in Contemporary Egypt', *Cairo Papers in Social Science* 27, nos. 1–2 (2006): 57–62; Gunvor Mejdell, 'The Use of Colloquial in Modern Egyptian Literature – A Survey', in *Current Issues in the Analysis of Semitic Grammar and Lexicon II*, ed. Lutz Edzard and Jan Retsö (Wiesbaden: Harrassowitz Verlag, 2006), 195–213.
66. Walters, 'Fergie's Prescience', 101.
67. Alexander Elinson, 'Darija and Changing Writing Practices in Morocco', *International Journal of Middle East Studies* 45, no. 4 (2013): 715–30.
68. Gabriel Rosenbaum, 'Egyptian Arabic as a Written Language', *Jerusalem Studies in Arabic and Islam* no. 29 (2004): 281.
69. Elinson, 'Darija and Changing Writing Practices in Morocco', 726.
70. Gunvor Mejdell, 'What Is Happening to "Lughatunā L-Gamīla"? Recent Media Representations and Social Practice in Egypt', *Journal of Arabic and Islamic Studies* 8 (2008): 115, 119.
71. Mariam Aboelezz, 'Latinised Arabic and Connections to Bilingual Ability', in *Papers from the Lancaster University Postgraduate Conference in Linguistics and Language Teaching* (2009), http://www.ling.lancs.ac.uk/pgconference/v03/Aboelezz.
72. Hirschkind, 'New Media and Political Dissent in Egypt', 137–53; Jon Nordenson, 'The Language of Online Activism: A Case from Kuwait', in *The Politics of Written Language in the Arab World*, ed. Jacob Høigilt and Gunvor Mejdell (Leiden: Brill, 2017), 266–89.
73. Reproduced from Kristian Takvam Kindt and Tewodros Aragie Kebede, 'A Language for the People? Quantitative Indicators of Written Darija and ʿammiyya in Cairo and Rabat', in *The Politics of Written Language in the Arab World*, ed. Jacob Høigilt and Gunvor Mejdell (Leiden: Brill, 2017), 24.
74. Reproduced from ibid., 27.
75. Interview with the author, Cairo, 11 December 2012.
76. Interview with the author, Cairo, 10 December 2012.
77. Interview with the author, Beirut, 14 November 2015.
78. Ahmad al-'Isili, quoted in Håland, 'Adab Sakhir (Satirical Literature) and the Use of Egyptian Vernacular', 157.
79. Mark Sebba, 'Writing Switching in British Creole', in *Language Mixing and Code-Switching in Writing: Approaches to Mixed-Language Written Discourse*, ed. Mark Sebba, Shahrzad Mahootian and Carla Jonsson (New York: Routledge, 2012), 97–102.
80. Interview with Marwa ʿAwad, Cairo, 24 June 2014.
81. Tewodros Aragie Kebede, Kristian Takvam Kindt and Jacob Høigilt, *Language Change in Egypt: Social and Cultural Indicators* (Oslo: Fafo, 2013), 88–92.
82. Latifa al-Najjar, اللغة العربية بين أزمة الهوية وإشكالية الاختيار' (The Arabic Language Between the Crisis of Identity and the Problem of Choice)', in *Language and Identity in the Arab World: Historical, Cultural and Political Problematics* (Beirut: Arab Center for Research and Policy Studies, 2013), 185–201.
83. Karen Gammelgaard, 'Czech Code-Mixing 1990–2010: From Domain Specialization Toward Graded Registers', in *High vs. Low and Mixed Varieties: Status, Norms and Functions Across Time and Languages*, ed. Lutz Edzard and Gunvor Mejdell (Wiesbaden: Otto Harrassowitz, 2012), 179–97.
84. Ibid., 183.
85. Sayahi, Diglossia and Language Contact, 94.
86. Brustad, 'Diglossia as Ideology', 47.

87. James Milroy and Lesley Milroy, *Authority in Language: Investigating Standard English* (London, UK; New York: Routledge, 1999), 30, http://public.eblib.com/EBLPublic/PublicView.do?ptiID=169661.

88. Alan Hudson, 'Outline of a Theory of Diglossia', *International Journal of the Sociology of Language*, no. 157 (2002): 8.

89. Gunvor Mejdell, '"High" and "Low" Varieties, Diglossia, Language Contact, and Mixing: Social Processes and Linguistic Products in a Comparative Perspective', in *High vs. Low and Mixed Varieties: Status, Norms and Functions Across Time and Languages*, ed. Lutz Edzard and Gunvor Mejdell (Wiesbaden: Otto Harrassowitz, 2012), 19.

90. Boussofara-Omar, 'Diglossia', 635.

91. Gammelgaard, 'Czech Code-Mixing 1990–2010', 184–5.

92. M. A. K. Halliday, Language as Social Semiotic: The Social Interpretation of Language and Meaning (London: Edward Arnold, 1978), 32.

93. El-Said M. Badawi, Michael G. Carter and Adrian Gully, *Modern Written Arabic: A Comprehensive Grammar* (London: Routledge, 2004).

Bibliography

Primary sources

The following is a complete list of the comics and other magazines I perused and/or analyzed for the purposes of this book. It is not a complete list of Egyptian and Lebanese adult comics or graphic novels, however; already there are so many works that I was not able to include in this book. In the case of magazines, I have specified which issues I have read. In the case of edited volumes and graphic novels, I have listed the editor and author(s), respectively.

Abirached, Zeina. *A Game for Swallows: To Live, to Die, to Return*. Minneapolis and New York: Graphic Universe, 2012 (graphic novel). Translated from French by Edward Gauvin. Original title: *Jeu des hirondelles*.

Amin, Rania (ed.). خارج السيطرة [*Out of Control*]. Cairo: Dar al-ʿAyn, 2011 (anthology).

Fut ʿAlayna Bukra [Pass by Us Tomorrow] 1–3 (Egyptian satirical science fiction magazine).

جراج - ممنوع الوقوف [*Garage – No Parking*], no. 0 (magazine).

al-Hanaʾi, Shirin and Hanan al-Kararji. الموت يوما آخر [*Death Another Day*]. Cairo: Comics Publishing, 2012 (graphic horror story).

إحنا: صوت جيل بحاله [*Ihna: The Voice of an Entire Generation*], various issues from 2006–2012 (monthly youth magazine).

Kerbaj, Mazen. 2006 بيروت لن تبكي: يوميات حرب تموز [*Beirut Won't Cry: Diaries from the 2006 July War*]. Beirut: Editions Snoubar Bayrout, 2016 (comics/graphic arts book).

Khoury, George (JAD). أبو شنب [*Abu Shanab*] (comic strip, featured in the Lebanese *al-Nahar* newspaper in the 1980s).

Khoury, George (JAD). *Carnaval*. Beirut: Mediterranean Press, 1980 (graphic novel).

كلمتنا [*Our Word*]. Various issues from 2012–2015 (monthly youth magazine).

Macaron, Raphaëlle. *Souffles Courts*. Unknown place and publisher: 2015 (graphic short story).

مجنون [*Mad*], 1–3 (magazine).

Merhej, Lena. مربى ولبن أو: كيف أصبحت أمي لبنانية [*Murabba wa-Laban, Aw: Kayfa Asbahat Ummi Lubnaniyya*]. Beirut: Samandal, 2011 (graphic novel).

Samandal, 1–15 (magazine).

al-Shafiʿi, Magdi. مترو [*Metro*]. Cairo: Dar al-Malamih, 2008 (graphic novel).

Shakmagiya, 1 and 2 [only released digitally] (magazine).

Shennawy, Muhammad (ed.) حدث بالفعل [*It really happened*], Cairo: al-Fann al-Tasiʿ, 2015 (anthology).

Tawfiq, Ahmad Khalid and Hanan al-Kararji. تأثير الجرادة [*The Grasshopper Effect*]. Cairo: Comics Publishing, 2014 (graphic novel).

توك توك، محطة القصص المصورة [*Tuk-Tuk: Graphics Stories Station*], nos. 1–14 (magazine).

ʿUbay, Muhammad Hisham and Hanan al-Kararji. يما 18 [*18 Days*]. Cairo: Comics Publishing, 2011 (graphic novel).

212

References

Abd al-Al, Ghada. عايزة أتجوز. Cairo: Dar al-Shuruq, 2008.

'Abd al-Hamīd, Tāmir. 'الكومكس.. تحليق إبداعي.. على ارتفاع منخفض.' Ibdāᶜ magazine, nos. 36–7 (2015): 145-149.

'Abd al-Rahman, Muna, and al-Shayma Hamid. 'إحنا اللي اتأخرنا!' Shakmagiya, 2014.

Abdallah, 'Sharīt/Strip', Tuk-Tuk no. 4 (2011): 26–7.

Abirached, Zeina. A Game for Swallows: To Die, to Leave, to Return. Single Titles edition. New York: Graphic Universe, 2012.

Aboelezz, Mariam. 'Latinised Arabic and Connections to Bilingual Ability.' In Papers from the Lancaster University Postgraduate Conference in Linguistics and Language Teaching (2009). http://www.ling.lancs.ac.uk/pgconference/v03/Aboelezz.

Abouelnaga, Shereen. 'Reconstructing Gender in Post-Revolution Egypt.' In Rethinking Gender in Revolutions and Resistance: Lessons from the Arab World, edited by Maha El Said, Lena Meari and Nicola Pratt, 35–59. London: Zed Books, 2015.

Abu-Lughod, Lila. 'Do Muslim Women Really Need Saving? Anthropological Reflections on Cultural Relativism and Its Others.' American Anthropologist 104, no. 3 (2002): 783–90. https://doi.org/10.1525/aa.2002.104.3.783.

Abu-Rish, Ziad. 'Garbage Politics.' Jadaliyya.com, 2016. http://www.jadaliyya.com/pages/index/24713/garbage-politics.

Al Kharouf, Amal, and David Weir. 'Women and Work in a Jordanian Context: Beyond Neo-Patriarchy.' Critical Perspectives on International Business 4, nos. 2/3 (2008): 307–19. doi:10.1108/17422040810870060.

'Al-Sisi Takes on "Sexual Terrorism" and Orders the Minister of Interior to Confront the Phenomenon of Harassment.' Al-Hayat, 11 June 2014. http://www.alhayat.com/Articles/2892577/الإرهاب-الجنسي-ويأمر-وزير-الداخلية-بمواجهة-ظاهرة-التحرش السيسي-يتحدى.

Al-Wer, Enam. 'Arabic Between Reality and Ideology.' International Journal of Applied Linguistics 7, no. 2 (1997): 251–65. doi:10.1111/j.1473-4192.1997.tb00117.x.

Amar, Paul. 'Turning the Gendered Politics of the Security State Inside Out?' International Feminist Journal of Politics 13, no. 3 (2011): 299–328.

Amnesty International. 'Circles of Hell': Domestic, Public and State Violence Against Women in Egypt. London: Amnesty International, 2015. http://www.amnestyusa.org/sites/default/files/mde_120042015.pdf.

Andeel. 'Ahl al-Qimma' (those at the summit). Tuk-Tuk no. 5.

———. 'The Evils of Men.' Tuk-Tuk no. 8.

Andeel and Hicham Rahma. 'Girls and Hormones.' Tuk-Tuk no. 3.

Anwar, Muhammad. 'داني الأحمر فتى الحي اللاتيني.' Ibda' magazine nos. 36-37 (2015), 8–11.

Armbrust, Walter. Mass Culture and Modernism in Egypt. Cambridge: Cambridge University Press, 1996.

The Asfari Institute. Gender Dimensions of the Protests. Protest Series. https://soundcloud.com/the-asfari-institute/police-brutality-panelwav (accessed 18 August 2016).

Ashwal, Ismail al-. 'المواطنون الشرفاء. حين يكون «الشرف» وصمة «عار» – بوابة الشروق.' Al-Shuruq, 5 May 2016. http://www.shorouknews.com/news/view.aspx?cdate=05052016&id=8edcc4ce-2653-467e-b1a3-921f391893ce.

Aswany, Alaa al-. 'Egypt's "Honorable Citizens".' World Affairs Journal, 6 January 2012. http://www.worldaffairsjournal.org/blog/alaa-al-aswany/egypts-honorable-citizens.

Ayubi, Nazih N. Over-Stating the Arab State: Politics and Society in the Middle East. London; New York: I.B.Tauris, 1996.

'Background on Case No. 173 – The "Foreign Funding Case".' Egyptian Initiative for Personal Rights, 21 March 2016. http://eipr.org/en/pressrelease/2016/03/21/2569.

Badawi, As-Said Muhámmad. Mustawayat al-arabiyya al-muasira fi Misr. Cairo: Dar al-maarif, 1973.

Badawi, El-Said M., Michael G. Carter and Adrian Gully. Modern Written Arabic: A Comprehensive Grammar. London: Routledge, 2004.

Comics in Contemporary Arab Culture

Bakhat, Islah. 'Arab Comic Strips Experience Their Own Spring.' *SWI Swissinfo.ch*, 2013. http://www.swissinfo.ch/eng/culture/picture-power_arab-comic-strips-experience-their-own-spring/35337848.
Barker, Martin. *Comics: Ideology, Power, and the Critics*. Manchester University Press, 1989.
Bayat, A. 'Islamism and the Politics of Fun.' *Public Culture* 19, no. 3 (2007): 433–59.
Bayat, Asef. *Life as Politics: How Ordinary People Change the Middle East*. Stanford, CA: Stanford University Press, 2010.
Bellin, Eva. 'Reconsidering the Robustness of Authoritarianism in the Middle East: Lessons from the Arab Spring.' *Comparative Politics* 44, no. 2 (2012): 127–49. https://doi.org/10.5129/001041512798838021.
———. 'The Robustness of Authoritarianism in the Middle East: Exceptionalism in Comparative Perspective.' *Comparative Politics* 36, no. 2 (2004): 139–57. https://doi.org/10.2307/4150140.
Berteloot, Tristan. 'Academic: Are the Smurfs Crypto-Fascists?' *Time*, 8 June 2011. http://content.time.com/time/world/article/0,8599,2076353,00.html.
Bhabha, Homi K. *The Location of Culture*. Oxford; New York: Routledge, 2004.
Bhatt, Rakesh M. 'In Other Words: Language Mixing, Identity Representations, and Third Space.' *Journal of Sociolinguistics* 12, no. 2 (2008): 177–200. doi:10.1111/j.1467-9841.2008.00363.x.
Blommaert, Jan. 'Bernstein and Poetics Revisited: Voice, Globalization and Education.' *Discourse & Society* 19, no. 4 (2008): 425–51.
———. *Discourse: A Critical Introduction*. New York: Cambridge University Press, 2005.
Bourdieu, Pierre. *The Field of Cultural Production*. New York: Columbia University Press, 1993.
Boussofara-Omar, Naima. 'Diglossia.' In *Encyclopedia of Arabic Language and Linguistics*, edited by Kees Versteegh. Leiden: Brill, 2006.
Brownlee, Jason. '… And Yet They Persist: Explaining Survival and Transition in Neopatrimonial Regimes.' *Studies in Comparative International Development* 37, no. 3 (2002): 35–63. https://doi.org/10.1007/BF02686230.
Brumberg, Daniel. 'The Trap of Liberalized Autocracy.' *Journal of Democracy* 13, no. 4 (2002): 56–68. https://doi.org/10.1353/jod.2002.0064.
Brustad, Kristen. 'Diglossia as Ideology.' In *The Politics of Written Language in the Arab World*, edited by Jacob Høigilt and Gunvor Mejdell, 41–67. Leiden: Brill, 2017.
———. 'The Story of Al-'Arabiyya, or: How the Abbasids Got a Standard Language Ideology.' Leuven: Tenth Conference of the School of Abbasid Studies, 2010. http://www.abbasidstudies.org/?page_id=341.
Brynen, Rex, Peter W. Moore, Bassel F. Salloukh and Marie-Joëlle Zahar. *Beyond the Arab Spring: Authoritarianism and Democratization in the Arab World*. Boulder; London: Lynne Rienner Publishers, 2012.
Carter, Michael G. 'Language Control as People Control in Medieval Islam: The Aims of the Grammarians in the Cultural Context.' *Al-Abhath* 31 (1983): 65–84.
Caubet, Dominique. 'Morocco: An Informal Passage to Literacy in Darija (Moroccan Arabic).' In *The Politics of Written Language in the Arab World*, edited by Jacob Høigilt and Gunvor Mejdell, 116–41. Leiden: Brill, 2017.
Chaaban, Jad. *Job Creation in the Arab Economies: Navigating Through Difficult Waters*. Arab Human Development Report Research Paper Series. United Nations Development Programme Regional Bureau for Arab States, 2010. http://www.arab-hdr.org/publications/other/ahdrps/paper03-en.pdf.
Chalcraft, John. *Popular Politics in the Making of the Modern Middle East*. Cambridge, UK: Cambridge University Press, 2016.
Cortsen, Rikke Platz, Erin La Cour and Anne Magnussen. *Comics and Power: Representing and Questioning Culture, Subjects and Communities*. Cambridge Scholars Publishing, 2015.

214

Bibliography

Coulmas, Florian. *Writing and Society: An Introduction.* New York: Cambridge University Press, 2013.

Delisle, Guy. *Jerusalem: Chronicles from the Holy City.* Translated by Helge Dascher. Montreal, QC: Drawn and Quarterly, 2012.

Di Ricco, Massimo. 'Drawing for a New Public: Middle Eastern 9th Art and the Emergence of a Transnational Graphic Movement.' In *Postcolonial Comics: Texts, Events, Identities,* edited by Binita Mehta and Pia Mukherji, 187–204. New York: Routledge, 2015.

Dorfman, Ariel, and Armand Mattelart. *How to Read Donald Duck: Imperialist Ideology in the Disney Comic.* New York: International General, 1984.

Doss, Madiha. 'Cultural Dynamics and Linguistic Practice in Contemporary Egypt.' *Cairo Papers in Social Science* 27, nos. 1–2 (2006): 51–68.

Doss, Madiha, and Humphrey Davies. المصرية المكتوبة العامية (*Written Egyptian Dialect*). Cairo: The General Egyptian Book Organization, 2013.

Douglas, Allen, and Fedwa Malti-Douglas. *Arab Comic Strips: Politics of an Emerging Mass Culture.* Bloomington: Indiana University Press, 1994.

Duncan, Randy, and Matthew J. Smith. *The Power of Comics: History, Form and Culture.* New York; London: Continuum, 2009.

Dunn, Michael Collins. 'MEI Editor's Blog: Why Is a Taboo Word Taboo? The Curious Case of أحا (a7a)', 2014. http://mideasti.blogspot.com/2014/01/why-is-taboo-word-taboo-curious-case-of.html.

Eagleton, Terry. *Ideology: An Introduction.* London; New York: Verso, 1991.

Egypt: Keeping Women Out. Sexual Violence Against Women in the Public Sphere. Cairo: FIDH, Nazra for Feminist Studies, New Women Foundation, Uprising of Women in the Arab World, 2014. https://www.fidh.org/IMG/pdf/egypt_women_final_english.pdf.

Eisele, John. 'Myth, Values, and Practice in the Representation of Arabic.' *International Journal of the Sociology of Language* 2003, no. 163 (2003): 43–59. doi:10.1515/ijsl.2003.045.

El Chazli, Youssef. 'Alexandrins en fusion: Itinéraires de musiciens égyptiens, des milieux alternatifs à la révolution.' In *Jeunesses arabes,* edited by Laurent Bonnefoy and Myriam Catusse. Paris: La Découverte, 2013.

El Feki, Shereen. *Sex and the Citadel: Intimate Life in a Changing Arab World.* London: Vintage, 2014.

El-Khazen, Farid. *Lebanon's First Postwar Parliamentary Election, 1992: An Imposed Choice.* Oxford: Centre for Lebanese Studies, 1998.

Elinson, Alexander. 'Darija and Changing Writing Practices in Morocco.' *International Journal of Middle East Studies* 45, no. 4 (2013): 715–30.

Ensor, Josie. 'Thousands of Lebanese Mass in "You Stink" Rally', *The Telegraph,* 29 August 2015, World sec. http://www.telegraph.co.uk/news/worldnews/middleeast/lebanon/11833292/Thousands-of-Lebanese-mass-in-You-Stink-rally.html.

Estren, Mark James. *A History of Underground Comics.* Berkeley, CA: Ronin Publishing, 1993.

Fahmy, Ziad. *Ordinary Egyptians: Creating the Modern Nation Through Popular Culture.* Palo Alto: Stanford University Press, 2011.

Farfán, José Antonio Flores, and Anna Holzscheiter. 'The Power of Discourse and the Discourse of Power.' In *The SAGE Handbook of Sociolinguistics,* ed. Ruth Wodak, Barbara Johnstone and Paul E. Kerswill. London: Sage Publications Ltd, 2010.

Ferguson, Charles A. 'Diglossia.' *Word* 15, no. 2 (1959): 325–40.

———. 'Diglossia Revisited.' *Southwest Journal of Linguistics* 10, no. 1 (1991): 214–34.

Filiu, Jean-Pierre. *The Arab Revolution: Ten Lessons from the Democratic Uprising.* 1st edition. Oxford; New York: Oxford University Press, 2011.

———, and David B. *Best of Enemies: A History of US and Middle East Relations, Part One: 1783–1953.* London: Harry N. Abrams, 2012.

Fishman, Joshua A. 'Who Speaks What Language to Whom and When?' In *The Bilingualism Reader*, edited by Li Wei, 55–71. London; New York: Routledge, 2007.

Gal, Susan, and Kathryn Ann Woolard. *Languages and Publics: The Making of Authority*. Manchester: St. Jerome Publishing, 2001.

Gammelgaard, Karen. 'Czech Code-Mixing 1990–2010: From Domain Specialization Toward Graded Registers.' In *High vs. Low and Mixed Varieties: Status, Norms and Functions Across Time and Languages*, edited by Lutz Edzard and Gunvor Mejdell, 179–97. Wiesbaden: Otto Harrassowitz, 2012.

García, Santiago. *On the Graphic Novel*. Translated by Bruce Campbell. Jackson: University Press of Mississippi, 2015.

Geertz, Clifford. *The Interpretation of Cultures: Selected Essays*. New York: Basic Books, 1973.

Ghannam, Farha. *Live and Die Like a Man: Gender Dynamics in Urban Egypt*. Stanford, CA: Stanford University Press, 2013.

'Government Shuts Down 3rd Library Owned by Rights Activist Gamal Eid.' *Mada Masr*, 20 December 2016. https://www.madamasr.com/en/2016/12/20/news/u/government-shuts-down-3rd-library-owned-by-rights-activist-gamal-eid/.

Gravett, Paul. *Comics Art*. London: Tate Publishing, 2013.

Groensteen, Thierry. *The System of Comics*. Jackson: University Press of Mississippi, 2007.

Guyer, Jonathan. 'Arabs of the Future: Beirut in the Present Tense.' *Institute of Current World Affairs* (blog), 13 January 2015. http://www.icwa.org/arabs-of-the-future-beirut-in-the-present-tense/.

———. 'The Case of the Arabic Noirs.' *Paris Review Daily* (blog), 20 August 2014. http://www.theparisreview.org/blog/2014/08/20/the-case-of-the-arabic-noirs/.

———. 'Inside the Strange Saga of a Cairo Novelist Imprisoned for Obscenity.' *Rolling Stone*, 24 February 2017. http://www.rollingstone.com/culture/features/cairo-novelist-imprisoned-for-obscenity-in-egypt-tells-story-w468084.

———. 'On the Arab Page.' *Le Monde Diplomatique*, 1 January 2017. http://mondediplo.com/2017/01/15cartoons.

———. 'Understanding Arab Comics.' *Los Angeles Review of Books*, 9 July 2016. https://lareviewofbooks.org/article/understanding-arab-comics/.

———. 'Yes and No!' *Oum Cartoon* أم كرتون, 14 January 2014. http://oumcartoon.tumblr.com/post/73306371896/yes-and-no-as-egyptians-head-to-the-polls-today.

Haddad, Emmanuel. 'Ebullition.' *Le Courrier*, 1 April 2016. http://www.lecourrier.ch/137895/ebullition.

Haeri, Niloofar. *Sacred Language, Ordinary People: Dilemmas of Culture and Politics in Egypt*. New York: Palgrave Macmillan, 2003.

Håland, Eva Marie. 'Adab Sakhir (Satirical Literature) and the Use of Egyptian Vernacular.' In *The Politics of Written Language in the Arab World*, edited by Jacob Høigilt and Gunvor Mejdell, 142–65. Leiden: Brill, 2017.

Halliday, M.A.K. *Language as Social Semiotic: The Social Interpretation of Language and Meaning*. London: Edward Arnold, 1978.

Hanafi, Hasan. 'Identity and Alienation in the Arab Consciousness.' In *Language and Identity in the Arab World: Historical, Cultural and Political Problematics*, 185–201. Beirut: Arab Center for Research and Policy Studies, 2013.

Hanf, Theodor. *Coexistence in Wartime Lebanon: Decline of a State and Rise of a Nation*. London: I.B.Tauris, 1993.

Hanna, Nelly. *In Praise of Books: A Cultural History of Cairo's Middle Class, Sixteenth to the Eighteenth Century*. Syracuse, NY: Syracuse University Press, 2003.

Haqq, Sally al-, and Mustafa Shawqi. *Comics in Arabic: The Egyptian Scene (in Arabic)*. Cairo: Association for the Freedom of Thought and Expression, 2016. http://afteegypt.org/freedom_creativity/2016/02/02/11609-afteegypt.html.

Hatfield, Charles. *Alternative Comics: An Emerging Literature*. Jackson: University Press of Mississippi, 2005.

Bibliography

Haugbølle, Sune. 'The Leftist, the Liberal, and the Space in Between.' *Arab Studies Journal* 24, no. 1 (2016): 170–93.

Herrera, Linda. 'Young Egyptians' Quest for Jobs and Justice.' In *Being Young and Muslim: New Cultural Politics in the Global South and North*, edited by Asef Bayat and Linda Herrera. New York: Oxford University Press, 2010.

Herrera, Linda, and Asef Bayat, eds. *Being Young and Muslim: New Cultural Politics in the Global South and North*. New York: Oxford University Press, 2010.

Heydemann, Steven. 'Upgrading Authoritarianism in the Arab World.' Brookings Institution, Analysis Paper no. 13, October 2007.

Hinnebusch, Raymond. 'Authoritarian Persistence, Democratization Theory and the Middle East: An Overview and Critique.' *Democratization* 13, no. 3 (2006): 373–95.

Hirschkind, Charles. 'New Media and Political Dissent in Egypt.' *Revista de Dialectologia Y Tradiciones Populares* 65, no. 1 (2010): 137–53.

Hofheinz, Albrecht. '#Sisi_vs_Youth: Who Has a Voice in Egypt?' *Journal of Arabic and Islamic Studies* 16 (2016): 327–48.

Hudson, Alan. 'Outline of a Theory of Diglossia.' *International Journal of the Sociology of Language*, no. 157 (2002): 1–48.

Hymes, Dell. *Ethnography, Linguistics, Narrative Inequality: Toward an Understanding of Voice*. Exeter: Taylor & Francis, 2003.

Høigilt, Jacob, and Gunvor Mejdell, eds. *The Politics of Written Language in the Arab World: Writing Change*. Leiden; Boston: Brill, 2017.

Iskandar, Adel. 'Big Words on Art: The School Playground and the Cloud of Bollocks.' *Status Hour*, 22 December 2014. http://www.statushour.com/andeel.html.

Ismail, Salwa. 'Confronting the Other: Identity, Culture, Politics, and Conservative Islamism in Egypt.' *International Journal of Middle East Studies* 30, no. 2 (1998): 199–225.

———. *Rethinking Islamist Politics: Culture, the State and Islamism*. London: I.B.Tauris, 2003.

———. *Political Life in Cairo's New Quarters: Encountering the Everyday State*. Minneapolis: University of Minnesota Press, 2006.

Jacquemond, Richard, and David Tresilian. *Conscience of the Nation: Writers, State, and Society in Modern Egypt*. Cairo, Egypt; New York, NY: American University in Cairo Press, 2008.

Kandiyoti, Deniz. 'Bargaining with Patriarchy.' *Gender & Society* 2, no. 3 (1988): 274–90. doi:10.1177/089124388002003004.

Karl, Don STONE, and Basma Hamdy. *Walls of Freedom: Street Art of the Egyptian Revolution*. Malta: From Here to Fame, 2014.

Kawar, Mary, and Zafiris Tzannatos. *Youth Employment in Lebanon: Skilled and Jobless*. Beirut: The Lebanese Center for Policy Studies, 2013. http://www.lcps-lebanon.org/publications/1368538726-youth_enemployment.pdf.

Kebede, Tewodros Aragie, Kristian Takvam Kindt and Jacob Høigilt. *Language Change in Egypt: Social and Cultural Indicators*. Oslo: Fafo, 2013.

Khoury (JAD), George. 'La Bande Dessinée D'expression Arabe de 1950 À Nos Jours.' *Takam Titou*, 2011. http://takamtikou.bnf.fr/dossiers/dossier-2011-la-bande-dessinee/la-bande-dessinee-d-expression-arabe-de-1950-a-nos-jours.

Kienle, Eberhard. *A Grand Delusion: Democracy and Economic Reform in Egypt*. London; New York: I.B.Tauris, 2001.

Kindt, Kristian Takvam, Jacob Høigilt and Tewodros Aragie Kebede. 'Writing Change: Diglossia and Popular Writing Practices in Egypt.' *Arabica* 63, nos. 3–4 (2016): 324–76.

———, and Tewodros Aragie Kebede. 'A Language for the People? Quantitative Indicators of Written Darija and 'ammiyya in Cairo and Rabat.' In *The Politics of Written Language in the Arab World*, edited by Jacob Høigilt and Gunvor Mejdell, 18–40. Leiden: Brill, 2017.

Kirkpatrick, David D. 'Egypt's New Strongman, Sisi Knows Best.' *The New York Times*, 24 May 2014. http://www.nytimes.com/2014/05/25/world/middleeast/egypts-new-autocrat-sisi-knows-best.html.

——. 'Human Rights Groups in Egypt Brace for Crackdown Under New Law.' *The New York Times*, 26 December 2014. http://www.nytimes.com/2014/12/27/world/middleeas t/human-rights-groups-in-egypt-brace-for-crackdown-under-new-law.html.

Klee, Katie de. 'Egyptian Twins Bring Comic Love to Cairo.' *Design Indaba*, 30 April 2015. http://www.designindaba.com/articles/point-view/egyptian-twins-bring-comic-love-cairo.

Klemm, Verena. 'Different Notions of Commitment (Iltizam) and Committed Literature (Al-Adab Al-Multazim) in the Literary Circles of the Mashriq.' *Arabic & Middle Eastern Literature* 3, no. 1 (2000): 51–62.

Kloss, Heinz. '"Abstand Languages" and "Ausbau Languages".' *Anthropological Linguistics* 9, no. 7 (1967): 29–41.

Krayem, Hassan. 'The Lebanese Civil War and the Taif Agreement.' In *Conflict Resolution in the Arab World: Selected Essays*, edited by Paul Salem, 411–36. American University of Beirut, 1997. http://ddc.aub.edu.lb/projects/pspa/conflict-resolution.html.

Kristiansen, Tore, Peter Garrett and Nikolas Coupland. 'Introducing Subjectivities in Language Variation and Change.' *Acta Linguistica Hafniensia* 37, no. 1 (2005): 9–35. doi:10.1080/03740463.2005.10416081.

'Lebanese Cronyism: Hire Power.' *The Economist*, 23 July 2016.

Lebanon National Human Development Report: Toward a Citizen's State. UNDP, 2009. http://www.lb.undp.org/content/lebanon/en/home/library/democratic_governance/the-national-human-development-report-2008-2009–toward-a-citize0.html.

Lentin, Jérôme. 'Middle Arabic.' In *Encyclopedia of Arabic Language and Linguistics*, edited by Kees Versteegh. Leiden: Brill, 2008.

——. 'Reflections on Middle Arabic.' In *High vs. Low and Mixed Varieties: Status, Norms and Functions Across Time and Languages*, edited by Lutz Edzard and Gunvor Mejdell, 32–53. Wiesbaden: Otto Harrassowitz, 2012.

LeVine, Mark. *Heavy Metal Islam: Rock, Resistance, and the Struggle for the Soul of Islam*. New York: Three Rivers Press, 2008.

Lillis, Theresa M. *The Sociolinguistics of Writing*. Edinburgh: Edinburgh University Press, 2013.

McAllister, Matthew P., Edward H. Sewell and Ian Gordon. 'Introducing Comics and Ideology.' In *Comics & Ideology*, 1–15. New York: Peter Lang, 2006.

McCloud, Scott. *Understanding Comics: The Invisible Art*. Reprint. New York: William Morrow Paperbacks, 1994.

McKee, Alan. *Textual Analysis*. London: SAGE Publications Ltd, 2003. http://srmo.s agepub.com/view/textual-analysis/SAGE.xml.

Maila, Joseph, and Fida Nasrallah. *The Document of National Understanding: A Commentary*. Oxford: Centre for Lebanese Studies, 1992.

Makhlouf, 'عن البكباشي ناصر.. توثيق تاريخي في قصة مصورة'. *al-Fann al-Tasi'* 5 (2012): 5.

——. 'al-Sanafir ḥa'irun.' *Tuk-Tuk* no. 3 (2011): 16–21.

Mehrez, Samia. *Egypt's Culture Wars: Politics and Practice*. Routledge Advances in Middle East and Islamic Studies, 13. London; New York: Routledge, 2008.

Mehta, Binita, and Pia Mukherji, eds. *Postcolonial Comics: Texts, Events, Identities*. New York: Routledge, 2015.

Mejdell, Gunvor. 'Diglossia, Code Switching, Style Variation, and Congruence.' *Al-'Arabiyya*, nos. 44–5 (2012): 29–39.

——. '"High" and "Low" Varieties, Diglossia, Language Contact, and Mixing: Social Processes and Linguistic Products in a Comparative Perspective.' In *High vs. Low and Mixed Varieties: Status, Norms and Functions Across Time and Languages*, edited by Lutz Edzard and Gunvor Mejdell, 9–24. Wiesbaden: Otto Harrassowitz, 2012.

——. *Mixed Styles in Spoken Arabic in Egypt: Somewhere Between Order and Chaos*. Leiden: Brill, 2006.

Bibliography

———. 'The Use of Colloquial in Modern Egyptian Literature – A Survey.' In *Current Issues in the Analysis of Semitic Grammar and Lexicon II*, edited by Lutz Edzard and Jan Retsö, 195–213. Wiesbaden: Harrassowitz Verlag, 2006.

———. What Is Happening to "Lughatunā L-Gamīla"? Recent Media Representations and Social Practice in Egypt.' Journal of Arabic and Islamic Studies 8 (2008): 108–24.

Merhej, Lena Irmgard. 'Men with Guns.' In *Postcolonial Comics: Texts, Events, Identities*, edited by Binita Mehta and Pia Mukherji. Kindle edition. New York; Oxford: Routledge, 2015.

———. 'Wasfat Lubnaniyya li l-Intiqam.' *Samandal* no. 7 (2009): 79–87.

Mhanna, Elias. 'The Fate of a Joke in Lebanon.' *The New Yorker*, 26 September 2015. http://www.newyorker.com/news/news-desk/the-fate-of-a-joke-in-lebanon.

Michaelson, Ruth. 'Egyptian Court Quashes Deal to Transfer Red Sea Islands to Saudi Arabia.' *The Guardian*, 21 June 2016, World News sec. https://www.theguardian.com/world/2016/jun/21/egyptian-court-quashes-transfer-red-sea-islands-saudi-arabia.

Miller, Catherine. 'Contemporary Darija Writings in Morocco: Ideology and Practices.' In *The Politics of Written Language in the Arab World*, edited by Jacob Høigilt and Gunvor Mejdell, 90–115. Leiden: Brill, 2017.

Milroy, James, and Lesley Milroy. *Authority in Language: Investigating Standard English*. London, UK; New York: Routledge, 1999. http://public.eblib.com/EBLPublic/PublicView.do?ptiID=169661.

Moawad, Nadine. 'The Bigger Struggle for Women in Municipalities.' *Sawt Al Niswa | صوت النسوة*, 16 May 2016. http://www.sawtalniswa.org/article/557.

Mokhtari, Rym. 'Shawk.' *Tuk-Tuk* no. 7 (2012): 35–8.

Moore, Alan, and Dave Gibbons. *Watchmen*. New York: DC Comics, 2005.

———, and David Lloyd. *V for Vendetta*. New York: DC Comics, 2005.

Morayef, Soraya. 'Arab Comic Artists Discuss Adversity and Censorship.' *Middle East Eye*, 19 August 2015. http://www.middleeasteye.net/fr/node/45520.

Muhammad, Dina. Introduction to story 'A Critical Painting.' *Shakmagiya* online, 2016. Online magazine available at http://kotobna.net.

Muhiy, Mustafa. 'Interview with Muzn Hasan: One Should Not Judge the Women's Movement Without Considering the Context Around Them (in Arabic).' *Mada Masr*, 13 October 2016. http://www.madamasr.com/ar/2016/10/13/feature/حوار/حوار-مُزن-حسن-لا-يجب-أن-نحاسب-الحركة-ال.

Nabki, Qifa. 'An Interview with Omar Khouri.' *Qifa Nabki*, 6 November 2014. https://qifanabki.com/2014/11/06/an-interview-with-omar-khouri/.

Najjar, Latifa al-. 'اللغة العربية بين أزمة الهوية وإشكالية الاختيار' 16 (The Arabic Language Between the Crisis of Identity and the Problem of Choice).' In *Language and Identity in the Arab World: Historical, Cultural and Political Problematics*, 185–201. Beirut: Arab Center for Research and Policy Studies, 2013.

Nasr, Joseph. 'You Asked for Democracy? There You Go!' *Ihna* 11 (2011).

Nordenson, Jon. 'The Language of Online Activism: A Case from Kuwait.' In *The Politics of Written Language in the Arab World*, edited by Jacob Høigilt and Gunvor Mejdell, 266–89. Leiden: Brill, 2017.

Palva, Heikki. *Artistic Colloquial Arabic: Traditional Narratives and Poems from Al-Balqa' (Jordan)*. Vol. 69. Studia Orientalia. Helsinki: Federation of Finnish Learned Societies/Bookstore Tiedekirja, 1992.

Parkinson, Dilworth B. 'Knowing Standard Arabic: Testing Egyptians' MSA Abilities.' In *Current Issues in Linguistic Theory*, edited by Mushira Eid and Clive Holes, 101:47. Amsterdam: John Benjamins Publishing Company, 1993. https://benjamins.com/#catalog/books/cilt.101.05par/details.

———. 'Searching for Modern Fusha: Real-Life Formal Arabic.' *Al-'Arabiyya* 24 (1991): 31–64.

———. 'Verbal Features in Oral Fusha Performances in Cairo.' *International Journal of the Sociology of Language* 2003, no. 163 (2003): 27–41. doi:10.1515/ijsl.2003.044.

'The People VS Samandal Comics.' *Indiegogo*, 2015. https://www.indiegogo.com/projects/1512356.

'Permission to Speak, Sir.' *The Economist*, 23 April 2016.

Płonka, Arkadiusz. 'Le Nationalisme Linguistique Au Liban Autour de Saʿīd ʿAql et L'idée de Langue Libanaise Dans La revue "Lebnaan" en Nouvel Alphabet.' *Arabica* 53, no. 4 (2006): 423–71.

Qualey, M. Lynx. 'Another Pop-Literary Comics Magazine Launches in Egypt: "Garage".' *Arabic Literature (in English)*, 31 August 2015. http://arablit.org/2015/08/31/garage/ (accessed 7 September 2015).

Rahma, Hicham. 'Al-ʿar bi l-zayt al-ḥarr.' *Tuk-Tuk* no. 7 (2012): 48–58.

Richards, Alan, and John Waterbury. *A Political Economy of the Middle East*. Boulder, CO: Westview Press, 1996.

Riches, Adam, Tim Parker and Robert Frankland. *When the Comics Went to War: Comic Book War Heroes*. Edinburgh: Mainstream, 2009.

Ricoeur, Paul. *From Text to Action: Essays in Hermeneutics, II*. Translated by Kathleen Blamey and John B. Thompson. Continuum, 2008.

Rima, Barrack. 'ضهر قبل قيلولة.' *Samandal* no. 8 (2010): 11–21.

Rosenbaum, G.M. 'Fushammiyya: Alternating Style in Egyptian Prose.' *Zeitschrift Für Arabische Linguistik* no. 38 (2000): 68–87.

——. 'Egyptian Arabic as a Written Language.' *Jerusalem Studies in Arabic and Islam* no. 29 (2004): 281–340.

Rosenkranz, Patrick. *Rebel Visions: The Underground Comix Revolution, 1963–1975*. Seattle, WA: Fantagraphics Books, 2002.

Roushdy, R., C. Krafft, C. Harbour, G. Barsoum and S. El-Kogali. *Survey of Young People in Egypt: Final Report*. Cairo: Population Council, 2010. http://www.popline.org/node/217332.

Sabin, Roger. *Adult Comics*. London: Routledge, 2013.

Sacco, Joe. *Footnotes in Gaza: A Graphic Novel*. New York: Metropolitan Books, 2010.

——. *Palestine*. 1st edition. Seattle, WA: Fantagraphics, 2001.

——, and Christopher Hitchens. *Safe Area Gorazde: The War in Eastern Bosnia 1992–1995*. Seattle, WA: Fantagraphics, 2002.

Salloukh, Bassel, Rabie Barakat, Jinan S. Al-Habbal, Lara W. Khattab and Shoghig Mikaelian. *The Politics of Sectarianism in Postwar Lebanon*. London: Pluto Press, 2015.

Sami, Hala G. 'A Strategic Use of Culture: Egyptian Women's Subversion and Resignification of Gender Norms.' In *Rethinking Gender in Revolutions and Resistance: Lessons from the Arab World*, edited by Maha El Said, Lena Meari and Nicola Pratt, 86–109. London: Zed Books, 2015.

Satrapi, Marjane. *Persepolis: The Story of a Childhood*. 1st edition. New York: Pantheon, 2004.

Sattouf, Riad. *The Arab of the Future: A Childhood in the Middle East, 1978–1984: A Graphic Memoir*. New York: Metropolitan Books, 2015.

Saxena, Mukul. 'Reified Languages and Scripts Versus Real Literacy Values and Practices: Insights from Research with Young Bilinguals in an Islamic State.' *Compare: A Journal of Comparative and International Education* 41, no. 2 (2011): 277–92. doi:10.1080/03057925.2011.547290.

Sayahi, Lotfi. *Diglossia and Language Contact: Language Variation and Change in North Africa*. 1st edition. New York: Cambridge University Press, 2014.

Scott, James C. *Domination and the Arts of Resistance: Hidden Transcripts*. New Haven: Yale University Press, 1992.

Sebba, Mark. 'Societal Bilingualism.' In *The SAGE Handbook of Sociolinguistics*, edited by Ruth Wodak, Barbara Johnstone and Paul E. Kerswill, 445–60. London: SAGE Publications, 2013.

——. 'Writing Switching in British Creole.' In *Language Mixing and Code-Switching in Writing: Approaches to Mixed-Language Written Discourse*, edited by Mark Sebba, Shahrzad Mahootian and Carla Jonsson, 89–106. New York: Routledge, 2012.

Bibliography

Shafy, Samiha. "'Horribly Humiliating": Egyptian Woman Tells of "Virginity Tests"'. *Spiegel Online*, 10 June 2011, International sec. http://www.spiegel.de/international/world/horribly-humiliating-egyptian-woman-tells-of-virginity-tests-a-767365.html.

Shahine, Selim H. 'Youth and the Revolution in Egypt.' *Anthropology Today* 27, no. 2 (2011): 1–3. doi:10.1111/j.1467-8322.2011.00792.x.

Sharabi, Hisham. *Neopatriarchy: A Theory of Distorted Change in Arab Society*. New York: Oxford University Press, 1988.

Sheehi, Stephen. 'Failure, Modernity, and the Works of Hisham Sharabi: Towards a Post-Colonial Critique of Arab Subjectivity.' *Critique: Critical Middle Eastern Studies* 6, no. 10 (1997): 39–54. doi:10.1080/10669929708720099.

Shehadeh, Lamia Rustum. 'Coverture in Lebanon.' *Feminist Review* 76, no. 1 (2004): 83–99. doi:10.1057/palgrave.fr.9400133.

Shehata, Samer S. 'The Politics of Laughter: Nasser, Sadat, and Mubarek in Egyptian Political Jokes,' Folklore, vol. 103, no. 1 (1992), 75–91.

Shenker, Jack. *The Egyptians: A Radical History of Egypt's Unfinished Revolution*. New York; London: The New Press, 2017.

Shimi, Rowan El. 'Women Artists Do Well as CairoComix Launches.' *Mada Masr*, 1 October 2015. http://www.madamasr.com/sections/culture/woman-artists-do-well-cairocomix-launches.

Shinnawī and Makhlouf, 'حجازي أبو التنابلة المجتهد.' *Tuk-Tuk* no. 1 (2011): 9–11.

Singerman, Diane. 'The Economic Imperatives of Marriage: Emerging Practices and Identities Among Youth in the Middle East.' Wolfensohn Center for Development and Dubai School of Government, 2007. http://www.shababinclusion.org/content/document/detail/559/.

'Sisi: Don't Listen to Anyone but Me.' *Mada Masr*, 24 February 2016. http://www.madamasr.com/news/sisi-dont-listen-anyone-me.

Skinner, Quentin. *Visions of Politics: Regarding Method, Volume 1*. Cambridge, UK: Cambridge University Press, 2002.

Soueif, Ahdaf. 'Foreword.' In *Walls of Freedom: Street Art of the Egyptian Revolution*, edited by Don STONE Karl and Basma Hamdy, 4–6. Malta: From Here to Fame, 2014.

——. 'Image of Unknown Woman Beaten by Egypt's Military Echoes Around World.' *The Guardian*, 18 December 2011, Comment is Free edition. http://www.theguardian.com/commentisfree/2011/dec/18/egypt-military-beating-female-protester-tahrir-square.

Stein, Daniel, and Jan-No L. Thon, eds. *From Comic Strips to Graphic Novels*. Berlin; Boston: de Gruyter, 2013.

Stråth, Bo. 'Ideology and Conceptual History.' In *The Oxford Handbook of Political Ideologies*, edited by Michael Freeden and Marc Stears, 3–20. Oxford: Oxford University Press, 2013. //www.oxfordhandbooks.com/10.1093/oxfordhb/9780199585977.001.0001/oxfordhb-9780199585977-e-013.

Suleiman, Yasir. *The Arabic Language and National Identity: A Study in Ideology*. Edinburgh University Press, 2003.

——. *Language and Identity in the Middle East and North Africa*. Richmond, Surrey: Curzon Press, 1996.

——. *A War of Words: Language and Conflict in the Middle East*. Cambridge: Cambridge University Press, 2004.

Taher, Menna. 'New Wave of Comic Books Flourishes in Egypt.' *Ahram Online*, 24 October 2011. http://english.ahram.org.eg/NewsContent/5/25/25015/Arts–Culture/Visual-Art/New-wave-of-comic-books-flourishes-in-Egypt.aspx.

Taine-Cheikh, Catherine. 'Arabe(s) et Berbère En Mauritanie : Bilinguisme, Diglossie et Mixité Lingistique.' In *High vs. Low and Mixed Varieties: Status, Norms and Functions Across Time and Languages*, edited by Lutz Edzard and Gunvor Mejdell, 88–109. Wiesbaden: Otto Harrassowitz, 2012.

Tawfiq. 'Rabab.' In *Hadatha Bi L-Fi'l (It Really Happened)*, edited by Muhammad Shennawy, 197–211. Cairo: al-Fann al-Tasi' (the ninth art), 2014.

Thompson, John. *Ideology and Modern Culture: Critical Social Theory in the Era of Mass Communication*. 1st edition. Stanford, CA: Stanford University Press, 1991.

'Timeline of Egypt's Escalating Campaign Against Civil Society | Project on Middle East Democracy (POMED).' http://pomed.org/blog-post/egypts-escalating-campaign-against-the-ngo-community/?utm_source=Project%20on%20Middle%20East%20Democracy%20-%20All%20Contacts&utm_campaign=6ea204fec0-Egypt_Coup_Resources&utm_medium=email&utm_term=0_75a06056d7-6ea204fec0-215935721 (accessed 3 July 2016).

UNDP. *Arab Human Development Report 2003: Building a Knowledge Society*. Arab Human Development Report. Amman: UNDP, 2003. http://www.arab-hdr.org/publi cations/other/ahdr/ahdr2003e.pdf.

United Nations Development Programme. *Arab Human Development Report 2016: Youth and the Prospects for Human Development in a Changing Reality*. New York: UNDP, Regional Bureau for Arab States, 2016.

Usta, Jinan, JoAnn M. Farver and Christine Sylva Hamieh. 'Effects of Socialization on Gender Discrimination and Violence Against Women in Lebanon.' *Violence Against Women*, vol. 22, no. 4 (2016), 415-431.

Valfret. 'Ecce Homo.' *Samandal* no. 7 (2009): 258–66.

Walby, Sylvia. *Theorizing Patriarchy*. Oxford, UK; Cambridge, MA: Wiley-Blackwell, 1990.

Walters, Keith. 'Fergie's Prescience: The Changing Nature of Diglossia in Tunisia.' *International Journal of the Sociology of Language* 2003, no. 163 (2003): 77–109. doi:10.1515/ijsl.2003.048.

———. 'Language Attitudes.' In *Encyclopedia of Arabic Language and Linguistics*, edited by Kees Versteegh. Leiden: Brill, 2007.

Wedeen, Lisa. *Ambiguities of Domination: Politics, Rhetoric, and Symbols in Contemporary Syria*. Chicago: University of Chicago Press, 1999.

Woolard, Kathryn A., and Bambi B. Schieffelin. 'Language Ideology.' *Annual Review of Anthropology* 23 (1994): 55–82.

'متابعات. "محيط | والي: المرأة المصرية الوتد وعمود الخيمة لحماية المجتمع'. *Moheet*, 2 June 2016. http://www.moheet.com/2016/06/02/2433673/والي-المرأة-المصرية-الوتد-وعمود-الخي.html.

Index

References to images are in *italics*.

Index

Index

Plate 1 Cover art of *Tuk-Tuk* 5, 2012 and *Samandal* 1, 2007.

Plate 2 Ahmad 'Ukasha, 'Cairo is a Wicked City, [al-Qahira Madina Sharira], *Tuk-Tuk* 11, 44–5.

Plate 3 Magdi al-Shafee, *Metro*, cover page.

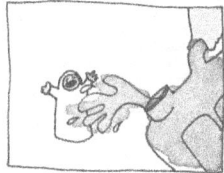

Plate 4 Lena Merhej, 'Lebanese Recipes for Revenge' [al-Wasfat al-lubnaniyya li-l-intiqam], *Samandal* 7, 83.

Plate 5 *Tuk-Tuk* 2 cover image (poster from launch at The French Institute in Cairo).
Reproduction of poster advertising the launch of the second issue on 10 April 2011.

Plate 6 *Shakmagiya* 1, cover image and extract from the story 'The Evolution of the Egyptian Woman', 39.

Plate 7 Duʿa al-ʿAdl, 50 *Cartoons and More on Women*, self-published booklet, Cairo 2016.

Plate 8 Muna Abd al-Rahman and al-Shayma Hamid, 'It Is We Who Are Late', *Shakmagiya* 1, 21.

Plate 9 EGYCon 2016, Cairo, photograph by the author.

Plate 10 Muhammad Shennawy, 'The Sponge Bob Gang', *Tuk-Tuk* 6, 8.

Plate 11   Cover image, *Skefkef* 4.

Plate 12   Cover image, *LAB619 6*.

www.ingramcontent.com/pod-product-compliance
Lightning Source LLC
Chambersburg PA
CBHW050421280326
41932CB00013BA/1945